Sehnsucht # 4

WAR OF THE FANTASY WORLDS

WAR OF THE FANTASY WORLDS

*C. S. Lewis and J. R. R. Tolkien
on Art and Imagination*

Martha C. Sammons

PRAEGER
An Imprint of ABC-CLIO, LLC

A B C ☰ C L I O

Santa Barbara, California • Denver, Colorado • Oxford, England

Library of Congress Cataloging-in-Publication Data

Sammons, Martha C., 1949–
    War of the fantasy worlds : C. S. Lewis and J. R. R. Tolkien on art and imagination / Martha C. Sammons.
        p. cm.
    Includes bibliographical references and index.
    ISBN 978-0-313-36282-8 (hard copy : alk. paper) — ISBN 978-0-313-36283-5 (ebook)
        1. Fantasy fiction, English—History and criticism—Theory, etc.
2. Lewis, C. S. (Clive Staples), 1898–1963—Knowledge—Fantasy literature.
3. Tolkien, J. R. R. (John Ronald Reuel), 1892–1973—Knowledge—Fantasy literature. 4. Creation (Literary, artistic, etc.)   I. Title.
    PR888.F3S36   2010
    823'.0876609—dc22   2009032313

ISBN: 978-0-313-36282-8
EISBN: 978-0-313-36283-5

14   13   12   11   10   1   2   3   4   5

This book is also available on the World Wide Web as an eBook.
Visit www.abc-clio.com for details.

Praeger
An Imprint of ABC-CLIO, LLC

ABC-CLIO, LLC
130 Cremona Drive, P.O. Box 1911
Santa Barbara, California 93116-1911

This book is printed on acid-free paper ∞

Manufactured in the United States of America

Contents

Introduction

C. S. Lewis remarked to J. R. R. Tolkien, "There is too little of what we really like in stories. I am afraid we shall have to write some ourselves." The result was a new type of novel that presents the spiritual and "mythopoeic" in a popular format. Their books have been described as "theologized science fiction," "alternative theology," "religious fantasy," and so on. Religious fantasy integrates aspects of Christianity with elements of fantasy and science fiction. However, the "religious" element varies, as well as the forms. Lewis and Tolkien disagreed about the role and nature of the writer and degree to which religious elements should appear in a story.

It is estimated that *The Lord of the Rings* and *The Chronicles of Narnia* have each sold more than 100 million copies of their numerous editions. Tom Shippey places *The Lord of the Rings* in the top tier of most influential books of the century, including both Tolkien's influence on the fantasy genre and as a literary classic. Tolkien's works have made modern fantasy both a popular and "respectable" genre for adult audiences. The release of Peter Jackson's movie trilogy *Lord of the Rings*, planned production of the film *The Hobbit* and 2007 publication of Tolkien's book *The Children of Hurin* have also renewed interest in Tolkien's works.

Similarly, Lewis's Chronicles are considered classics of children's literature. The release of Disney's movie version of the first book in the series, *The Lion, the Witch and the Wardrobe,* in December 2005 has increased interest in Lewis's fantasy fiction. The movie of the second book, *Prince Caspian,* was released in May 2008. There are plans to release additional films in *The Chronicles of Narnia,* in addition to his nonfiction books *The Screwtape Letters* and *A Severe Mercy.*

Most scholarship about Tolkien and Lewis describes their shared faith and academic interests or analyzes each writer's fantasy works. However, no books focus solely on their contrasting views about fantasy, and Tolkien's views about fantasy are rarely discussed in detail. Yet Tolkien's and Lewis's views of art and imagination are not only central to understanding the themes, value, and relevance of their fantasy fiction but are also strikingly different. Tolkien himself was interested in studying mythological invention and the mystery of literary "sub-creation." He thus offers his work as an experimental subject for observation.[1]

There has been some debate whether the Inklings—a literary group consisting of Lewis, Tolkien, and their colleagues—were uniform in their goals and writing because of their shared Christian views and interest in myth, language, fantasy literature, and history. However, they had unique points of view. It is possible to find similarities between elements of Lewis's and Tolkien's novels, including the influence of Norse mythology, their creation myths, and imagery. Yet their fantasy works are dissimilar, particularly with regard to the amount of detail and development of the secondary world, their style and narrative methods, and Christian references.

Their contrasting approaches to fantasy literature are evident both in their essays about the genre and as themes within their fantasy works. In their essays and letters, they provide key insights about the artistic process, their goals as writers, characteristics of successful fantasy literature, and the value and purpose of fairy tales and fantasy. Understanding their views about fantasy, in turn, helps us better understand and appreciate their works.

Both writers had similar literary interests and influences, including Norse mythology and fairy tales. Their theories about imagination were also influenced by Christian writers such as George MacDonald and G. K. Chesterton. They returned to fairy tales and classical mythology, as well as medieval models and metaphors, and disliked most modern literature. Both also believed in the value of myth, especially the ability of pagan mythology to convey kernels of Truth. The Christian story, they believed, is myth become fact. In fact, Tolkien's argument with Lewis about Christianity and myth was influential in Lewis's conversion. Because the Fall has separated man from the spiritual, they acknowledged the importance of both reason and imagination. Their shared love and respect for the created world of nature and animals and intense dislike of the effects of industrialization and modern culture are especially evident in their writings. They agreed that fantasy can provide "recovery," regaining a clear view of the world as it was meant to be seen.

Differences in their writing methods also provide valuable insights into the artistic process. Tolkien wrote and revised meticulously, sometimes for years, while Lewis wrote quickly and effortlessly. Tolkien began with invented languages and then developed an elaborate mythology to create a world where his languages could exist. Lewis's works began with mental pictures; he would then find the appropriate "form" to tie together the images. Tolkien felt the stories arose in his mind as "given things" that were revealed to him. Tolkien sets his secondary world on earth in an imaginary time. His penchant for historical and linguistic detail is unparalleled. In contrast, Lewis's worlds are always "parallel" to ours. Both characters and readers enter the world, only to return to reality, hopefully changed. Lewis uses just enough language, geography, and science to make his novels believable. Although their creative processes and portrayals of their secondary worlds differ, both chose the fairy tale tradition as the ideal form for their fiction. Tolkien, in fact, considers fairy tales one of the highest forms of art. The fairy tale genre contributes many of the elements and stylistic features found in both writers' works. The association of fairy tales and children, they believed, was accidental. In fact, it is adults who "need" the fairy tale sense of wonder.

Both writers claim that their books are not allegorical, using words such as *applicability* and *supposition* to describe their writing. Tolkien, whose goal was to "elucidate truth," presents Christian morals through actions. Lewis's works are more obviously didactic. Both, however, use elements from the real world within their fantasy worlds in order to teach truths about our world. They believe the world has been drained of enchantment by placing higher value on science and reason rather than imagination and feeling. Fantasy has the power of enchantment, thus changing readers' views of the primary world as they return to it with a restored vision. Advantages of fantasy are recovery, escape, fulfillment of desires—especially the desire to escape death and communicate with animals—and *eucatastrophe*, Tolkien's term for the happy ending. Myth has the power to communicate truths that cannot be discovered or expressed in any other way. More than simply plot, myth is a "net" to catch something else. However, pride results in seeking to possess created objects and using them to wield power over others. The created object therefore cannot be hoarded or possessed. Rather, it must be released to set the bird free from the net, leading the reader outside the self to an encounter with the "Other."

Ironically, although Tolkien and Lewis are usually associated with one another as both friends and academic colleagues, they claim they did not influence what each other wrote. Tolkien's famous line "It really won't do, you know!" was his reaction to *The Lion, the Witch and the Wardrobe*. But he was more favorable toward *Out of the Silent Planet*. In general, Lewis had nothing but praise for Tolkien's works. As research for the documentary *C. S. Lewis, Beyond Narnia* revealed, they argued about a number of topics. Despite their differences of opinion, Tolkien and Lewis greatly influenced one another and even impacted the completion and publication of many of their works.

Tolkien and Lewis primarily disagreed about the relation of art to God's Truth. In his classic study of Romanticism and literary theory,

The Mirror and the Lamp, M. H. Abrams studies the changing views of the mind as a "mirror" of outside reality compared to the mind as a "lamp" or a "fountain" that determines what it knows. Tolkien and Lewis exemplify these contrasting viewpoints. Abrams classifies critical theories based on their orientation toward one of the following four elements related to a work of art: the Universe, the Work, the Artist, and the Audience. Tolkien and Lewis write about the relationship of fantasy to "reality," characteristics of good fantasy, the creative process, and the effects of fantasy on readers. Their theories about art reflect differences in literary theories from Plato to the Romantic poets. Tolkien was especially influenced by Coleridge's theories about fantasy, fancy, art, and imagination. Tolkien and Lewis drew on this rich background of literary theory, as well as medieval models of the universe, for their own metaphors for art. Believing the artist is created in God's image and adds to creation, Tolkien uses "Romantic" images of trees and light. Lewis, believing the artist imitates and rearranges God's materials, uses analogies such as mirror and reflection.

Tolkien took a more liberal view of the idea of man being made in God's image by calling the artist a "sub-creator," i.e., a creator of images not found in our world. To Tolkien, fantasy is a human right because we are made "in the image and likeness of a Maker." As a sub-creator, Tolkien believes that his art is the splintered, refracted light of God's Truth and an act of worship. The chief purpose of life, he writes, is to increase our knowledge of God by contemplating the world and then be moved to a chorus of praise and thanks, calling on all created things to join us.[2]

In his letters, Tolkien explains that *The Lord of the Rings* is essentially about the relation of creation to sub-creation. Sub-creation is freed from the channels the Creator has already used. Thus certain things not theologically sound are acceptable with an imaginary world and, in fact, can present Truth. Fantasy is made out of simple, fundamental things from the primary world but rearranges primary matter in secondary patterns. By defining fantasy as sub-creation with an inner consistency of reality, Tolkien makes it a reality apart from ours. Tolkien not only expands on and rewrites the Genesis story but considers his myth a supplement to the Bible because writ-ers of the Bible and of fairy stories become coworkers with the Great Author.

Tolkien looks forward to the Truth as a story still in the making, while Lewis looks back to the One Story already written by God. According to Lewis, while man can create, he cannot do so from nothing as God can. Stories can only rearrange or retell what al-ready exists. Lewis's view of reality, involving man's separation from his heavenly potential, can be described as Platonic, and he devel-ops this concept of art in his fantasy fiction. Lewis writes that all theists must believe that the "world was modeled on an *idea* existing in God's mind," that God invented or thought of matter just like Dickens thought of Mr. Pickwick.[3] Because Lewis believes every-thing originates with God, imaginative inventions must reflect God's Truth. Poets, musicians, and inventors never "make," only build from, rearrange, and recombine elements and materials that already exist from the Creator. Thus the word *creation* cannot really be applied to human writing. Art and imagination are, however, a path to understanding God. Lewis's art that began with "mental pictures" can merely reflect this Truth. Lewis uses "living pictures" in his sto-ries to represent the eternal Truth that art conveys through static images.

Tolkien's theories about fantasy are found in his essay "On Fairy Stories," which he originally presented as the Andrew Lang Lecture on March 8, 1938, at the University of St. Andrews. It was later published in *Essays Presented to Charles Williams* in 1947. This essay is both a major contribution to theories about fantasy literature and a framework for understanding his writing. Many of Lewis's views about fantasy, fairy tales, and science fiction are found in his essays collected in *On Stories*. The following chapters focus on Tolkien's and Lewis's theories about fantasy found primarily in their essays and letters, as well as themes and examples from their fantasy fiction.

This book is not a critical analysis of *The Silmarillion*, *The Hobbit*, *The Lord of the Rings*, *The Chronicles of Narnia*, or the Space Trilogy. Rather, it examines only elements that relate to Tolkien's and Lew-is's views about art or implementation of their theories. This book is also not intended to review information that is covered well by other authors. Rather, it touches on many topics as they relate specifically to the theme of Tolkien's and Lewis's views about fantasy and creativity.

For more information about their lives and friendship, there are several well-known biographies, particularly those by Humphrey Carpenter (*Tolkien*), Walter Hooper and Roger Green (*C. S. Lewis: A Biography*), and by Lewis himself in his autobiography, *Surprised by Joy*. Tom Shippey's *J. R. R. Tolkien: Author of the Century* reviews Tolkien's contribution to literature and philology. In addition, Colin Duriez examines their relationship in *Tolkien and Lewis: The Gift of Friendship*.

This book begins by describing how Tolkien and Lewis met and influenced each other. It discusses how they began writing their works and the processes they used, including their attitudes about the artist as creator. Both Tolkien and Lewis wrote essays and letters describing their theories about fairy tales and fantasy. Their definitions of key terms related to fantasy fiction are presented here, along with an examination of their views about the fairy tale form, audience, qualities of good fantasy, the science fiction and fantasy genres, imagination, and sub-creation. Tolkien's and Lewis's views about creativity are exemplified in their fantasy works. Thus it is important to study the theme of art and creation in Tolkien's *The Silmarillion* and Lewis's *Chronicles of Narnia* and Space Trilogy as well as their depiction of Elves, eldila, evil, and magic. Literary history and theorists influenced Tolkien and Lewis, and each writer illustrates a different tradition with regard to their views of creativity. Therefore, this book outlines the literary theories and medieval models and metaphors of the universe that affected both writers. It then explores Tolkien's and Lewis's own metaphors for art used in both their essays and fiction. The final chapter looks at how Tolkien and Lewis implemented secondary worlds. It compares their purposes as well as techniques, including style and invented languages.

1

The Artist

Tolkien and Lewis share many interests and influences, yet differ in their creative processes. This chapter provides a brief background on their relationship as colleagues and how their fantasy works were developed, then compares their creative processes.

INFLUENCES

In 1926, Tolkien and Lewis met at a faculty meeting to discuss curriculum for the Oxford English School. In his autobiography, Lewis jokes that he was warned to never trust a Papist or a philologist, and Tolkien was both. Lewis was a fellow of Magdalen College, Oxford, from 1915 to 1954, and then became Professor of Medieval and Renaissance English at the University of Cambridge. Tolkien was the Rawlinson and Bosworth Professor of Anglo-Saxon at Pembroke College, Oxford, from 1925 to 1945, and then became Merton Professor of English Language and Literature at Merton College,

Oxford, in 1945. They met regularly at the Coalbiter's Club that Tolkien founded to read Icelandic sagas and the Eddas. Eventually, they began the Inklings, a literary society where friends would read their unpublished works aloud and receive praise and criticism. The Inklings inspired both Lewis and Tolkien to get their works published. While it is not the intent of this book to review in detail the biographies of both writers, it is interesting to compare the "soil" of experience, as Tolkien calls it, that contributed to their mutual interests.

Lewis attributes his similarity to Tolkien to their temperaments and the fact that they were both Christians. In addition, they shared similar tastes in literature. Both, for example, disliked modern novels.[1] They were also influenced by the novels of William Morris, especially *The Earthly Paradise* (1913) in which mariners searching for a land that gives immortality arrive at a land where they hear mythic tales. Tolkien owned almost all of Morris's works. Lewis compares the subject matter and languages of Morris and *Le Morte d'Arthur*, which he considers the greatest work he ever read. However, he calls Morris genuine and *Morte* artificial reproduction.[2] He was "ravished" by *The Well at the World's End*; Morris also taught him the idea of unsatisfied desire, a theme that runs throughout Lewis's novels.[3]

Both liked the works of George MacDonald, particularly *Phantastes* and *The Princess and the Goblin*.[4] Tolkien was especially influenced by MacDonald's Curdie books but disliked the moral allegory of most of his works.[5] Although he thought "The Golden Key" was poorly written and incoherent, Tolkien was asked to write a preface to a new edition of it.[6] While writing the preface, however, Tolkien wrote his own *Smith of Wootton Major*. Lewis was a strong admirer of the fairy tale quality, melodrama, and direct preaching of MacDonald's works.[7] In reading MacDonald's *Phantastes*, he sensed a "bright shadow."[8] Lewis contrasts MacDonald with Charles Kingsley's *The Water-Babies*, describing it as the difference between imagination and fancy, holiness and morality.[9]

Tolkien and Lewis also shared common sources used in their own fantasy: Norse mythology, Homer, Beowulf, and medieval romances.[10] Both loved "northernness" and Celtic myths, even when they were young. Tolkien was especially influenced by the Norse Prose Edda and Icelandic myth and legend. He is well-known for his translation of *Beowulf* and influential essay "Beowulf: The Monsters and the Critics," which contains many of his theories about writing. *Siegfried and the Twilight of the Gods* with Arthur Rackham's illustrations gave Lewis a sense of pure "northernness" and longing.[11] In 1913, Lewis wrote "Loki Bound," a poetic tragedy about the Norse gods. Even as an adult, for relaxation he enjoyed reading boys' books about distant lands and strange adventures.[12] Love for the ancient contrasts their dislike of the modern: Both writers shunned most contemporary literature, industrialization, capitalism, and politics.

Their love of Norse mythology and "northernness" was not the only thing they had in common. Both, for example, grew up with a deep despondency. The death of Tolkien's mother when he was twelve and his unhappiness at school made him pessimistic and insecure.[13] Similarly, Lewis's mother died of cancer when he was just ten. Her death removed his security like the sinking of the continent of Atlantis and gave him a "deeply ingrained pessimism."[14] In addition, both writers have been described as having divided selves: the rational, scholarly, and analytical side versus an imaginative, artistic side.

Tolkien and Lewis also served in World War I as junior line officers. By 1918, writes Tolkien, all but one of his close friends had died. Trench fever gave Tolkien time to begin *The Book of Lost Tales*. In "On Fairy Stories," Tolkien says that war awakened his interest in fantasy. He would later advise his son Christopher serving in World War II to use writing to convey his feelings about good and evil and prevent them from festering.[15] After six months of service, Lewis was seriously injured by a British shell.

Tolkien and Lewis thus turned to imaginary lands as the ideal way to escape the loss of their mothers and friends, the results of the war, and to express their attitudes toward modern society.

INKLINGS

Their shared love for similar types of literature contributed to their own writing. Because there was no fantasy or mythic literature for adults, their goal was to write mythopoeic stories disguised as popular "excursionary" thrillers. In 1936, Lewis said, "Tollers, there is too little of what we really like in stories. I am afraid we shall have to try and write some ourselves."[16] Tolkien writes that the type of literature he wanted to read was scarce and "heavily alloyed."[17] Lewis compares what they wanted to write and read to *The Hobbit*.[18] They agreed to each write a story: one on time and one on space, flipping a coin to decide.

The result was that Tolkien would write about time travel, and Lewis would write about space travel. Tolkien's book was to be called "Númenor, the Land in the West." It was to be about the island of Atlantis, which he repeatedly dreamed about, and would use memory as the vehicle for time travel.[19] However, Tolkien wrote only a few chapters and was slow at completing what has become known as *The Lost Road*, about a boy who loves language and dreams about the land of Númenor, which can only be reached by time or space travel. But Tolkien never completed it, partially due to his work finishing up *The Hobbit*. Lewis did write his space books: *Out of the Silent Planet*, *Perelandra*, and *That Hideous Strength*. Tolkien believes Lewis's "immense power and industry" allowed him to finish his trilogy quickly, whereas he was "slower," "meticulous," "indolent," and "less organized."[20] Tolkien reminisces that because they were both amateurs, neither of them expected success. The reward of their efforts was that they provided each other with stories that they generally liked, although there were some parts of each other's fiction that they disliked.[21]

TOLKIEN'S WORK

Tolkien's own work—some completed and some not completed—is extensive, spanning his entire career. The twelve-volume *The Silmarillion*, which contains the history of Middle-earth, was Tolkien's grand work that began in 1917. But he describes his great mythology as always being with him, even at birth. It is a blend of his love of language, growing things, and northern legends.[22] His heart and mind, he says, were always in *The Silmarillion*.[23] Tolkien wanted *The Silmarillion* published together with *The Lord of the Rings*, but it was published after his death by his son Christopher in 1977.

Tolkien was especially influenced by the nineteenth-century Finnish epic the *Kalevala*, which Elias Lönnrot wrote from Finnish and Karelian folklore. His dream was to write a similar mythology for England, a body of connected legend ranging from the "large and cosmogonic" to "romantic fairy-story."[24] He also wanted it to have a high, cool, clear tone and quality; British "air"; and Celtic beauty. Not only was there a dearth of myth, fairy stories, and heroic legends, but he also knew of no songs or stories in ancient English about Elves and dwarves.[25] In addition, Tolkien did not believe that the Arthurian legend satisfied what England lacked. The "faerie" elements are too "fantastical, incoherent, and repetitive" and the Christian religion too explicit. Tolkien took characters, setting, and elements from other ancient literatures and traditional fairy tales but blended them to create his own mythology.

Another goal was to create a history for his languages. Tolkien began constructing languages as a boy and wrote legends to fit them.[26] His mother gave him German lessons and was interested in etymology, alphabets, and handwriting, arousing her son's interest in them.[27] Welsh especially attracted him by its style and sound. After seeing it on coal trucks, he always wanted to know what it was about. As a philologist, Tolkien was, of course, inspired by linguistics, and inventing languages was the foundation of his writing; in fact, he describes all his work as philological.[28] The story of Kullervo in the *Kalevala* provided Tolkien with the basis for the legends in *The Silmarillion* that, in turn, would provide a world for his private languages.[29]

His work took a somewhat different turn when *The Hobbit* began in 1930. Tolkien was grading papers when he found that one of the students had "mercifully" left a page blank. He scribbled "In a hole in the ground there lived a hobbit" but did nothing about it for a long time.[30] Tolkien writes that when his children were young, he invented and told children's stories to amuse them. He intended *The Hobbit* to be one of these.[31] In an interview, however, he said that he did not write *The Hobbit* specifically for children or for his own children's private enjoyment.[32] In his letters, he writes that he did not know why he wrote it but that the story was derived from his passion for epic, heroic legend, mythology, and fairy stories.[33] He wrote fairy stories not to address children but because he wanted to write that kind of story.[34] Later, he discovered what the story referred to.[35] That is, it began as a children's story but was torn from the mythology—*The Silmarillion*—that already existed.[36] As the book developed, it became more connected to his grander "mythology" and more heroic.[37] Other influences for *The Hobbit* include epic, myth, fairy stories, *Beowulf*, and *The Silmarillion*.[38] After much urging, Tolkien published the book in 1937 with great success. He revised the text twice.

Lewis found *The Hobbit* uncanny: "It is so exactly like what we would both have longed to write (or read) in 1916: so that one feels he is not making it up by merely describing the same world into which all three of us have the entry."[39] He describes *The Hobbit* as a new and unforgettable saga for both children and adults that may become a classic. The illustrations, maps, names, and characters such as dwarves are atypical of children's stories.[40] Lewis also writes that Tolkien knows more about hobbits than he needs to for the story. It is not only for children; after numerous readings, readers will grow to appreciate the scholarship and reflection that went into it.

After the success of *The Hobbit*, Tolkien's publisher Stanley Unwin wanted a sequel, while Tolkien wanted "heroic legends and high romance," resulting in *The Lord of the Rings*.[41] Tolkien saw the allure of hobbits and decided to put "earth under the feet of 'romance.'"[42] Beginning the new book with the chapter "A Long-Expected Party," he did not know how to proceed. He was still more interested in and preoccupied with the fairy stories and pure mythology of *The Silmarillion*.[43] Tolkien describes the beginning as more suited for adults and not as allegory but rather about the "darkness of present days."[44] Eventually, after much struggle to move the story

along, Tolkien found the link between *The Hobbit* and his background mythology: the One Ring.[45]

In the foreword to *The Lord of the Rings*, Tolkien says his main
motive was to tell a long tale that would hold readers' attention, as
well as amuse, delight, excite, and deeply move them. It is also important to note that, unlike *The Hobbit*, it was intended for an adult
audience.[46] While *The Silmarillion* was essentially written in the high
style of detailed history as Tolkien's "private hobby," *The Lord of the
Rings* was written for a specific audience and as the result of the urging of his publisher. Their styles and purposes thus differ. Tolkien
identifies several other purposes of *The Lord of the Rings*: to create a
world for his languages, to please himself, to experiment with
writing a long narrative, and to induce secondary belief.[47] He also
notes that, as literature, the story has a literary effect and purpose
rather than being real history—despite his extreme efforts to portray
it as real.

Lewis was Tolkien's "only audience" for a long time.[48] He heard
The Lord of the Rings read aloud and was often moved to tears.[49] In
contrast to Lewis's positive opinions, several members of the Inklings disliked *The Lord of the Rings*, including Owen Barfield, John
Wain, R. E. Havard, and especially Hugo Dyson. Lewis served as
"midwife" for Tolkien, encouraging and nagging him to write with
gravity and at length.[50] When Tolkien was "stuck" and could not
seem to move forward, Lewis pressured him to finish.[51] He acknowledged the debt he owed Lewis for "sheer encouragement" and the
idea that his works could be more than just a hobby. Without Lewis's "interest and unceasing eagerness for more," he would have
never finished it.[52] *The Lord of the Rings* was finally published in
1950.

Nevertheless, Lewis writes that he and Tolkien did not influence
what each other wrote: "No one ever influenced Tolkien—you
might as well try to influence a bandersnatch."[53] Likewise, Tolkien
claims that they were "too 'set'" and "too different."[54] But they
clearly did affect each other's works. Lewis, for example, suggested
that Tolkien reduce the amount of conversation and "hobbit talk,"
and the publisher confirmed the opinion. Despite the fact that

Tolkien could write indefinitely about hobbit food and jokes, he deferred to this criticism by reducing the dialogue.[55] Lewis also urged Tolkien to write more seriously because he found the hobbits most amusing in "unhobbitlike situations."[56] Lewis would comment, "You can do better than that. Better, Tolkien, please!" Then Tolkien would rewrite the section.[57] For example, one passage that Tolkien did revise is Gandalf's confrontation with Saruman at Isengard.

Lewis writes that the book "will break your heart"; it is like "lightning from a clear sky," a "heroic romance for adults" and "glorious sea" successful among the most unlikely readers and unlike anything ever written.[58] He also describes Gimli's love of Galadriel and the departure from Lothlórien as "unbearable."[59] The book is "almost unequalled in the whole range of narrative art" and ranks with the Aeneid as an "immediately sub-religious" book. It excels in sheer sub-creation, and the eucatastrophe (happy ending) reminds us of victory. On the other hand, there were a few passages Lewis wished had been rewritten or omitted.[60] Although he particularly disliked the first chapter because it contains fragments of the hobbit story that was adapted for children, the rest of the book is the "real stuff."[61]

Lewis wrote to publisher Stanley Unwin that no imaginary world like that in *The Lord of the Rings* had ever been created. It has diverse elements and is still true to its own internal laws; is objective, independent of the author's own psychology, and relevant to the real world but free from allegory; and varies in style to fit diverse scenes and characters (comic, epic, monstrous, etc.).[62]

LEWIS'S WORK

While Tolkien never really wrote his book about time travel, Lewis did write his "space book." By the 1930s, so many major changes had taken place in science fiction that Lewis decided it was time to react against them. What had developed was the pulpy "scientification" story begun by writers such as the American Hugo Gernsback, who developed the magazine *Amazing Stories*. Such science fiction dealt with the weird, amazing, romantic, and technological.

But the main purpose was to concentrate on science—to disseminate new hypotheses and speculations—rather than on plot or character. In contrast, Lewis wanted to write about space travel to refute J. B. S. Haldane's views in *Possible Worlds and Other Essays* (1927) that interplanetary travel was vital to mankind's future and in response to science's hope of defeating death.

By September 1937, Lewis completed *Out of the Silent Planet*. The first publisher, J. M. Dent, rejected it, but Tolkien advised him to submit it to Allen and Unwin, who had published *The Hobbit*. Tolkien also sent two long letters of support. Despite the fact that they too rejected it, the editor sent it to *The Bodley Head*, and it was published in the autumn of 1938.

Lewis probably had an idea of writing a sequel long before *Out of the Silent Planet* was published, but no one is sure what he intended. The end of the novel leaves the way open for a sequel by suggesting that eternal cosmic forces behind Weston will play an important role in the next centuries and will be dangerous if not stopped. The letter at the end of the book, which is also pure fiction, was a way to prepare for a sequel because it ends: "If there is to be any more space travelling, it will have to be time-travelling as well."[63]

Lewis wrote only part of a possible sequel—"The Dark Tower," published in *The Dark Tower and Other Stories*. This fragment, written in 1938 or 1939, is about time travel, beginning with a line that links well with the conclusion of *Out of the Silent Planet*: "'Of course,' said Orfieu, 'the sort of time-travelling you read about in books—time-travelling in the body—is absolutely impossible.'" Ransom appears in the story, described as "the hero, or victim, of one of the strangest adventures that had ever befallen a mortal man."

The next book in Lewis's Space Trilogy, *Perelandra*, began in the spring of 1941 after he completed his book *Preface to Paradise Lost*. Again, it was probably not intended as part of a trilogy because he apparently never planned one. But *Perelandra* arose partly as a result of *Preface to Paradise Lost* when Lewis started thinking about the purpose of the forbidden fruit in the Garden of Eden and realized it was to instill obedience. He also became interested in the nature of an unfallen Adam and Eve.

The book grew as well out of recurring mental pictures of floating islands, an image he most likely got from Olaf Stapledon's *Last and First Men*: "In the early days of Venus men had gathered foodstuffs from the great floating islands of vegetable matter." Next, says Lewis, he built up a world in which floating islands could exist.[64] Then the story about an averted fall developed. As we shall see, mental images are the process Lewis used to begin almost all of his fiction. By November 9, 1941, he was through the first conversation with the Green Lady, and he finished the entire book by May 11, 1942. The novel was published in 1943.

In 1943, Lewis delivered his lecture "The Abolition of Man" at the University of Durham and had also become influenced by his friend Charles Williams, whose works he called "theological shockers." He describes *The Place of the Lion* as Christian fantasy with layers of fantasy, theological stimulus, and edification. But his own romanticism differed from Williams's by finding revelation in mythology and nature, or the "mythically apprehended."[65] Both served as major influences on *That Hideous Strength*. In this novel, Lewis merges the two worlds of Britain and Logres. However, the other two books in the Space Trilogy take place on other planets. In the preface, Lewis writes that the book is subtitled a "fairy tale" because it uses traditional fairy tale techniques, such as "hum-drum scenes and persons."

That Hideous Strength was finished by December 20, 1943, and was published in July 1945, thereby completing the "trilogy"; however, Lewis says it can be read on its own. The book sold well, but Lewis still thought the reviewers and critics hated it, predominantly because they saw the National Institute of Co-ordinated Experiments (N.I.C.E.) as a fantastic absurdity.

When Lewis was in his fifties, he turned to writing children's stories. In autumn 1939, evacuees from London came to Lewis's home to escape the bombing. Lewis notes that he never appreciated children until the war brought them to him. Because he wanted to entertain them and noticed that people weren't writing the kinds of imaginative books he wanted, he decided to write some himself. He thus began making notes for *The Lion, the Witch and the Wardrobe*.

In 1948, Lewis talked about finishing a children's book in the tradition of Edith Nesbit but having a difficult time with it.[66] He had always enjoyed the works of Nesbit and Beatrix Potter. *Squirrel Nutkin*, for example, gave him a glimpse of joy and the sense that something of great importance was being communicated.[67] When he was young, he delighted in fairy tales and fell under the spell of dwarves, desiring marvels and the supernatural.[68] In his letters, Lewis even describes seeing woods and imagining dwarves marching alongside him and longing for a world where this was true.[69]

Lewis began writing his own stories before he was six years old and up until he was twelve. His stories were about a medieval country called Animal-Land. He also created a mythical land called Boxen, for which he systematically recorded its 700-year history and then its geography, complete with detailed maps, steamship routes, and elaborate illustrations. Although we can see how this might have been the embryo of what later would grow into Narnia, Lewis emphasized that none of the Narnian stories or characters was drawn from these childhood tales. Animal-Land only shared anthropomorphic beasts with Narnia. It was "astonishingly prosaic," having no "hint of wonder," poetry, or romance.[70] The stories deal mainly with politics rather than with the more imaginative events and the sense of joy that pervade Narnia.

On March 10, 1949, Lewis read two chapters of the book to Roger Lancelyn Green, who encouraged Lewis to finish the book.[71] Lewis had only this one book in mind, and he says he had no notion of writing any others. A "hazy sequel" only came to mind long after the idea for this book was conceived. *Prince Caspian* (1951) took only six months to complete. Next, *The Voyage of the "Dawn Treader"* (1952) was ready. Lewis liked his first draft of the story, and it came to him quickly and easily; in fact, he wrote it in only three months. He then completed *The Silver Chair* (1953), which also took three months to write. *The Horse and His Boy* (1954) soon followed. Finally, he wrote *The Magician's Nephew* (1955) and *The Last Battle* (1956) simultaneously. At Green's suggestion, the series was called "The Chronicles of Narnia." As a result of his series, Lewis achieved almost instant success. The time lines for both the

Space Trilogy and the Chronicles illustrate the apparent ease and speed with which Lewis wrote, compared to Tolkien's many years of careful writing and revision.

"IT REALLY WON'T DO"

Much has been written about Tolkien's reaction to the Narnia books. In spring 1949, two months after he finished writing it, Lewis read part of the manuscript of *The Lion, the Witch and the Wardrobe* to Tolkien but received a thoroughly unenthusiastic, negative response. He flatly detested the book and thought it unsalvageable—"about as bad as can be."[72] Tolkien told Roger Lanceyln Green, "It really won't do, you know!"[73] Lewis, in turn, was deeply distressed at Tolkien's opinion, not only because he was a valued friend and fellow scholar, but also because it weakened his own confidence in a book he was insecure about. He was "hurt, astonished, and discouraged when Tolkien said that he thought the book was almost worthless."[74]

There are numerous theories as to why Tolkien disapproved. First, Tolkien believed a good book should be written slowly to create a consistent and convincing secondary world. Tolkien seemed annoyed at the swiftness at which Lewis could write, with little revision. In contrast, Tolkien took years to write and he revised endlessly.[75] In fact, Lewis says Tolkien was never satisfied with a manuscript. If someone suggested that Tolkien publish something, he would reply that he needed to look through it, and that meant starting over.[76] Tolkien not only thought the book was hastily written but also that the mythology lacked development and had careless, inconsistent details.[77] For example, if it is always winter, where do Mr. and Mrs. Beaver get their food?

Next, Tolkien told Lewis that there were too many discordant elements, especially Father Christmas. (Roger Lancelyn Green agreed with the Father Christmas criticism.) The book is a blend of Greek, Roman, and Norse mythology, as well as elements from the books of Edith Nesbit, Kenneth Grahame, and Beatrix Potter. Tolkien asked, "'Nymphs and their Ways, the Love-Life of a Fawn.'

Doesn't he know what he's talking about?"[78] He also did not like Lewis's treatment of mythical creatures by sanitizing, sentimentalizing, and misrepresenting their natures.[79] According to George Sayer, Tolkien so "strongly detested" the way Lewis merged mythological characters in the series that he gave up reading them.[80] As a person who adamantly disliked allegory and popular theology, Tolkien believed the Christian meaning in the Narnia books was blatant, especially the allegorical battle between good and evil. He was so unenthusiastic about Lewis's apologetics and Broadcast Talks that he called Lewis an "Everyman's theologian."[81] He felt Lewis was not trained in the theological subjects he was writing and speaking about. Other theories about Tolkien's negative attitude focus on his jealousy of Lewis's success and the fact that Lewis broke their agreement to write for adults rather than children.

Tolkien was more favorable toward *Out of the Silent Planet* because there are numerous philosophical and mythical implications that do not detract from the adventure. He was so "enthralled with the book" that he did nothing else until he finished it. With its underlying myth of the fall of the angels and mankind, the novel is a successful and irresistible blend of *vera historia* and *mythos*.[82] He also describes the language and poetry as well done and interesting.

On the other hand, he had several criticisms. First, to be marketable, a story must pass as the true history of a journey to a strange land, but the novel is too short with inconsistent details. For example, the Pfifltriggi as the third species needs more attention. In addition, the visit to Eldilorn is reached too soon artistically, and there should be more narrative passages in the Malacandran portion to balance the opening and details about the journey. Finally, the narrative style uses "creaking stiff-jointed passages," and the philology is unappealing.[83]

Tolkien worked on a story called the "Notion Club Papers" between 1944 and 1946. It is considered a critique of Lewis's Space Trilogy because it presents the minutes of a group of Oxford dons who meet to discuss Lewis's novels. Tolkien criticizes science fiction writers who use spaceships as devices to convey humans and provide less credibility than if they had a wizard wave a wand. A poor science fiction world is not made credible by using scientific jargon or principles.

Ironically, Lewis uses names loosely based on some of Tolkien's. Lewis heard *The Silmarillion* read aloud and was impressed by it but vaguely remembered names. Tolkien believes the name *Eldila* was based on his *Eldar*, *Numinor* was based on *Númenor*, and that *Tor* and *Tinidril* are echoes of *Tuor* and *Idril*. Some critics believe that Ransom as a philologist was actually based on Tolkien. But Tolkien calls Lewis's actual mythology "different," "incipient and never fully realized."[84] Lewis added a postscript written by Ransom to Lewis himself. Diana Glyer suggests that this postscript essentially contains Tolkien's criticisms of the book.[85] For example, Ransom expresses disappointment with Lewis's manuscript. He criticizes the omission of much of the philology and the eldil speech account of the shutter jamming, as well as two key scenes.

Tolkien also liked *Perelandra* but not *That Hideous Strength*, owing to the influence of Charles Williams on the plot.[86] Colin Duriez believes when Williams joined the Inklings, Tolkien felt neglected by Lewis. Tolkien read many of Williams's books and found them "inpenetrable" and "distasteful"; he was "wholly unsympathetic" to his way of thinking.[87] Tolkien also believed Lewis was too impressionable and thus "bowled over" by Williams. Even after Williams died in 1945, Tolkien and Lewis's friendship never recovered.

Eric Seddon believes that Tolkien's objections to Lewis's Narnia books should be true for the Space Trilogy as well, yet Tolkien did not have as many objections. In a letter, Tolkien mentions that much of Lewis's work was outside his "range of sympathy"—as his was outside Lewis's. The key is Tolkien's attitude toward Lewis's last book, *Letters to Malcolm*, which he calls "distressing" and "in parts horrifying."[88] Seddon concludes that this link explains Tolkien's attitude toward Lewis. Tolkien was not only rejecting Narnia as a work of literature but also rejecting Lewis's feelings about God. According to Seddon, his problems with the book became obvious to Tolkien in 1949 as he examined *Letters to Malcolm* and recognized the "incompatibility of Lewis's subjective Anglicanism with his own objective Catholicism."

Letters to Malcolm is set up as a dialogue with an imaginary partner, Malcolm. By making the book appear to be real correspondence, Lewis is able to comment on controversial subjects and be less subject to criticism. In the book, he attacks Roman Catholicism, thus contrasting his and Tolkien's beliefs. For example, Lewis labels the recitation of prayers learned in childhood a childish practice. Seddon suggests that Tolkien perhaps wondered what happened to the Lewis he had known as a colleague for so many years and who had joined him in fighting the idea that mythopoeic literature should be abandoned when one becomes an adult.

Despite their differences, Tolkien writes that he and Lewis were closest friends from 1927 to 1940, and he was dear to him even after that. However, over the years, Tolkien's dislike of Narnia and Lewis's apologetics contributed to their cooling relationship.[89] In addition, Tolkien believed Lewis's romance with Joy Gresham came between him and his friends. In fact, Tolkien refused to write an obituary for Lewis or to contribute to a memorial volume.[90] But Lewis's death preoccupied Tolkien, and he acknowledged their debt to each other and deep affection.[91] Both Tolkien's daughter Priscilla and his son Christopher consider Tolkien's relationship with Lewis profoundly important.[92]

Although it is evident that Tolkien both encouraged and criticized Lewis's works, Tolkien, in turn, was a major influence on his conversion to Christianity, as well as on his success as a writer. Gareth Knight observes that "in addition to the later impact on his own work, it could be said that without Tolkien there might well have been no C. S. Lewis as Christian apologist and writer of the science or children's fiction!"[93] Their mutual feedback was unquestionably influential on their works, although their actual writing processes differed.

TOLKIEN'S PROCESS

In his letters, Tolkien provides insight into how he wrote. For example, he never deliberately thought out any episode. Rather, he would have an imperfect glimpse of the "thing" in a preliminary outline, and then once he got started, the episode would write itself.[94] A study of Tolkien's manuscripts indicates that he did not use a master plan but rather felt his way along, working out the story by trial and error.[95] According to his son Christopher, Tolkien wrote in stages or "phases," creating rough sketches and then filling in more and more details or making changes.

Tolkien always began writing with a name; it then produced a story. He discovered that legends depend on language and language depends on legends.[96] Essentially, he wrote "backward" by beginning with names and objects, such as the Ring. He would then determine what a name meant or invent a believable world where the object could exist.

Tolkien describes himself as not inventing but waiting until he knew what happened or the book wrote itself.[97] He insisted that stories arose in his mind as "given things." In an interview, Tolkien said, "My stories seem to germinate like a snowflake around a piece of dust."[98] As the "given things" arose in his mind, they would separate, and then links between them grew. He drew some tales fully, and others were sketched.[99] Cycles should be linked to a "majestic whole" but leave room for "other minds and hands, wielding paint and music and drama."[100] The process was a "branching acquisitive theme," a key metaphor for his art, as will be seen later.

He would also meet things and characters along the way that surprised him. For example, the Ents presented themselves as he wrote Book Three Chapter IV without his premeditation or conscious knowledge.[101] When Boromir came along, Tolkien did not "invent" or "want" him.[102] In addition, he was astonished by people and places he "met" on the way, such as Bree, Strider, the Mines of Moria, Lothlórien, Fangorn Forest, Sauron, and the Palantíri.[103]

Tolkien told Clyde Kilby several times that he had been given the story as an answer to prayer.[104] Instead of inventing, he had the sense that events were revealed to or through him.[105] Thus he was simply recording, reporting, or discovering what was already there.[106] Tolkien talked about his book as a chronology of actual events rather than fiction and himself as a historian.[107] In fact, he believed he was "meant" to write the story in the same way that Frodo was "meant" to have the Ring.[108] Furthermore, he refers to the Writer of the Story as someone other than himself.[109] It is not surprising, then, that when Tolkien was visited in Oxford by a man who asked him if he really thought he had written the entire book by himself, Tolkien replied that he no longer supposed so.[110]

Once he completed *The Lord of the Rings*, he did not believe it belonged to him; rather, it had "been brought forth" and "must go its appointed way in the world."[111] The work, which he typed several times himself and was seven feet high, was written in his "lifeblood."[112] He wrote to his publisher that he desired the work to be published because solitary art is not art, and it is important to complete one's work.[113]

LEWIS'S PROCESS

Lewis used a different writing process than Tolkien. Material for a story formed in his mind by beginning as "mental pictures."[114] All his fiction, including *The Chronicles of Narnia* and three science fiction books, began with pictures in his head. He didn't know how or why they came, but he wrote stories about them.[115] Then ideas began to "bubble up" into story form.[116] His plans for books lay in drawers; later, he would come across an idea and realize he could write the story.[117] Like Tolkien, he would return to stories he had begun earlier, for much of his best work was rewriting things he had abandoned years before.[118] Lewis almost never wrote more than one draft of his novels, and then he would write rapidly.[119] However, he would make revisions, most notably to *The Magician's Nephew* and *That Hideous Strength*.

The Lion, the Witch and the Wardrobe began with a picture of a Faun carrying an umbrella and parcels in a snowy wood and a queen on a sledge. Lewis had this picture in his mind since he was about sixteen; then when he was forty, he decided to try writing a story about it. At first, he had little idea where the story would go until Aslan came bounding into it. He didn't know where the Lion came from except that he had been having nightmares about lions.[120] Once Aslan was there, he pulled not only this story together but also the other six Narnia stories.[121]

Lewis's works began as pictures but later developed as an expression of his worldview. In "Sometimes Fairy Stories May Say Best What's to Be Said," Lewis describes two sides of the writer: the Author and the Man. The Author writes to release his creative impulse, beginning with an image and then longing for the appropriate form. The Man then enters, desiring to direct the writing toward some end: to please, instruct, or communicate. Lewis claims he never began a book with a message or moral and then invented the story to explain it because he couldn't work like that. Instead, he discovered the moral by writing the story.[122] After the stories began with pictures coming into his head, the thoughts accompanied the writing. For example, *Perelandra* is about the fall resulting from an avoidable free act of sin; *That Hideous Strength* is about scientific ethics.[123] *Perelandra* began with a mental picture of floating islands with no story or location. Then Lewis created a world where they could exist. It was not created with a didactic purpose; the averted fall later came into the story.

According to Lewis, he never "made" a story. Rather, he compares the process to bird watching. The images always come first. Some of them have a common flavor or smell, which groups them. A set might join to create a complete story. But because there are usually gaps, the author needs to deliberately invent things to explain why characters are where they are doing certain things.[124] Inventions take hold of the pictures that arise from somewhere and then connect them to build a "thing."[125]

The writer has a "plastic impulse" to make something and give it shape: "unity, relief, contrast, pattern."[126] The "ferment" of bubbling mental pictures leads nowhere unless it is accompanied by "the longing for a Form." This form may be verse, prose, short story, novel, or play, and it determines the shape or pattern of events and the work's effect. For example, a poem has both thought and form: "The matter inside the poet *wants* the form: in submitting to the Form it becomes really original, really the origin of great work."[127] When the bubbling and the form click, the impulse is complete.[128]

Lewis always distinguishes between content and form, and the form must contain Truth. Lewis uses his description of his artistic

Figure 1.1 Lewis's writing process

process to defend criticism of his Narnia books as presenting Christianity to children under the guise of fairy tales. Some imagined that he researched child psychology, picked an age group, listed Christian truths, and then hammered out allegories to embody them. Lewis calls this "pure moonshine." As shown in Figure 1.1, the images came first. There wasn't even anything Christian about them at first; rather, that element pushed itself in as part of the bubbling. The images then sorted themselves into events to become a story. Next came the form—the fairy tale—because it seemed ideal "for the stuff I had to say."[129] He wanted a form that would bridge the gap between the supernatural and the realm of experience. The form that both he and Tolkien chose was based on the fairy tale tradition, as described in the next chapter.

2

Art

In their essays and letters, Tolkien and Lewis describe their views about the value and purpose of fairy tales and fantasy. This chapter reviews each author's opinions about the fairy tale form and the appropriate audience, as well as their attitudes toward the science fiction genre. It also presents their definitions of terms such as *fantasy*, *imagination*, and *sub-creation*.

TOLKIEN ON FAIRY TALES

Many of Tolkien's theories about fantasy that essentially describe his own works are found in his essay "On Fairy Stories," which was presented as the Andrew Lang Lecture on March 8, 1938, at the University of St. Andrews. It was eventually expanded and published in *Essays Presented to Charles Williams*. This essay is both a major contribution to theories about fantasy literature and a framework for understanding his writing. Even Tolkien himself believed it is an important work.[1]

Tolkien writes that he loved fairy stories ever since he could read but never studied them. One of his goals was to defend fairy tales against the theories of folklorists, philologists, and anthropologists. The philological and anthropological studies of fairy tales attempted to explain their barbarities such as cannibalism, murder, and incest. For example, Max Müller attributed these elements to changes in words and meaning. Calling mythology a "disease of language," Müller believed mythological gods derived from celestial events and eventually became stories. Andrew Lang attributed fairy tales to totemism and ritual of primitive tribes. Ancient mythic heroes became the heroes of epic poetry, then characters in fairy tales, thus devolving into a "lower mythology."

It was widely believed that folktales and myths were derived from nature myths. For example, the Norse gods were personifications of elements in nature; these are really allegories, says Tolkien. Eventually, epics and legends made these stories localized by using real places and heroic men. Finally, these legends became nursery tales. For Tolkien, nature myths and allegories are uninteresting. In contrast, he affirms the value of the fairy tale genre and its effect on today's readers. In fact, a theme throughout Tolkien's works is man's trivialization of and disrespect for fairy tales and legends.

In his essay, Tolkien describes fairy stories rather than defining what they are. They tell of Faërie, a realm or state where fairies live. But they are not about the small creatures traditionally called fairies. He especially dislikes fairy tales such as Michael Drayton's "Nymphidia," a dull story with "fluttering sprites," "prettiness," and a palace with walls of spider's legs. Rather, most stories are about mankind's adventures in the "Perilous Realm" and the air that blows there.[2] Here Tolkien uses the Romantic metaphor of the wind as a creative power that is felt but not seen.

Throughout the essay, Tolkien lists many of the things that Faërie contains: elves, fays, dwarves, witches, trolls, giants, dragons, stepmothers, and mortal men; the sun, moon, stars, sky, and earth; trees, birds, water, and food; beauty, joy, and sorrow; and "mortal men, when we are enchanted." It contains beauty that is both enchanted and perilous, and "both joy and sorrow as sharp as swords."[3]

In Faërie there is also enchantment or magic. Enchantment (casting under a spell) is what primarily distinguishes fairy stories from other types of tales such as traveler's tales, dream stories, or beast fables. Fairy tales are appealing because of their age and because they free us from time. Successful fantasy allows the reader to go into another time outside our own, or even outside Time itself.[4]

A major element of fairy tales is prohibition. For example, a locked door is an eternal temptation. These prohibitions have been preserved in tales because of their significance. In "The Ethics of Elfland," G. K. Chesterton describes this element as the Doctrine of Conditional Joy. Fairy tales always contain an "if": You may do this *if* you do not do that. All "wild and whirling" things depend upon one forbidden thing. "In the fairy tale an incomprehensible happiness rests upon an incomprehensible condition. . . . An apple is eaten, and the hope of God is gone."[5]

Tolkien then describes the complicated history of the development of fairy tales. The web of a story is affected by the author's independent *invention*, as well as *inheritance* (borrowing in time) and *diffusion* (borrowing in space).[6] Tolkien identifies three elements that fairy tales may focus on: Nature, the Supernatural, and Man. These three "faces" of fairy tales vary depending upon the teller. The essential face of Faërie is the Magical toward Nature. The focus of this face is what Tolkien calls Recovery, regaining a clear view of the world. The Mystical toward the Supernatural is the face of fantasy that provides "eucatastrophe," the sense of joy. The Mirror of Scorn and Pity toward Man mocks mankind and is often seen in beast fables and dystopias, which Tolkien does not consider true fantasy (Figure 2.1).

Tolkien compares fairy tales to a cauldron of soup. The soup contains dainty and undainty bits of history, folktales, legends, myths, and other tales or things the author remembers. Cooks add to this soup and dip in their ladles, carefully selecting what they want. Although the essence of the soup remains the same, the flavor and ingredients change with cultures and readers. Thus it is difficult to determine their origin. He also compares a story to a tapestry. While you can unravel single threads, you cannot analyze the effect of all

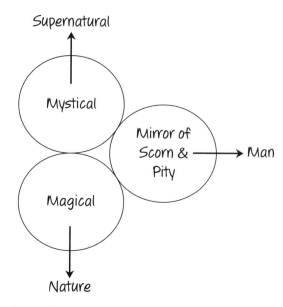

Figure 2.1 Three elements of focus for fairy tales

the threads as a whole tapestry. The picture is greater than the sum of the parts.

LEWIS AND THE FAIRY TALE FORM

In his letters, but especially in the essays collected in *On Stories and Other Essays on Literature*, Lewis presents some of his views on fairy tales and writing for children. He also refers to Tolkien's essay "On Fairy Stories," which he calls one of the most significant works on the subject.

Lewis claims he is not "representing" the real (Christian) story in symbols; instead, he chose fairy tales as the form for his stories because they don't lend themselves to analysis. Lewis writes, "I am not quite sure what made me, in a particular year of my life, feel that not only a fairy tale, but a fairy tale addressed to children, was exactly what I must write—or burst."[7]

However, in other writings, he gives several reasons for choosing this genre. First, it was the form that best fitted what he had to say and that ideas and images in his mind demanded.[8] He did not ask children what they wanted and adapt stories to them; instead, the "imaginative man" in Lewis led him to use the fairy tale genre because it fitted his ideas.[9] Lewis observes that fairy tales already have the Spirit in them. For example, "Cinderella" illustrates exalting the humble while "Sleeping Beauty" illustrates Redemption.[10]

The only real effect this form had on his style was on the level of his vocabulary, lack of erotic love or analytical passages, and composition of chapters of almost equal length for reading aloud. His style is remarkably clear and vivid, like that of many fairy stories. For example, who can forget the many long-awaited meals the Pevensie children sit down to eat, like the "nice brown eggs, lightly boiled . . . sardines on toast, and then buttered toast, and then toast with honey, and then a sugar topped cake." Lewis also gives us the tiniest details, down to the dead bluebottle on the windowsill or the slight blister on Susan's heel.

According to Lewis, fairy tales are well-known for having the following common elements:[11]

- Begin with "Once upon a time"
- Are set in a castle, forest, or town
- Portray clearly defined good and bad characters and royalty
- Include giants, elves, talking animals, witches, and fairies
- Contain magic
- Use numbers such as three or seven
- Have a problem that is solved, with the good side winning
- Teach a lesson or moral
- End with "they lived happily ever after"

In addition, Lewis identifies several distinct advantages of fairy tales:[12]

- Can be brief, by both permitting and compelling the author to leave things out
- Require a limited vocabulary, little description, and chapters of equal length
- Cannot be analyzed

- Cut down on reflective, expository, digressive, and descriptive passages
- Concentrate on action and conversation
- Can be both general and concrete
- Make experience palpable
- Give new experiences
- Add to life
- Are flexible and traditional

AUDIENCE

Both Tolkien and Lewis affirm that fairy stories are not only for a child audience. The association of fairy stories with children was accidental.[13] In fact, they were not originally intended for any particular audience.[14] Unfortunately, stories were relegated to the nursery like old furniture because adults didn't want them or like them.[15] If fairy stories are left in the nursery, they can become ruined, just like good furniture or paintings.

Fairy tales were first told orally based on rituals and were intended to explain natural events. In the fifteenth century, the printing press and increased literacy created changes in the fairy tale form and themes. Late seventeenth-century French writers made tales appropriate for the aristocracy by focusing on appropriate social behavior. Literary fairy tales were first written and published for adults. Because they were symbolic and contained "subversive" language and themes, they were not approved for children. At the end of the eighteenth to early nineteenth century, fairy tales were published for children but still considered vulgar. Some were "sanitized" versions of adult tales; others were "moralistic." By the end of the nineteenth century, fairy tales became less communal and presented the individual author's values. For example, the Brothers Grimm used tales to present German culture.

Victorian writers wrote tales for private reading by the elite.[16] Fairy tales and children's literature of the Victorian period are noted as well for their moralizing. Charles Kingsley's *The Water-Babies* (1863), for example, includes sermons in the narrative. Tom, a chimney sweep, turns into a river creature and learns moral lessons through characters such as Mrs. Bedonebyasyoudid. Kingsley tried to make both children and adults recognize the "miraculous and divine element underlying all physical nature" and "wrapped up" his "parable in seeming Tom-fooleries" to "get the pill swallowed."[17]

In the nineteenth century, a magical quality was reborn in children's fantasy. Up to this time, children's books had been seen as instructional and moral, whereas fairy tales were seen as foolish lies. Matthew Arnold was one of the earliest opponents of religious fairy tales and the writing of MacDonald in particular, calling for an emphasis on conduct. Consequently, there was a need for the rise of fantasy in "de-mythologized" England, as Chesterton calls it. According to Stephen Prickett, the Romantic period influenced children's fantasy in the nineteenth century by reviving "religious mysticism and a renewed feeling for the numinous—the irrational and mysterious elements in religious experience."[18]

Tolkien calls modern attitudes about fairy stories and children "contemporary delusions." While people treat children as a separate race, fairy stories should not be associated only with children. Instead, both children and adults can like fairy tales because of personal taste. Fairy tales are actually an adult genre for which a "starving audience" exists.[19] A fairy story worth reading "is worthy to be written for and read by adults."[20] They can be read by either audience as a legitimate type of literature. Liking fairy tales can begin in childhood and actually increase with age. So growing up does not mean losing innocence and wonder. Furthermore, children are not a "class" but immature people who vary in tastes and abilities. The author thus cannot limit the reader's vocabulary, because he or she needs to challenge gifted readers by extending their reach.[21] Tolkien also cautions not to write down to the audience; at any age, we are moved by works "above our measure."[22] For example, in his children's story *Roverandom*, Tolkien uses words such as *paraphernalia* and *phosphorescent*, as well as puns and literary allusions.

Both Tolkien and Lewis agree that one's enjoyment of fairy tales is affected by taste rather than age. When Lewis was ten, he read fairy tales in secret and would have been ashamed if he had been caught. But when he was fifty, he read them openly: "When I became a man I put away childish things, including the fear of childishness and the desire to be very grown up."[23] As an adult, he still liked books he read as a child (although his imagination was asleep during the desert teen years).[24] Similarly, readers may go through stages when they are first attracted to fairy tales, then ashamed of reading them, and finally perhaps return to them as adults. In the dedication to Lucy Barfield in *The Lion, the Witch and the Wardrobe*, Lewis writes, "Some day you will be old enough to start reading fairy tales again."

Tolkien classifies his own works as fairy stories, not because of the child audience but because that's the kind of story he wanted to write.[25] While he did not write *The Hobbit* with the intent of addressing children, he was influenced by the tradition of directing fairy stories to children. This convention was also a result of his making up stories for his own children. Because he wrote it in a hurry, there were unfortunate results in his style. In contrast, he wrote *The Lord of the Rings* with more consideration and did not address it to children or any other specific audience. In fact, he had no interest in writing for children or for any kind of person, only writing "for itself." If the book is childish, it is because he is childish, he says. He actually describes *The Lord of the Rings* as a long, complex, bitter, terrifying romance, a monster "quite unfit for children."[26]

In *An Experiment in Criticism*, Lewis defends fairy tales by arguing that children are not deceived by them. Some forbid fairy tales because they deceive readers by giving a false picture of life. Rather, it is realistic stories that are confusing and improbable because they may give the reader false expectations. Such stories are "contrived to put across some social or ethical or religious or anti-religious 'comment on life.'"[27] In contrast, no one expects life to be like fairy stories. Tolkien believes that children are more interested in a story's Truth, such as whether a character is good or wicked, rather than whether the story really happened.[28]

According to G. K. Chesterton, *make-believe* is a misleading term. A child is not deceived or confused by words such as *fact*, *fable*, and *falsehood* but knows the difference between reality and fiction: "This is the beginning of all sane art criticism. Wonder combined with the complete serenity of the conscience in the acceptance of such wonders."[29] He feels children would make up such things for themselves even if they had no fairy tales. Lewis notes that a number of mothers and teachers believed *The Lion, the Witch and the Wardrobe* would frighten children. But children liked it, very young ones understood it, and few children were frightened by it.[30] Violence in fairy tales will not cause children fear: "Let there be wicked kings and beheadings, battles and dungeons, giants and dragons, and let villains be soundly killed at the end of the book."[31] Along with terrible characters, there are comforters and protectors. Narnia contains ogres, spirits, cruels, hags, incubuses, wraiths, horrors, efreets, sprites, orknies, wooses, ettins, ghouls, boggles, minotaurs, spectres, people of the toadstools, and other creatures. The narrator refuses to describe them because if he did "the grown-ups would probably not let you read this book."

Fairy tales do not produce fear in a child or the idea of evil or the ugly: "The fear does not come from the fairy tales, the fear comes from the universe of the soul."[32] These things are in the child already because they are in the world. But they do give the child a clear idea of the possible defeat of evil, a Saint George to kill the dragon he has already had in his imagination. When the child sees brave heroes, he learns that terrors have a limit and "that there is something in the universe more mystical than darkness, and stronger than strong fear."[33]

Instead of being banned, Lewis reasons, fairy tales should be required reading. For example, Lewis was surprised that a five-year-old visitor named Michael had never been read to or told a story. He feared the child's poor imagination had essentially been starved. He also wondered what that generation of children would grow up like without fairy tales or nursery rhymes.[34] Madeleine L'Engle writes that even today, children are taught about the tangible world—called the "real" and "practical"—but that there has been no emphasis on imagination (fantasy, myth, fairy tale), which will give Truth.[35] Lewis suggests that the fantastic or mythical can be used for readers of all ages and has the power to be both general and concrete, as well as present "whole classes of experience" and experiences we never had before. Instead of just commenting on life, it can add to it.[36]

It is no wonder, then, that a theme running throughout the Narnia books is the importance of reading the right kinds of books, such as those that feed the imagination and contain adventure. Some children, like Shasta (*The Horse and His Boy*), read no books at all. Children like Eustace (*The Voyage of the "Dawn Treader"*) read the wrong kinds of books. At his school, for example, Eustace reads only books of information with "pictures of grain elevators or of fat foreign children doing exercises in model schools." They discuss "exports and imports and governments and drains" in great detail but say little about dragons. Because Eustace has read none of the right books, he has no idea what a dragon is and consequently must turn into one before he learns. And because he has no idea how to tell a story straight, Eustace even has difficulty in describing his experience.

GOOD FAIRY TALES

Lewis identifies three ways of writing for children:[37]

- Give them what they want.
- Write as if the story were told by an adult to a child.
- Use a children's story as the best form for what you have to say.

He also identifies two kinds of writers for children. One treats them as a distinct race and literary species by writing what they believe children like. But children do not have common literary taste and may like the same types of works as adults. The other and best kind of writers use the common human ground they share with children and countless adults.[38]

A good story, says Lewis, should not be written "down" as if told to a child. When he wrote the Narnia tales, he did not begin by first asking what children want and then trying to dish it out to them. Instead, the author should use the same rules to write for either adults or younger audiences, speaking to the reader simply as one person speaking to another. Because only poor stories are enjoyed just by children, a good work should not be written for one audience.[39] "No book is really worth reading at the age of ten which is not equally (and far more) worth reading at the age of fifty—except, of course, books of information."[40]

Lewis wrote for children only in the sense that he omitted things they would not like or understand. Although he thought they would unconsciously understand the theology, the many letters he received from children indicated that they saw it more clearly than many adults.[41] Lewis uses *The Hobbit* as an example of what is considered a children's book only because children can read and enjoy it. However, years later, after reading it multiple times, the reader can truly appreciate the Truth, scholarship, and reflection behind it.[42]

Lewis accuses critics who think the term *adult* is a term of approval of being concerned about being grown up and afraid to be childish. They pity a 53-year-old man like himself who cherishes dwarves, giants, talking animals, and witches because he suffers from "arrested development" rather than perpetual youth.[43] Instead, Lewis reasons, we should grow by adding a taste for new things, not by losing old pleasures like fairy stories. As Lewis says in *The Silver Chair*, "Even in this world, of course, it is the stupidest children who are most childish and the stupidest grownups who are most grown-up."

There is a difference between being "childlike" and "childish." For example, George MacDonald, whose own stories influenced the Narnia tales, claims he wrote not for children but rather for the "childlike, whether of five, or fifty, or seventy-five."[44] Similarly, Madeleine L'Engle believes only the most mature can be childlike, which involves memory—not forgetting "any part of ourselves."[45] *Childish* is not a bad term if it means keeping one's curiosity, imagination, ability to suspend disbelief, and wonder. One should never lose a taste for marvels and adventures.

SCIENCE FICTION

In *An Experiment in Criticism*, Lewis judges books by the way people read them. Science fiction and fantasy, he observes, can appeal to different types of audiences. Fantasy and science fiction differ basically in that rational, instead of supernatural, explanation is used in the latter. Science fiction traditionally is distinguished from other types of fantasy in that it is more limited by the laws of science or what might be scientifically feasible in the future. Thus "magical" occurrences must be given rational explanation.

Lewis identifies different types of science fiction:

- Science fiction as a backdrop for a story (the fiction of Displaced Persons). Lewis observes that some science fiction is about technology, satire, myth, or planets used as a backdrop for a story that could just as well have taken place elsewhere. He dislikes science fiction writers who take an ordinary story about spies, shipwrecks, or gangsters and put it in another world setting.[46]
- Stories interested in possibilities, how things might be done (the fiction of Engineers), space travel, or other undiscovered techniques. An example of this type of book is Jules Verne's *20,000 Leagues Under the Sea*.
- Scientific but speculative fiction. With the rise of realism throughout the eighteenth and nineteenth centuries, only external, perceivable reality was considered important. The division of phenomena into the natural and real versus the supernatural gave rise to "sentimental" and "speculative" fiction. Speculative fiction considers what a certain planet or experience is like. It is a reaction to realism, treating the supernatural as real and establishing enough history and background to make the supernatural credible. The power of the supernatural impels the story: "In the primary world, the existence and activity of such powers are a matter of religious faith," whereas in the "fantasy's secondary world, their existence and activity are subject to

material proof."[47] An example of speculative fiction is H. G. Wells's *The First Men in the Moon* (1901), which Lewis claims was the best of this sort he had read and Wells's best novel.[48] Although he praises the "pure fantasy" of these novels, Lewis criticizes the sermonizing and didacticism.[49] But Wells's story, which has much in common with *Out of the Silent Planet*, was inspiration for Lewis's book.

Lewis was not interested in the scientific side of his own planetary novels or following the typical trends of science fiction.[50] Thus he used enough popular astronomy in his stories to create in the "common reader" a "willing suspension of disbelief."[51] Another difference is that traditional writers of science fiction seem always to show aliens as monsters or ogres and terrestrial invaders as good and ever in the right. For Lewis, his trilogy began the trend of showing the opposite to be true.[52]

- Stories about the future, such as the destiny of our species. Here Lewis found the greatest influences on his own books. What spurred him to write was Olaf Stapledon's *Last and First Men* (1930) and an essay in J. B. S. Haldane's *Possible Worlds* (1927), both of which have the "immoral outlook" he tries to pillory in Weston. He liked the interplanetary idea as a mythology and wanted to use his Christian viewpoint instead of the opposite point of view, which had usually been used.[53]
- Fantasy stories about not only space travel but also "gods, ghosts, ghouls, demons, fairies, monsters, etc." This type of science fiction can do the following:[54]
  - Represent the intellect free from emotion
  - Present the moral without didacticism
  - Present the marvelous, thereby adding to life

This last type of science fiction was most desirable to Lewis because it is necessary only to provide "superficial plausibility" rather than probability. Lewis describes his "planetary romances" as the "exorcism" of his "fierce curiosity" subject to his imaginative impulses.[55] Strange worlds require only wonder, beauty, or suggestiveness. For example, he placed canals on Mars even though science had proved they don't exist.[56] While *Out of the Silent Planet* has no factual basis, Lewis uses science fiction as a form for imaginative purposes and to provide a "Christian critique of our age."[57] The only details Lewis includes about the means of space travel are that Weston, Devine, and Ransom journey for twenty-eight days in a spherical metallic spaceship with crystal and wire instruments. Because the center is always down in this sphere, the floor you are standing on feels flat and horizontal, and the wall you lean against feels vertical. In *Perelandra*, Ransom is simply transported in a white coffin moved by the Oyarsa in a sort of state of suspended animation.

After World War II when attitudes toward science changed, there was a shift in emphasis in science fiction, and it began to consider religious themes. It is an ideal form to deal with such ideas because it is, by nature, more interested in concepts such as the future of mankind or ethical implications of science. It is thus a natural genre in which to speculate about religion on other planets or in the future. Madeleine L'Engle writes that she seeks theological insights in science fiction because the genre is suited to exploring "the nature of the Creator and creation" and because thinking about other worlds and modes of being is a "theological enterprise."[58]

Although Lewis was influenced by H. G. Wells, Olaf Stapledon, J. B. S. Haldane, and Rider Haggard, the "father" of his Space Trilogy was David Lindsay. *Voyage to Arcturus* combines two types of fiction: that of Novalis and George MacDonald with H. G. Wells and Jules Verne. While Lewis describes the style as appalling, a "ghastly vision comes through." In this novel, Lindsay expresses the idea that the Creator is the Devil and therefore all creation is evil and an illusion. Only the soul is good in some way. Tolkien describes the book as more "powerful" and "mythical" than *Out of the Silent Planet*, but it contains more religion and morals in it than story.[59]

Lindsay was the first writer to use other planets in fiction effectively, showing Lewis that other planets are good for *spiritual* adventures and that he could combine "scientification" with the supernatural.[60] Tormance is "a region of the spirit." Lewis writes: "The idea of other planets exercised upon me then a peculiar, heady attraction."[61] In science fiction containing other planets and stars, Lewis found an ideal genre for depicting beauty and awe unlike that found in our world.[62]

However, to give readers the sense of "otherness," the writer cannot simply use the strange or distant: "To construct plausible and moving 'other worlds' you must draw on the only real 'other world' we know, that of the spirit."[63] In addition, Lewis firmly advises that the writer should never break the spell or bring the reader back to earth with a "bump." Instead, he should make the reader feel instead of simply telling him, as well as make something "happen" once the reader has gotten to the other world.[64]

Lewis expresses irritation with people (in Interplanetary Societies) who take fantasy as 100 percent real and possible in this world.[65] For this reason, many have argued that Lewis's books are not properly science fiction at all. Science fiction, after all, is usually defined as a projection of what science knows or where theories may lead, whereas Lewis admittedly was uninterested in scientific accuracy. Still, he considers science fiction important because it can deal with key issues, such as human destiny, far more seriously and effectively than "realistic" fiction can.

Morality is also important, and this is a key issue for both Tolkien and Lewis. In modern science fiction stories, Lewis observes, alien species usually accept science but are devoid of moral standards. The implication is that scientific thought is objective and universal, but morality is not.[66] Popular thought tends to distinguish between scientific and moral or metaphysical thought. The former is believed to "put us in touch with reality," whereas the latter does not. And certainly his books, whatever the genre, fulfill that goal. Eventually, Lewis became less interested in science fiction because he believed one could not find out the really interesting things about planets and solar systems.[67] Instead, he turned to the fairy tale form.

In "On Fairy Stories," Tolkien distinguishes science fiction from fantasy by simply showing man on other planets building more

towns like those on earth and then continuing to play with mecha-
nized toys. While he read science fiction and fantasy, he found that
modern books did not hold his attention. However, he read all of
E. R. Eddison's works and describes them as some of the best
invented worlds. Eddison was a member of the Inklings for about
two years. But Tolkien disliked his characters and invented names.[68]
Two science fiction authors he did enjoy were Isaac Asimov and
Mary Renault.[69]

FANTASY

Tolkien considers fairy stories one of the highest forms of art
because they can create images not found in the primary world.[70]
What are the values and functions of these tales?

Fantasy, or the fantastic, he defines as freedom from observed fact
or the primary world.[71] It is both Sub-creative Art and its Expression derived from the Image; it has a quality of strangeness and wonder that is essential in fairy stories. "We make because we are made
in the image and likeness of a Maker."[72] Fantasy is thus "a natural
human activity."

Fancy is image making; it is analogous to understanding and is a
form of memory freed from space and time.

Imagination is analogous to reason and the power of image-
making.

Art is the link between imagination and its final result, *sub-creation*, which gives the "inner consistency of reality."[73] It produces
Secondary Belief (Figure 2.2).

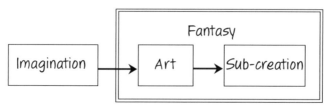

Figure 2.2 The relationship among imagination, fantasy, art, and sub-
creation

While Tolkien provides definitions of these terms, Lewis defines different types of fantasy and what he means by imagination. Lewis apparently believed much of Tolkien's theory of sub-creation and recommended "On Fairy Stories" to those who asked him about his own fantasy.[74]

First, there is a difference between *literary* and *psychological* fantasy. Literary fantasy is a narrative that is about "impossibles and preternaturals."[75] Psychological fantasy, on the other hand, is an imaginative construction that may or may not be mistaken for reality. If it is mistaken for reality, it is *morbid castle-building*. If it is imaginative construction used moderately and briefly, it is *normal castle-building*. This type of fantasy is either egoistic or disinterested, depending upon whether or not the day-dreamer is the hero. If an unliterary reader reads fantasy for egoistic castle-building, then he will dislike it because he demands superficial realism.[76]

Lewis also distinguishes between *realism of content* and *realism of presentation*. Lewis praises literary works that combine both morality and strong religious principles with fullness of presentation. For example, George MacDonald's fantasy hovers between allegory and myth. According to Lewis, if a reader wants "egoistic castle building," he will dislike the fantastic because events cannot really happen.[77] "Realism of Presentation" can be found in stories that are not "realistic." This technique makes something palpable and vivid by using "sharply imagined detail." For example, in *Beowulf*, the dragon is described as "sniffing along the stone."[78] The writer, Lewis suggests, must not rely on adjectives or adverbs but rather must make the reader feel. The art lies in "making us believe we have imagined the unimaginable."[79]

IMAGINATION

Lewis identifies the purpose of imagination as helping us understand others and respond to or produce art. However, it should not be a substitute for virtues or successes that should be sought in the real world.[80]

Lewis's "Great War" with his friend Owen Barfield was a written debate about whether imagination can be a vehicle of Truth.

Tolkien's view of sub-creation was strongly influenced by Barfield's book *Poetic Diction*. The thesis of his book is that poetic language comes from the nature of language and the poetic imagination. Thus by studying language, we can understand the evolution of human consciousness. Barfield believed certain kinds of metaphors can provide a material image with immaterial content. They can expand the reader's consciousness, thus providing new knowledge about the world. Studying the history of words similarly reveals that words that once had one fused meaning have now become abstract, splitting their meanings and reflecting man's split from nature. In the past, words had both literal and metaphorical meanings that were not separated. The evolution of language and consciousness are consequently parallel.

Both Lewis and Owen Barfield agreed that imagination is the source of meaning.[81] Lewis writes that "reason is the natural organ of truth; but imagination is the organ of meaning. Imagination, producing new metaphors or revivifying old, is not the cause of truth, but its condition."[82] Because the imagination works on material from the senses, the mind can never perceive an object until the imagination has worked on it. Cognition synthesizes percept (sense-datum) and concept (what the person brings to sense-datum), thus creating the world of experience and participating in the cosmic Intelligence. Language is a source of knowledge because concepts are inseparable from language. Knowledge involves recognizing relationships, which is expressed in metaphor.

In his essay "The Harp and the Camera," Barfield uses two metaphors derived from inventions of seventeenth-century German Jesuit Athanasius Kircher. Kircher invented both the wind harp—strings in a box that the wind blows through— and the camera obscura— a box with an aperture and mirror. The harp's medium is air, which is both inside and outside us. It is thus similar to inspiration. The camera's medium is light, which does not enter the body. The camera can only present a replica or internal reproduction of the world. Thus the Aeolian wind harp is an "emblem" for the Romantic movement, and the camera is an "emblem" for the Renaissance. These two symbols contrast two types of perception: inspiration and a caricature of imagination. Barfield asks, "Is it fanciful . . . to think of a sort of mini-harp stretched across the window of the eye—an Apollo's harp if you will—as perhaps not a bad image for the joy of looking with imagination?"[83] He identifies this joy with the Joy Lewis spent his life searching for.

The Aeolian harp was also used by Novalis, the German poet, who compares it to the Märchen or adult fairy tale: "A fairy story is like a disjointed dream-vision, an ensemble of wonderful things and occurrences, for example, a musical fantasy, the harmonic sequences of an Aeolian harp, nature itself." George MacDonald, in turn, uses this passage as the motto for his book *Phantastes*, which influenced Lewis. Barfield says that the "Romantic theologians" Tolkien, Lewis, and Williams wrote about the place of myth, imagination, and Märchen today. They show that writers of myth are both signing their own names, as well as the name of "the Author and Lord of the archetypes themselves."[84]

Both Barfield and Tolkien were influenced by Samuel Taylor Coleridge's theories about imagination. Coleridge recognized imagination's role in constructing the physical world. That is why he distinguished between primary and secondary imagination. *Primary imagination* is involuntary, whereas the *secondary imagination* is the act of the will. The primary imagination half perceives and half creates the physical world. The secondary imagination is more sophisticated but uses the same kind of operation.[85] Besides inventing new words, metaphor invents meaning. In fact, any new use of a word is metaphor because it arouses our cognition of the unknown by using the known.[86] The poet "creates and recreates by the magic of new combinations. . . . Thus, the poet's relation to terms is that of maker."[87]

Lewis cautions that imagination is not the presence of mental images; rather, they are pointers to something that can only be communicated by similes and metaphors.[88] Likewise, thinking is a different process from imagining because whatever we think or say is different from our mental picture. And mental images are always different from the real thing.[89] The act of imagination is the cause; a mental picture is the result. But they begin at the same time.[90] Real imagining can come only when images come quickly and are then dropped: "If any one of them becomes static and grows too clear and full, imagination proper is inhibited."[91]

In his Great War debate with Owen Barfield about imagination, Lewis wonders whether the valuable state is the "image-less and wordless state before the images come."[92] Mental images helped Lewis most when they were "fugitive and fragmentary—rising and bursting like bubbles in champagne or wheeling like rooks in a windy sky." If you hone in on one of them, it dies.[93] Lewis contrasts the image-making faculty and its uses by the Holy Spirit in visions, dreams, wishes, and hallucinations.[94] In contrast, the inventive faculty is seen in *hom faber*, or man the toolmaker. This faculty creates things from any plastic material, including stone, metal, wood, cloth, memory, and imagination, inside or outside the mind.[95]

Tolkien describes how literature works as pictures in the mind. For example, if a writer says "hill" or "river," a reader will picture it himself out of all hills or rivers he has seen and the one that first embodied the word.[96] Fantasy is thus best as literature rather than painting or drama. The latter are visual presentations and thus offer only one form. Drama, for example, relies on the visual and a substitute magic rather than letting the imagination create images. But literature is more universal. When, for instance, Pauline Baynes, who illustrated many of Tolkien's and Lewis's books, asked Tolkien about some details, Tolkien replied that the "inwardly seen picture" was most important to him.[97]

What is the value of imagination? For both writers, art and imagination are an act of worship and a path to understanding God. Lewis believes the artist's duty is to lavishly create, because if he invents a world, he is worshipping God more effectively than a realist analyzing the external world.[98] While God sends beauty into nature, it will perish unless man appreciates it through worship, which sends it back to God.[99] Each individual was created to worship God by communicating a unique vision.[100]

Part of man is not nature and therefore unsatisfied by it. Reason is inadequate to perceive the spirituality of real things.[101] But the symbols of imagination can present super-intelligible reality.[102] To talk about things not perceived by the senses, however, we must use metaphors and mental images.[103] While Heaven is beyond our experience, descriptions must be within our experience. Thus descriptions must be symbolic; even the Scripture uses imagery.[104]

Lewis coins the term *transposition* to describe the restatement of ideas in news terms, just as piano music can be transposed into a new key for other instruments. It is an attempt to take a lower medium and try to express the transcendent and supernatural. For example, we can draw pictures of sun or snow, but if properly done, they can give the sensation of sunshine or cold. Thus images can provide some expression of the supernatural.[105]

SUB-CREATION

Tolkien calls the highest form of creativity *sub-creation*. Fancy and imagination are linked through art and made manifest in sub-creation: "making immediately effective by the will the visions of 'fantasy.'"[106] The will is the link between the indestructible mind and being and the realization of the imagination. In so doing, it uses up the spirit's energy.[107] The will's function is freedom from the "channels" God the creator has already used.[108] However, it is also a tribute to the variety and infinite possibilities of God's works. Coleridge similarly writes that the power of imagination is first put into action by the "will and understanding" and kept under their control. It balances or reconciles "opposite or discordant qualities."[109]

Tolkien says the mind can form mental images of things not present. It then arranges the images into a form and gives them an "inner consistency of reality." If the writer has achieved this consistency, then all the details of the secondary world are either derived from reality or flow into it. The form is *secondary world fantasy*. Because it can create images not found in our world, sub-creation is the most nearly pure, rare, and potent form of art. It is difficult to achieve, requiring labor, thought, special skill, and "elvish craft."[110] The sub-creative desire has no biological function and is separate from it.[111] The reader also becomes a sub-creator. Orson Scott Card believes that individual readers re-create Tolkien's story, creating a "collaboration between the Reader-at-This-Moment and Tolkien-at-the-Time-He-Wrote."[112]

Tolkien describes man as a sub-creator who fills the world with Elves and goblins. Tolkien undoubtedly was influenced by Maisie Ward's introduction to G. K. Chesterton: "Cheerful fantasy is the creation of a new form wherein man, become creator, co-operates with God."[113] Fantasy is a human right because we are made "in the image and likeness of a Maker" and make "by the law in which we're made."[114] On the other hand, fantasy can be poorly done, used for evil or to delude, or be carried to excess. It can create false gods or social and economic theories requiring sacrifice.[115]

These ideas come from Tolkien's poem "Mythopoeia," which was written in response to a conversation Tolkien and Lewis had in 1929. Despite the fact that Lewis believed myths were "breathed through silver," Lewis called them "lies" and therefore "worthless." "Mythopoeia" means "mythos" (myth) and "poiesis" (creation). Lewis also uses the term *mythopoeia* in his essay describing the mythopoeic gifts of George MacDonald and Rider Haggard.[116] "Mythopoeia" expresses the Platonic idea that the material world is a reflection of Truth. In addition, modern science and reason will never give us complete knowledge. The following is a summary of the points Tolkien makes in his poem.

Philomythus is speaking to Misomyths. Misomyths looks at trees and stars and labels them as such. A star has become "just matter in a ball" traveling along a mathematical course. God made all creation, including rocks, trees, earth, stars, and men. But trees are not trees until they are named. Creating involves both seeing and naming. For example, trees are not trees until man sees and names them because things truly come into existence by the act of naming. Speech also distinguishes man from animals. Still, speech is only an echo and dim picture of the world rather than a photograph.

The creative process is a stirring within that pans the "vein of spirit out of sense." Man digs out "foreknown" things from memory and brings out "great powers" that allow him to look back and behold the Elves.

Man can behold the world with renewed vision. Thus a person does not see stars until he sees them as living silver bursting with flames. There is no sky unless seen as a "jeweled tent" woven with myths and patterned by elves. There is no earth unless seen as Mother Earth. Man's heart gets wisdom only from the Wise. In "On Fairy Stories," Tolkien similarly writes that Pegasus enobled horses; Gram the sword in Norse mythology revealed cold iron. By using materials and simple, fundamental things from the primary world and by being free with nature, the fantasy writer makes them more wondrous in their new setting.

Although man is estranged from God, he is not lost, changed, or dethroned—just disgraced. He still keeps his "rags of lordship." The author will not worship the "great Artefact" of machines. God, the Creator, is the single White light; man is the sub-creator, the refracted light, the splintering of the single light into many hues and combined into "living shapes that move from mind to mind." It is our right to fill the world with elves, goblins, and dragons because we are following the laws by which we were made. Thus our dreams and wishes are not in vain.

The legend makers are blessed by creating poems about things not found on earth. Although they are aware of evil and death, they do not retreat but rather tell about things not recorded in time. They do not tell us to flee the world but tell us about victory and ultimate defeat. We have forgotten the past and become blind to the world around us. But artists illuminate our hearts with the light of suns no one has yet seen. The author wants to sing like the minstrels and sail on quests like the mariners.

In addition, the author does not agree with the theory of evolution. He also refuses to consider man an ape who walks on a flat, dusty path in an unchangeable world where the "little maker" has no part with the "maker's art." Technological progress is like a dark abyss. So he will not bow down before the Iron Crown of technology or lay down the golden scepter of art.

The scientific approach to the material world is limited, but true knowledge will come in Paradise. There we may stop gazing upon "everlasting Day" and instead see the day illuminated and renewed by being just like what is True rather than a mirror of Truth. We will see "all is as it is, and yet made free." Salvation will change but not destroy things. In Paradise, poets will "make anew" and "have flames upon their head."

This poem contains many of the themes about art, creativity, and imagination and distaste for modern technology that Tolkien and Lewis exemplify in their fiction, as described in the next chapter.

3

Applications

Tolkien and Lewis convey their theories about art not only in their essays and letters but also in their imaginary worlds. Even their views of evil draw on the idea of twisting what was created as good. This chapter compares the writers' created mythologies, as well as both the ideal and evil creatures central to their ideas about art.

THE SILMARILLION

In *The Silmarillion*, Tolkien tells the story of the creation, Fall, redemption, and apocalypse with his own modifications. He provides helpful commentary about *The Silmarillion* in his letters, particularly a letter to Milton Waldman in 1951. The focus of the following summary is the theme of sub-creation.

    The Silmarillion centers on the fate of primeval jewels called the Silmarilli ("radiance of pure light").[1] It is not about man but the Elves—their fall, exile from Valinor, entry into Middle-earth, and war with the Enemy.[2] There is no journey or quest to tie together the legends. Rather, they are pure mythology and for the most part tragic.[3]

Ainulindalë (which means music of the Ainur) is Tolkien's creation myth. He wrote "The Music of the Ainur" as one of the earliest stories in *The Book of Lost Tales*, which indicates that as early as 1917 he was working on a myth about the relationship between creation and sub-creation. While it contains hints of the biblical creation, it also draws on Norse and classical mythology. Because *The Silmarillion* is the history of Middle-earth and thus our Earth, it is a mythological account of our own history.

There is one God, Eru, also called The One or Ilúvatar, who is the source of and sovereign over everything. Eru is the only one who creates the world itself. However, he allows others to share in ordering and carrying out his Primeval Design. He begins a musical theme. Then he creates the Ainur, or the Holy Ones, who are angelic powers or rulers similar to gods in mythology.[4] They are created even before the physical world but are not incarnated.[5] Kindled with the Flame Imperishable, the Ainur are the offspring of his thought. Although they do not create, they exercise authority in their spheres.[6]

When the Ainur come into the Void, Eru declares, "Behold your Music!" After showing them a vision of the world, he invites the Ainur to adorn it, make it "a Great Music," and to create harmony. Their freedom to create is intrinsic to the creative process. After they interpret Eru's vision, they complete the Design the One "propounds" to them: first in musical or abstract form. They love the world and rejoice in creating with voices described as harps, trumpets, and choirs. Later, their work will become "historical vision."[7]

One of the Ainur, Melkor (later called Morgoth), introduces alterations that do not interpret Eru's mind. Because the individual will can become independent and take on the role of the Creator, there is an ability to fall. This concept is intrinsic to Tolkien's view not only about the creation of evil but also of evil's abuse of sub-creative power. Melkor shares the gifts of his fellow Ainur and has the greatest gifts of knowledge and power. Seeking the Imperishable Flame, he often goes alone into the void. Because Melkor tries to

weave his own music into the theme, he brings discord and disharmony. His music results in a turbulent sound compared to a storm,
drowning out the other music. It is a distortion or parody rather
than a new theme.

Eru then introduces new themes and events into the original design.
More themes follow. A second Theme begins that is both similar
and dissimilar from the first. Melkor's discord arises again. The third
Theme is different, and two conflicting songs emerge: one that is both
sorrowful and beautiful, and one that is loud and pompous. When
Melkor's discords arise, the themes of the Children of Ilúvatar (also
called Eruhín, the Children of God) are sung into being. These are
the Elves (Firstborn) and Men (Successors). As a separate addition to
the Design, they have a unique relationship to Eru.[8]

Finally, when Eru shows the results of the Ainurs' musical themes,
they behold a vision of their creation as a drama. Not only can they
see the entire unfolding of the World's history but also the part each
of them has played. Tolkien writes that a major part of his mythology is the gods' knowledge of the world's history and their part in
making it before it becomes "real."[9] After the vision ends, Eru says,
"Eä! Let these things Be!" The One thus presents the Music as visible History.[10] We are told that at the end of days, the choirs of the
Ainur and Children of Ilúvatar will make an even greater music
before Ilúvatar.[11] Men too will join in the Second Music of the
Ainur.[12]

The Music of the Ainur produces Arda, which contains Middle-
earth, and Aman, and those who hear it are permitted to enter into
it. Some fall in love with the vision, thus playing the most sub-
creative or artistic part in the Music. These Ainur choose to enter
and take on material form on earth by becoming Valar. The Valar,
then, are the fourteen most powerful spirits of the Ainur who enter
Arda after it is created. They are divine angelic powers who exercise
the authority delegated to them but not in creation, making, or
re-making.[13] They live in Valinor, a land across the sea in the West. Eru
appoints the Valar to prepare the world for the Children of Ilúvatar,
moral men, and immortal Elves. Because the Valar did not conceive of
or make Elves or Men, the Valar are forbidden to dominate them.[14]

Tolkien describes the Valar as sub-creative. Because they are allowed to create some elements of the universe, they thus participate in creation and contribute to Eru's artistry. But they cannot make fundamental changes of any kind.[15] Although they share in the world's making, it is not in the same way that we "make" a work of art or a story.[16] Those who enter the created world have varying amounts of knowledge. Some know the Creator's mind. Others become associated with major artists and gain knowledge through their minds.[17] But they must remain in Time until the End. Tolkien equates them with the "gods" in traditional mythology.[18] After Melkor is expelled from Arda, the Valar fight with Melkor and imprison him.

There are several types of Elves, who are central to Tolkien's views about creativity.[19] Eldar, the High Elves, hear the summons of the Valar to pass from Middle-earth over the Sea to the West; Lesser Elves do not. The High Elves journey across the sea to Valinor and have enhanced powers and knowledge. The Vanyar are the Highest of the High Elves. The second group is the Sindar, or Grey Elves, who do not cross to Valinor and go as far as Beleriand, the western part of Middle-earth.

Noldor are High Elves who return over the Sea to Middle-earth. Because they love machinery, science, and technology, they can produce things that can be used for evil.[20] They are the most skilled of Elves and learn from Aulë. As the artists, poets, and craftsmen, they delight in tongues, scripts, embroidery, drawing, carving, and making gems. Manwë, Chief of the Valar, loves the Vanyar best of all Elves; from him they receive song and poetry, which is his delight. The first Elves in Middle-earth make speech and give names to things they see. They are called the Quendi, signifying that they speak with voices.

Aulë, one of the Valar, is greatest of all craftsmen and makes beautiful, shapely works. He enjoys both making things that others have not thought of and being praised for his skill. His pride and delight is in making but not possessing things—a concept key to Tolkien's view of art. However, he becomes impatient for Ilúvatar to create living beings for the Ainur to take care of. He also desires to create those he can teach his craft. Usurping the Creator's power, he therefore tries to give independent life to his own creations, thirteen dwarves. But they do not have independent life.

When The One asks him why he has done this action beyond his power and authority, Aulë replies that making things is in his heart because he was made by Him. He remains faithful to Eru, submitting to his will. Thus Aulë tries to destroy his children with a hammer. But The One, appreciating his desire to create and his humility, allows them to become part of his design and free from Aulë's will.[21] Because Aulë, who is renowned for his crafts, created the dwarves, so too the dwarves become known for their crafts, working in metal, jewels, and stones.

Aulë loves the Noldor; so he and his people live among them, resulting in their increased knowledge and skill. Their thirst for knowledge and love of words fuel their desire to find appropriate names for things they see or imagine.[22] During the time Melkor is chained, the Noldor and Rúmil of Tirion, the loremaster, record speech and song on metal, stone, or drawings.

Sauron, another angelic spirit, becomes Aulë's servant and later instigates a revolt in Númenor. He convinces the Númenóreans to ignore the ban to cross forbidden waters and go to Aman the Blessed, thus becoming like the Valar and possessing everlasting life. As a result, Númenor sinks into the sea. As in the Flood story, only the faithful are saved and allowed to sail to Middle-earth.

During the Second Age, the Elves have a "second fall." Because they long to remain on earth rather than return to the West, their art becomes antiquated.[23] As Sauron tempts the Noldor to make western Middle-earth as beautiful as Valinor, they begin to succumb to magic and machinery. They create the Rings of Power that primarily slow decay but also cause lust for domination.

Men too are fallen. The descendants of Men who try to repent and flee west to avoid the Dark Lord and false worship renew their knowledge of Truth. Their world is monotheistic and their god The One, but he is "immensely remote."[24] On Middle-earth, the Númenóreans are descendants of the Edain of the First Age granted the island of Elenna. They are better and more noble Men who live within sight of the immoral land Eressëa. They speak Elvish and even look like the Elves. Although they are mortal, they have a triple life span but not immortality. This extra time allows them to achieve much in art and wisdom. But they become possessive, craving even more time and immortality. Thus the gods ban them from sailing to Eressëa. They fall from grace in phases. First, they take sea voyages and bring art and knowledge to Wild Men as benefactors. During the second stage, in their desire to escape death, they create a cult of the dead and lavish wealth and art on tombs and memorials.[25]

The Dúnedain, a race of men descended from the Númenóreans, use both their own speech and that of the Elves. They converse with the Eldar, and the loremasters learn the High Eldarin tongue of the Blessed Realm. Consequently, they learn the stories and songs and make their own letters, scrolls, and books containing "wisdom and wonder." They are craftsmen as well. Their gift from Ilúvatar is death, but Morgoth makes it seem to be a darkness to be feared. Tolkien writes that man's art and poetry is dependent upon or modified by that inherited from the Elves. The Elves represent part of human nature.[26]

ELVES

The Silmarillion is the tale of Elvish history and legend. Tolkien regretted using Elves because they have been depicted so differently in tradition, especially in Shakespeare.[27] In contrast to diminutive creatures, Tolkien's Elves are tall, fair-skinned, and gray-eyed; they have physical bodies but with keener senses than men. Their story, writes Tolkien, is about the effect of mortality on art and the sub-creative desire.[28] It is also about the relationship between Art and Primary Reality, and between Creation and Making (and sub-creation).[29] Tolkien usually uses the words *making* and *craft* rather than *creation* to describe human (and elvish) art because only God can "create." Creation is Eru's act of Will that gives Reality to conceptions; making is permissive.[30] Elves are the only creatures that Eru directly creates; others are created through sub-creation by lesser gods.

In "On Fairy Stories," Tolkien explains that the Elves desire sub-creative art, and from them we learn what fantasy aspires to and desires. He calls Enchantment an "elvish craft." Elves are the ideal artists and have the powers we would like to have. Not only do they have enhanced aesthetic, creative, and aesthetic faculties and longer life, but they are also more beautiful and noble than Men, despite their similar appearance.[31] The Elves desire to remain in Middle-earth, not just because they are fond of it and are the superior caste but because they can be artists.[32] The Elves put the thought of everything they love into what they make, such as beautiful leaves and stone, and they are "created to adorn the earth and heal it."[33] Tolkien contrasts Elves with hobbits by making them small to reflect the small reach of their imagination rather than their courage or power.[34]

Tolkien writes that one theme in the story is that man's art and poetry is derived from the Elves.[35] The story moves from that of the Elves to men—myth passing into history or the dominion of men.[36] By the time of Faramir and Boromir, men of Gondor value warriors over men with other skills. Gone are the time when Minas Tirith cherished "gentleness and the arts," as the Elves taught them. Elves and Men thus represent different aspects of the Humane. In the Second Age, the Men of Numenor who closely follow the Elves achieve a golden age but lose it in a fall similar to that of the Elves. Their long life helps them achieve much in art but also makes them possessive. Sauron exploits this attitude in making them rebel against the Valar. Fallen man has also stained the Elves.

During the Second Age, the Elves have a second "fall." They want to have memories of the West but also to remain on ordinary earth. They become obsessed with "fading" and stopping history. Although they want to be "artists," their art becomes antiquated, like "embalming."[37] Some of the Noldor go to Eregion. The Elven smiths and dwarves develop the closest friendship that ever existed between the two races, resulting in highly developed smithcraft.

However, Sauron convinces the Elves to create nineteen Rings of Power for use as creation. An alliance of Elven smiths led by

Celebrimbor and Sauron first creates the Seven and Nine rings, which are corrupted. After Sauron leaves, Celebrimbor forges the Three Rings of the Elves—Fire, Water, and Air. These rings are created by their own imagination; they have power to preserve and do not make one invisible.[38] While the rings prevent decay, they also enhance the possessor's powers, resulting in evil magic that dominates. The Elves' rings remain "unsullied" because Sauron never touches them. Because the rings reflect the character of each race they were made for, the Elven rings increase their ability to understand, make, heal, and preserve rather than making them desire to dominate or hoard wealth, as Elrond explains. With one of these rings, Elrond becomes master of healing; Galadriel uses another one to create the light of Lothlórien. Secret guardians maintain the Three Rings, and they preserve the memory of ancient beauty and peace. On the other hand, the Elves come near to falling into bad magic.

THE MYTH OF DEEP HEAVEN

In Lewis's Space Trilogy, the myth is told gradually throughout his stories. In contrast to Tolkien, the story has more biblical echoes but, like Tolkien, echoes the Book of Genesis. This is the history of the Field of Arbol: Maleldil the Young, who lives with the Old One—a spirit with no body or passions—first made and ruled the world. Maleldil—Creator of the Universe, Ruler, Law-giver—is "all a burning joy and strength."

Each planet was given an Oyarsa, an angelic spirit, to rule. During the years before there was life on Earth, the Oyarsa of Earth, who was brighter and greater than all the Oyeresu, became "bent" (evil), and these years were thus called the Bent Years. He not only wanted to be like Maleldil but also decided to destroy other worlds. With his left hand he smote the moon, so that one side turned away forever from Deep Heaven and toward Earth. Then he tried to invade Malacandra, a planet older than Earth. Once the air was warm and full of birdlike creatures, but he robbed it of its atmosphere, bringing cold death on the harandra, or high land. The planet thus suffered a sort of "fall" in the battle between Maleldil and the Bent Oyarsa. But Maleldil opened up the handramits (low ground) to release warm springs and prevent total death of the planet.

Although Malacandra was protected from evil, it is to some extent fallen and now dying. Lewis believed that there may be different sorts and degrees of fallenness. Malacandrians have no understanding of concepts of deceit, malice, war, slavery, prostitution, and revenge. When the Bent Oyarsa tried to make the inhabitants of Malacandra fear death approaching and make spaceships for invading other planets, Maleldil stopped him. They now do not fear death but welcome it. However, birds are extinct, the ice caps frozen, and the forests stone. Its "fall" was therefore different from that on earth.

Eldila are the intermediaries between Oyarsa, who rules the planet, and the three "hnau," or rational species with spirits. Lewis says this "angelocracy" is a thing of the past; only in ancient worlds do we find creatures like those of Malacandra, because the Incarnation changed everything. Because Maleldil took on the form of a man, reason must be in human form.

During the Great War that followed the invasion of Malacandra, Maleldil drove the Oyarsa of Earth out of the heavens and bound him in the air of Earth. Confined to this region below the moon are both he and those eldila who sold themselves to him and have made Earth their headquarters. Earth is therefore under a state of siege, an "enemy-occupied territory" cut off from the rest of Deep Heaven. Because no message comes from it, all Oyeresu call it the "silent planet." Yet because of the evil that grew on Earth, there Maleldil "dared terrible things" when he became a man.

The Bent Oyarsa, wanting to make war again on Deep Heaven, plans an attack on Perelandra but can only act through a human agent. Because Perelandra is the youngest of planets, its history is only beginning. It was the first world to waken after the coming of Christ and therefore has no eldila; it is not fallen but open to temptation. According to Lewis, if there are other rational species, it is not necessary to believe they have fallen. When Perelandra arose from Arbol, the Perelandrian Oyarsa "rounded" the planet, spun air about it, wove its roof, and built the floating islands. Because the King and Green Lady resist evil, they are given the planet to rule from Tai Harendrimar by their Oyarsa, although he will remain as counsel. When they ascend the throne, it is said that the "world is born" because for the first time two humans have actually gained Paradise. They now have a new and joyful relationship with angels and Nature. With no sense of passing time, they take charge of the seasons and growth, as well as the land, rivers, and beasts. They are to name all creatures, guide all natures to perfection, love all, and bear children. As in Narnia, nobler beasts will become "hnau" and speak. A temple will also be built to Maleldil's glory on the Fixed Land.

The year in which *That Hideous Strength* takes place (sometime after World War II) is prophesied to be one of great stirrings and changes, for the celestial year that began in the twelfth century is an evolutionary year. Lurga (Saturn) will descend in this age. He is the god of death, cold, and age. Thus when he visits St. Anne's, those in the house feel the sun dying, the Earth gripped in cold, the "heat-death" of the universe, then the blackness of nonentity. For the universe, says Lewis, has been at war—Earth's evil eldila warring against those of Deep Heaven—but the siege is now drawing to an end, the two sides becoming more defined.

The "rightful king" is Maleldil. According to the Seventh Law, Maleldil promised that he would not send powers to mar or mend Earth until the end times. Consequently, the dark eldila, knowing the moon's orbit provided a barrier, confidently believed Earth was blockaded from the powers of Deep Heaven reaching Earth. But when men such as Weston and Devine began sending spaceships to spread sin to other planets, they broke Maleldil's law, opening up a new relationship between men and Maleldil. Now the eldila from Deep Heaven are free to invade Earth. But they can only work through the agency of men such as Merlin, whose mind is to be taken over, and Ransom, an intermediary between Heaven and Earth. The whole history of Earth has led up to the crucial moments described in *That Hideous Strength*. If man shakes off the limitations of his powers imposed by mercy from the results of the Fall in the

Garden of Eden, Hell will reign incarnate. Evil men will then have the power of evil spirits, making Nature their slave.

Maleldil does not make worlds to live forever. Thus after Perelandra has made 10,000 revolutions round the sun, the "sky curtain" will be torn down, and the Perelandrians will at last see Deep Heaven and be free. Their bodies will take on eldilic form, and some of them, as well as the King, the Malacandran Oyarsa, and former hnau of Earth, will come to Earth to participate in its liberation. Earth will then be in final siege and its "black spot" cleared away. Maleldil himself will make war on Earth, breaking the moon, then blotting out its light. Fragments cast into the seas will cause smoke to arise and cover up the sun. There will be plagues and horrors. Yet all will ultimately be cleansed so that the memory of the Black Oyarsa is erased forever. Earth can at last be reunited to the Field of Arbol, its real name heard again. This, then, will be Earth's true beginning.

OYERESU, ELDILA, AND MALACANDRAN CREATURES

Lewis wanted to show the rich universe as being full of a variety of creatures different from humans.[39] His eldila, he explains, are angels or "longaevai" (long-livers), not fairies, whose habitat is space. They are always about Maleldil's business.[40] Aerial demons, like Lewis's Dark Eldila, were believed to live between the moon and Earth. Good and bad eldila wage a perpetual invisible warfare.

Medieval man believed each planet was controlled by a resident planetary intelligence or angelic spirit whom Lewis calls an Oyarsa. His responsibility was to keep his sphere moving by desire for God. Lewis's Oyeresu, the greatest of eldila, were put on the planets to rule when they were made and to keep the planets in their orbits. All Oyeresu speak together, except for Earth's, who is silent. But every Oyarsa still has a representative (wraith) on Earth, just as in every world there is an unfallen partner of the Black Archon. Earth's Oyarsa (Lucifer), who was brighter and greater than Malacandra's, became "bent" long before human life began on Earth. Although he was free, he desired to spoil other worlds beside his own. Malacandra's Oyarsa explains that during a great war, they drove him out of the heavens and "bound him in the air of his own world. . . . There doubtless he lies to this hour."

Tolkien thought that the eldila were inspired by the Eldar in *The Silmarillion*.[41] Ransom compares eldila to our traditional idea of albs, devas, gods, angels, and fairies. They are superior intelligences who do not eat, breed, breathe, or die. The "body of an eldil is a movement swift as light"; he can touch and bathe in what we call light, whereas things that are firm for us seem thin and ephemeral to him. To humans, the eldil is a thin, half-real body that can go through walls and rocks, but an eldil can go through them like a cloud because he is solid and firm. So to Ransom's eye, eldila appear only as "footsteps of light," variations of light and shade like a sunbeam or moving of the leaves. To his ear their voices seem a silvery sound. Conscious of his humanity, Ransom feels embarrassed and shy in their presence.

Because the Bent One, the Oyarsa who wants to become like Maleldil, rebels, he is driven from the heavens. Tellurian eldila are a different and hostile kind of eldil who chose to follow the Bent Oyarsa of Earth and are thus the reason for the "fatal bent" of Earth's whole history. "Darker ignorance" comes from doing evil, and its temptations repeatedly arise throughout the trilogy.

Malacandra's Oyarsa lives an enormous time, has no sense of duration, and does not die or breed. Though his habitat is space, he abides at Meldilorn and has ruled all hnau and everything in Malacandra since its creation. Like all hnau he is a copy of Maleldil, and like Maleldil he is a "terrible good."

In a personal letter, Lewis explains outright the "dark secret," as he calls it, to be found in the Space Trilogy: "You have the angels, the eldila. You have Maleldil 'who lives with the Old One'—i.e., God the Father and God the Son. . . . He did and suffered terrible things in retrieving Thulcandra (i.e., was incarnate and crucified on Earth) fighting against the Bent One, the eldil who had gone wrong (Satan, the rebel angel)."[42] Thus we can see many parallels between Lewis's myth and the biblical account of Lucifer, the Fall of man, and God's nature. However, according to Lewis, only two in sixty reviewers realized it was anything other than a "mere invention."

Like Tolkien, Lewis portrays his views of art and creativity in his other worlds. The planet of Malacandra is a world where heroism and poetry are at the bottom and "cold scientific intellect" is above it. The only animal life we meet on Malacandra are pale furry creatures somewhat like giraffes, only slenderer and higher. But there are three distinct, rational beings—hrossa, sorns, and pfifltriggi—seemingly representative of the various kinds of fauna on earth—animal, bird, and reptile/insect. These creatures represent different types of artistic skill.

The hrossa are a combination of seal, otter, and penguin. As Ransom learns and loves so well firsthand, the hrossa live in the handramits near the rivers in beehive-shaped huts made of stiff leaves. Their culture might be considered stone-age because they sleep on the ground and use stone knives and primitive vessels. They also eat only fish and boiled vegetables, for they are great fishermen and farmers. Yet the hrossa are talented speakers, singers, and poets. The hrossa have no art except poetry and music practiced every evening by a team of four. Like the Anglo-Saxons, they perform their poetry and music in a group: one chants while the others interpret with song. Ransom cannot understand their rhythm. Because they believe that writing destroys poetry, unfortunately they now have fewer books.

Lewis describes his "dear friends the hrossa" as theologians, in a sense, because they know the Old One (God) and Maleldil (Christ). However, they do not know the Third One (Holy Spirit) because they have never fallen "thence never been redeemed, thence never baptized, thence never received the gift of the Holy Ghost."[43] While those on earth fear death because of the Fall, the hrossa see it as entering a better world through spiritual rebirth into a life with Maleldil. Each who dies naturally dies at a predictable time (160 Earth years), when his full life span is over. Then the body is in a sense "unmade" or unbodied, scattered into nothing during the burial ceremony. They describe this as dropping the body into a still pool so the hnau can rise from the body into a second life.

Of all the hnau, sorns are the most like men, yet closest to the traditional "science fiction" outer space creature pictured in pulp magazines. Over two to three times the height of a man, sorns are white, spindly, flimsy, and "madly elongated." As the "intellectuals" of the planet, they are interested in such things as astronomy and history and are hopelessly inept at boating, fishing, swimming, and creating or understanding poetry. Perhaps that is why Lewis calls them "sorns," which, according to the *Oxford English Dictionary* means "those who depend on others for existence." Their language, called Surnibur, is spoken in booming voices.

Poetry has true meaning when both spoken and later remembered. Hyoi the Hross tells Ransom that "the most splendid line becomes fully splendid only by means of all the lines after it." If one goes back to read the line, he will not only find it less splendid but also kill it. One cannot long to hear a line over again. A pleasure is only full-grown when remembered. Pleasures of appreciation are the enjoyment of things for their own sakes, the "disinterested" love of the object itself, the feeling "which makes us glad of unspoiled forests that we shall never see; which makes us anxious that the garden or bean-field should continue to exist."[44] The eldila sing that fruit we have not plucked, water we have not floated on, Nature we have not seen do not exist for man or await his coming to be perfect. Thus Ransom's taste of the waters and fruits of Perelandra is like meeting a new genus of pleasure through all his senses at once. This concept of enjoying the "otherness" of things is central to both Lewis's and Tolkien's views of art.

Pfifltriggi are the nervous and amusing frog-, insect-, reptile-like creatures of Malacandra who enjoy making things that are pleasant to look at and not useful, such as sculpture. Sometimes they make useful things that the sorns think of, as long as they are difficult. With their delicate and many-fingered hands ideal for doing manual work, they dig and make crafts—things both useful and useless, the beautiful, and the intricate objects designed by the sorns. This artwork is often created out of stone with elaborate ornamentation, a mixture of pure line drawings, designs, and packed and empty surfaces. Through their art, they keep the historical records of the planet as well. Augray the sorn says that if Ransom had died trying to reach the sorns' caves on the handramit, the hrossa would have written a poem about it.

EVIL

Both Tolkien and Lewis depict the way evil can twist and mock ideal creation. Tolkien believes that evil in fantasy teaches us that we have an eternal element; it teaches us about ourselves and allows us to "experience" evil without actually having it affect us spiritually.[45]

A range of evil sub-creative urges is seen in *The Silmarillion* and *The Lord of the Rings*. In Tolkien's myth, no beings other than Eru (The One) can create souls or spirits. Eru gives special sub-creative powers to certain high created beings, so the urge to create begins as a gift. Ideal art comes from The One; the Enemy illustrates the wrong use of creative power. Just as we were given free will, so too the highest created beings are given sub-creative powers but within limits and subject to commands or prohibitions. The Enemy wasn't evil in the beginning; his fall was sub-creative. In this way, Tolkien's myth explains how God cannot create evil. Evil beings attempt to create independently of the Creator's will. When such creatures fall, the creatures they create for themselves are born of sin and thus are evil.[46] Evil also cannot make new things of its own; it can only mock and produce counterfeits.[47] These beings are consequently simply remodeled and corrupted or are like puppets filled with the minds of their makers.[48]

Morgoth is the prime sub-creative Rebel.[49] He breeds orcs during the First Age to mock Elves and conducts genetic experiments with creatures who already exist, ruining and twisting them. When Morgoth makes things for himself, he abuses his privilege, but his creations become a real part of the world. The Elves, who represent good sub-creation, are his enemies and the object of his hate.[50] The orcs, in turn, cannot make anything that is beautiful. They do not work with their hands any more than they have to and invent "clever" things such as killing machines. In addition, they cannot even invent their own language but must borrow it from others.

Aulë creates the dwarves from impatience, but his repentence results in Eru's allowing the dwarves to become independent creatures. Aulë then teaches the dwarves to mine for precious metals and jewels. Despite their skills as smiths, they also create armor and weapons. Shippey believes that Tolkien is using a tradition of identifying the Fall of man in Cain and Abel and the invention of metallurgy, which resulted in weaponry.[51] Fëanor illustrates possessiveness by refusing to sacrifice his art. He too creates weapons by using a secret forge to make swords. In *The Hobbit*, Bilbo hears the poem "over the misty mountains" and he begins to feel the desire of the dwarves for beautiful things created "by hands and by cunning and by magic."

Sauron loses his imaginative ability after his fall. His Ring of Power will be discussed in more detail in the next chapter. Saruman calls himself a "Ring-maker," but he is only imitating Sauron. Saruman illustrates the difference between two types of creative power. Saruman requires power to order things the way he wants. According to Treebeard, he is scheming to become a Power. Saruman has a "mind of metal and wheel" and cares for living things only insofar as he can use them. Although Isengard was once fair and beautiful, Saruman reshapes it to his evil purposes. The "arts and subtle devices" that he thought were his own came from Mordor.[52]

Lewis agrees that the Devil could make nothing but infected everything.[53] Because evil is "spoiled good," it cannot create but can ruin something Another has created—thus the term *bent*. Even scientists at N.I.C.E. were once good, says Ransom. Evil seeks to dominate and participate in "tyrannous re-forming of Creation." It can, however, arise from a seeming good desire to benefit the world quickly according to one's own plans. Evil results in coercing the wills of others, becoming possessive, and desiring to be lord of one's own creations.

This type of evil is illustrated in *The Chronicles of Narnia* through the witch Jadis, who battles her sister to gain the throne of Charn. In revenge, Jadis spoke the "Deplorable Word" that destroys all living things when spoken. She had learned this word in a "secret place" and paid a "terrible price" for it. With that word, she cast all of Charn and its inhabitants into a frozen enchantment. Under one of her spells, the Witch promises to sleep among them like a statue until someone strikes a bell to awaken her.

MAGIC

Some beings love the primary world but are dissatisfied with it. They may then become possessive of things they create, desiring to be lord of their private creations. First they rebel against the Creator's laws, especially morality, and then desire Power. This greed, in turn, leads to Magic.[54] Fantasy worlds always contain magic, usually in the form of characters with magical abilities or magical creatures and objects. Magic is an inherent power that men cannot possess, obtain, or achieve by spells. In fairy stories, says Tolkien, magic should always be treated seriously rather than satirized.

Tolkien distinguishes between creating a secondary world and Magic, which he calls a key element in the Perilous Realm that alters the primary world and seeks power. In "On Fairy Stories," Tolkien distinguishes between two kinds of magic: "magia" (good) and "goeteia" (bad); however, either can become good or bad depending on the motive, purpose, or use. Magia is used for certain beneficent purposes. An example is the magic of the Elves, whose art and sub-creation are not used for power or domination.[55] Knowing and appreciating people, objects, and nature are preferable to seeking power. For instance, Tom Bombadil is described as the spirit of pure science who desires to know the history and nature of things because they are "other" and is not interested in "doing" anything with the knowledge. He is called "master" but not lord because he does not seek to possess or dominate.[56]

In contrast, bad magic is a technique rather than an art that attempts to alter the primary world; it desires to dominate, enchant, delude, and enslave.[57] Tolkien describes such magic as "vulgar devices" used by the scientific magician. Evil art is used for power and "tyrannous re-forming of Creation."[58] For Tolkien, technology and the "machine" is a modern form of magic.

In *English Literature in the Sixteenth Century*, Lewis, tracing the use of magic in literature, distinguishes magic from witchcraft and Satanism.[59] Magic and astrology are opposites because the magician believes in human omnipotence. In medieval literature, magic had a "faerie" and romance quality, but by the Elizabethan period, magic was treated as reality. According to Lewis, good magic shows the link between the natural and supernatural. Magic and miracles such as talking trees, magic rings, beasts turning into men and vice versa are conveyed in fairy tales. While they illustrate nature being invaded by an alien power, in Christianity, miracles show invasion by God.[60] Lewis gives examples of fairy tale sentences such as, "This is a magic cave and those who enter it will renew their youth."

Magic is not "paltry and pathetic techniques" used to control nature. For example, in *The Silver Chair*, Jill wants to draw a circle on the ground and say an incantation using charms and spells to enter Narnia. But Eustace, calling such methods "rot," replies that they can't *make* Aslan do things. Instead, they can only ask him. Magic is usually the methods used by evil spirits, Lewis writes, whereas miracles are answers to prayer.[61] In *Looking for God in Harry Potter*, John Granger defines good magic as incantational, while bad magic is invocational. The former harmonizes with the Bible through imitation, but the latter calls upon evil spirits for power.[62] It is only through good magic—a magic wardrobe, magic horn, a magic picture, and magic rings—that the children of our world enter Narnia.

A theme in *The Magician's Nephew* is the bad use of magic to control other people. Both Uncle Andrew and Jadis claim that theirs is a "high and lonely destiny." Uncle Andrew, who only dabbles in magic, seeks to use the children and to exploit his discoveries in other worlds. Digory calls him "a wicked, cruel magician like the ones in the stories." Andrew describes Narnia as one of these secret countries that is real—"a really other world—another Nature— another universe," a place that cannot be reached except by magic. Jadis, like other tyrants, does not care for joy, justice, or mercy. She is not interested in things or people; rather, people exist only to do her will, and she is "terribly practical." She paid a "terrible price" for her knowledge and power.

According to Narnian history, the Emperor-Over-Sea sent a Deep Magic into the world from the "Dawn of Time." This magic permits the Witch to kill every traitor, and unless she has blood, Narnia will perish in water and fire. Quite simply, it is the moral law that demands justice for evil. But further back in time is a Deeper Magic about which the Witch knows nothing. This law states that when a willing victim who has committed no treachery is killed in the traitor's stead, the Stone Table will crack, and Death will start working backward. In fairy tales, spells are used to break and induce enchantments. "And you and I have need of the strongest spell that can be found to wake us from the evil enchantment of worldliness which has been laid upon us for nearly a hundred years."[63]

The Creator whom the fantasist imitates is often likened to a magician. In "The Ethics of Elfland," Chesterton says, "I had always believed the world involved magic: now I thought that perhaps it involved a magician."[64] The essential nature of fairy story is magic, and in the case of religious fantasy, the source of magic is usually the supernatural. The value of the magical element in Christianity is that Heaven is a "realm of objective facts." According to Chesterton, intellectuals attempt to remove this magic and replace it with the "spiritual element." Lewis describes God's existence as a "given" or "magical" fact rather than "spiritual": "One cannot conceive . . . a more 'magical' fact than the existence of God as *causa sui* [cause of itself]."[65]

Tolkien and Lewis, then, created secondary worlds that both contain and point to a Creator. Their contrasting metaphors depicting the relation of art to God's Truth are discussed in the next chapter.

4

Art Theories and Metaphors

While Tolkien's and Lewis's fiction depict their contrasting views about man's creativity, evil, and magic, their theories about art and metaphors for the creative process follow a long tradition of literary criticism and medieval views of the universe. This history is important, because while Tolkien and Lewis share many of the same ideas about the value of fantasy, their ideas about art as creation in God's image are quite different. This chapter briefly reviews literary theories, artists, and the medieval models that influenced Tolkien and Lewis. It also presents metaphors for art that they use in their fantasy fiction.

LITERARY THEORY

In *The Mirror and the Lamp*, M. H. Abrams outlines the history of critical theory that puts Tolkien's and Lewis's contrasting theories in perspective. Critical theories are oriented toward one of the following four elements "in the total situation of a work of art": the Universe, the Work, the Artist, and the Audience (Figure 4.1).

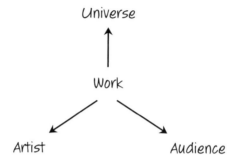

Figure 4.1 M. H. Abrams's four elements related to a work of art

The universe is "people and actions, ideas and feelings, material things and events, or super-sensible essences."[1] The work is the artistic product of the artist, or artificer. Its subject is derived from exciting things. The audience includes listeners, spectators, or readers. Of these four elements, the one that receives the most emphasis changes depending upon the critical theory.

Kathryn Hume believes that for fantasy works, Abrams's "universe" is an oversimplification. Not only is there a universe within a work but also the worlds surrounding both the author (World 1) and reader (World 2).[2] The author obtains material from World 1, and if successful, changes not only the audience but their world (World 2).

Tolkien's and Lewis's views of fantasy involve all four of these elements (Figure 4.2). First, the author has an impulse—the desire to create. He or she then chooses the appropriate form. The artist uses elements from the primary world to create the secondary world that the audience enters. The effect of the secondary world on the audience is important because fantasy works are both useful and relevant. For Lewis and Tolkien, the secondary world reflects Truths of the spiritual world. A more appropriate diagram, then, shows two other worlds: the secondary world found in the work itself and the spiritual world.

How and why a Christian fantasy writer achieves his expression of faith begins first with his concept of the relation of art to God's Truth. While the idea that poetry is inspired by the gods is ancient, Plato began the controversy by condemning art as an imitation that leads us away from reality. One of his most influential ideas in *The Republic* is the allegory of the cave—a story that seems to have influenced Tolkien's ideas. This story tells of people chained inside a cave looking at a wall and unable to turn around. They see only faint shadows on the wall and dim sounds coming from outside the cave, which are reflections of the world outside. If they do not become free and look outside the cave, they will never see reality but only incomplete reflections.

Explicit reference to the poet's invention being similar to God's creation of the universe is found in late fifteenth-century Florentine writers. For example, in his *Commentary on Dante* (1481), Cristofor Landino writes that "although the feigning of the poet is not entirely out of nothing, it nevertheless departs from making and comes very near to creating. And God is the supreme poet, and the world is His poem."[3] In 1561 Scalinger stated that while other arts represent things as in a picture, "the poet represents another nature and varied fortunes, and in so doing makes himself, as it were, another God."[4]

The use of a *mirror* as a metaphor for art was popular with literary critics beginning with Plato to the mid-eighteenth century.[5] The mirror analogy focused on the subject matter of art rather than the artist. What was important was art's "truth" and correspondence to reality. Art was also commonly compared to a *painting*, enforcing the idea that poetry reflects objects and actions.[6]

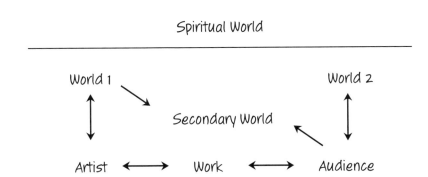

Figure 4.2 Elements related to a work of art in Tolkien and Lewis

A key concept from Aristotle through the eighteenth century was that art was an *imitation* of either actual or ideal objects. This term implied that art is a reflection, representation, counterfeit, copy, or image. While the theory that art is imitation and thus analogous to a mirror called for artistic realism, in neoclassic criticism, art imitates the ideal and thus must differ from the world.[7] Neoclassic theories viewed art as imitation but instrumental in producing an effect upon the audience.[8]

The concept of poet as creator in God's image began in English criticism with Sir Philip Sidney, who believed the poet is a second creator of a second Nature. Sidney's "pragmatic theory" viewed art as something made to achieve a reader response.[9] In "An Apology for Poetry" (1595), he describes the Roman name for poet as *vates* (prophet) and the Greek name *poeta* from *poiein*, "to make." While other arts use nature for their object, the poet, "lifted up with the vigour of his own invention, doth grow in effect another nature, in making things either better than Nature bringeth forth, or, quite anew, forms such as never were in Nature, as the Heroes, Demigods, Cyclopes, Chimeras, Furies, and such like."[10] Because man is made in God's likeness, man was set above works of second nature, which he shows most in poetry, "when with the force of a divine breath he bringeth things forth far surpassing her doings."[11] Because of the Fall, we know what perfection is but are unable to reach it. Poetry is the art of imitation with the goal of teaching and delighting.

Other writers believed that poets do not imitate God's created nature but rather a second one that the poet creates. In 1589, George Puttenham, in "The Art of English Poesy," called poets "creating gods." Abrams notes that this idea that the artist is a God-like creator of a second nature was kept alive by Italian and English neoplatonists who applied the word *creation*, though casually, to poets such as John Donne and Alexander Pope. They used the term to explain and justify supernatural elements in a poem copied from life. These elements, they said, belong to a second "supernature" created by the poet.[12] Poets are like God in that they use the same patterns God used to model the universe.[13] According to Lewis, neoplatonists such as Joseph Scaliger, Philip Sidney, Francis Bacon, and others presented a Christianized Platonic dualism, in which the material world is inferior to that of the soul: "The man who, in his 'feigned history,' improved on Nature and painted what might or ought to be, did not feel that he was retreating from reality into a merely subjective refuge; he was reascending from a world which he had a right to call 'foolish' and asserting his divine origin."[14]

In *The Spectator* (1712), Joseph Addison wrote that poets present fairies, witches, magicians, etc., with the nature the poet bestows on them. This type of writing is difficult because the writer must work from invention.[15] This second world is analogous to the primary world but is a new creation because it not only uses nature but also makes new worlds and creatures. Later critics carried on this idea of "creative imagination." Imagination was viewed as being above reason because it invents fantastic characters not existing in nature and is a mental process reenacting God's own method.[16] By 1740, the idea existed that the poem can be a second creation that is not a replica of this world but creates its own world subject to its own laws, thus giving it an inner coherence. There were seen to be two kinds of Truth: rational and poetic.

During the eighteenth century, art was considered a selective mirror and the perceiving mind reflective of the external world. Invention involved combining the familiar in new ways or reassembling ideas that replicate sensations.[17] Thus art was like a mirror presenting selected ordered images.[18] According to the theory of literary invention at the time, ideas are images in the mind that move sequentially across the mind's eye. If they recur in a different order or are combined into a new whole, we have fancy or imagination.[19] The process involves dividing and recombining "discretes" to form a whole that has a new order but not new parts.[20] Some critics developed a theory that God had an infinite number of possible creations and could not bring all into existence. So the poet is able to create other beings that are possible.[21]

ROMANTICISM

In *English Literature in the Sixteenth Century*, Lewis observes that empiricism eventually reduced nature to mathematical and mechanical elements so that nature was no longer viewed as genial and animistic. When the rise of secular rationalism destroyed the belief that the supernatural was part of the real world, this idea was also rejected in fiction. C. N. Manlove writes, "Gradually fantastic worlds could rely on less and less of an element of prior belief in their possibility: nature ceased to be accepted as involved with supernature, and became what one experienced, where supernature was relegated simply to what one believed—or imagined."[22] When fantasy eventually reappeared, it was as the Romantic "heterocosm," "the belief that the artist could create his own truth system which need have no empirical connection with our own."[23]

By the nineteenth century, the word *create* was routinely used to describe what the poet does. For example, in "A Defence of Poetry," Percy Bysshe Shelley writes, "Poetry lifts the veil from the hidden beauty of the world, and makes familiar objects be as if they were not familiar." In addition, it "makes us the inhabitants of a world to which the familiar world is a chaos. . . . It creates anew the universe after it has been annihilated in our minds by the recurrence of impressions blunted by reiteration."[24] Tolkien agrees with Shelley that imagination is an instrument of moral good and has the ability to penetrate the surface of reality.

With the Romantic poets, and especially William Wordworth's "Preface to the *Lyrical Ballads*" (1800), the emphasis shifted to the artist. Thus began the "expressive theories" of art.[25] A work of art is the "internal made external," the result of creative process, and is a combination of the poet's "perceptions thoughts and feelings."[26] Poetry results from the poetic impulse seeking expression, or the "compulsion of the 'creative' imagination which, like God the creator, has its internal source of motion."[27] The work of art, then, is not a reflection of nature but shows the poet's mind and heart.

Romantic theories of poetry used metaphors such as "overflow" because they considered poetry the expression of feeling. Thus metaphors changed from imitation to expression and from mirror to fountain, plant, and lamp.[28] These metaphors show the importance of the mind in perception. The Romantic writers describe the perceiving mind as a lamp projecting light that is active and made in God's image.[29]

COLERIDGE

Samuel Taylor Coleridge's views are important because Tolkien was directly influenced by his terminology. Coleridge and his contemporaries believed that emphasizing reason causes a separation of mind and nature, subject and object, resulting in a separation of the individual from others and the environment. Imagination is key in restoring unity, balance, and reconciliation.

In *Biographia Literaria* (1817), Coleridge defines three terms: *Fancy*, *Primary Imagination*, and *Secondary Imagination*. *Fancy* is a "mode of memory" free from time and space. It takes materials derived from the senses and moves them in time and space.[30] The *Primary Imagination* is involuntary and common to all men. It is "a repetition in the finite mind of the eternal act of creation in the infinite I AM."[31] This is God's creative Word in the human mind. Genuine creation synthesizes opposing forces into a new whole and does not mimic existing models or reassemble elements into a new pattern. The *Secondary Imagination* is a voluntary act of will found primarily in poets. It "dissolves, diffuses, dissipates, in order to recreate."[32] Coleridge also distinguishes between *phantasia* and *imaginatio*. Phantasia, the active function of the mind, comprehends; imaginatio, the passive function of the mind, receives impressions.

As will be discussed later, Tolkien's views differ from those of Coleridge. While both believed in the importance of reason, Tolkien reverses Coleridge's terminology. In addition, Coleridge did not believe imagination could grasp Truth beyond the scope of reason, as Tolkien does.

GEORGE MACDONALD

Besides these literary theorists, one of the chief influences on Tolkien's and Lewis's views about art and imagination was George MacDonald.

The *Kunstmärchen*, or art folktale, was the product of German Romantics who wanted to turn away from the rational. Writers such as E. T. A. Hoffmann, Friedrich de la Motte Fouqué, and Novalis strongly influenced MacDonald, giving him the idea of using the fairy tale form to express the mystical and supernatural. Specifically, MacDonald's prescription for constructing a fairy tale came from Novalis. MacDonald points to Fouqué's *Undine* (1811) as an example of what he means by a fairy tale. However, such works died out when they became vehicles for philosophical ideas rather than simply tales.

MacDonald saw fantasy's potential for showing the transcendent immanent in reality and how fantasy requires moral behavior from man. Symbols and images present these theological insights. In addition, instead of "telling" the message, MacDonald makes the moralizing a part of the story, depicting spiritual qualities working in people.[33] By illustrating that fantasy could deal with religious questions, he became an important influence on Lewis. Lewis calls MacDonald the first writer to blend holiness and magic.

MacDonald and Lewis share a conservative view of the artist, claiming it is better to use the word *creation* for "that calling out of nothing which is the imagination of God." Only God can create from nothing. "Everything of man must have been of God first."[34] The creation is "divine art" that humans can view with awe. But humans, created in God's image, receive creativity as a gift. Man simply rearranges and recombines elements God has made. However, by using materials from our world and drawing on reality, the author can express Truths that cannot be expressed or explained in other ways. For MacDonald, man may invent new worlds with their own laws because he delights in "calling up new forms," the nearest he can come to creation.[35] If they are mere inventions, they are Fancy. If they are new embodiments of old Truths, they are products of the imagination.

MacDonald defines imagination as "an imaging or a making of likenesses."[36] As the faculty most like God's, it is man's highest mental faculty, existing in the subconscious. God inhabits this area of the mind, controls what it does, and is the source of thoughts.

Imagination gives form to thought, form comes from nature, and nature comes from God. The artist, then, has no control over the products of his imagination. The imagination lights the form, thus making visible the thought within the form. It can present us with new thought-forms, or revelations of thought. However, it creates none of the material from which forms are made. Instead, it takes already-existing forms and groups, subordinates, and harmonizes them into a whole that can unveil thoughts. It is the artist's job to create anew hidden patterns in his own work.

Imagination is part of God's nature and comes from an overflow of love and a meaningful purpose. God's imagination flows into creation and, through humans who participate in creativity, it can flow back to God. Imagination is also the means by which humans can find meaning and purpose. MacDonald believes the main function of imagination is "to inquire into what God has made" and apprehend spiritual Truth. It refuses to consider science the only way to interpret nature.[37] MacDonald was influenced by the German Romantics, who said imagination and intuition receive Truth, and then reason apprehends it. Thus imagination and intellect must work together in harmony.

The work of art should have a "narrative surface bustling and incoherent, supported by an underlying musical harmony" deriving from "an orchestration of themes."[38] Because works of the creative imagination are formed by principles above our apprehension, and even though they may seem chaotic, incoherent, and dreamlike, they are about God, in God's language, and expressions of spiritual Truth. God invests nature with meaning but Truth is hidden; but man, through imagination, can come to know Truth if he is in harmony with God: "The 'harmony within,' the hidden unity and coherence of all things, is with God, whose meanings and purposes infuse the entirety of this apparent chaos with a higher order. The spiritually mature artist is able to catch glimpses of the true import of things."[39]

Creativity comes through both knowing God the Redeemer and the Creator.[40] Thus the closer the artist is to Christ, the better the imagination will be. It also requires a childlike vision of the world.

The imagination is "baptized" and participates in Christ's death and new life. This baptized imagination comes by cleansing and awakening the conscience in order to break down the barrier between sense and intellect, phenomenal and noumenal.[41]

MEDIEVAL MODELS

Tolkien and Lewis draw not only on the rich tradition of literary theory but also on medieval models of the universe. This background helps shape our understanding of their metaphors for fantasy and the imagery used in their fantasy fiction. Furthermore, medieval attitudes about the universe explain these authors' beliefs about the ability of fantasy to restore our relationship with nature and objects.

Lewis's *The Allegory of Love* (1936), *English Literature in the Sixteenth Century Excluding Drama* (1944), and *The Discarded Image* (1964) examine the sources and influences of the medieval worldview. Medieval theories about the planetary system and metaphors of the Music, the Great Dance, and hierarchy of beings (complete with supernatural creatures, beasts, and even inorganic matter) reflected a belief that there is a carefully and intricately patterned universe crafted by a Divine Artisan.

Planetary Model

In the Ptolemaic universe, the Earth is surrounded by a series of hollow transparent spheres. On each is a luminous body (Moon, Mercury, Venus, the Sun, Mars, Jupiter, Saturn). Next is the stellatum, or stars, followed by the sphere called the *Primum Mobile* (First Movable). God causes the Primum Mobile to rotate. Each sphere is an intellectual being called an Intelligence that moves out of love for God.

In contrast, in Dante Alighieri's planetary model, there are seven concentric circles revolving around a point. These are the various orders of angels circling around God as the center of light. Lewis says that while the ancient model was physically teleocentric and anthropocentric, it was spiritually theocentric. In other words, this spatial metaphor illustrates the spiritual universe where God, not man, is at the center. Being bent by sin, Earth is thus cut off from and remains outside the universe. Lewis encounters this same phenomenon in *The Great Divorce* as he climbs in a bus going to Heaven. He has a sense of being in a large space but also of having gotten "out" of Earth "in some sense which made the Solar System itself seem an indoor affair."[42]

Lewis's planetary creations come from tradition and from elements in his own vast imagination as well as an even more elaborate picture that comes to us from the Middle Ages. Scenes in *Perelandra* were meant to be enjoyable or to suggest sensuous happiness.[43] It was Lewis's favorite of the three books, and he especially enjoyed the imaginary world.[44] Ransom says the Malacandrians turn the solar system inside out. To them, the asteroids are Dancers on the edge of the planets or Great Worlds; Jupiter is the "center," as in ancient mythology, for it is associated with something of "vast importance." For this reason, the Oyarsa tells Ransom, earthlings must drop out of Heaven into a world because Earth is outside Heaven; space is the realm of myth and light. Lewis turns our own view of the universe inside out by explaining how even the Ptolemaic model with Earth at the center should really be turned around. For the spatial order is quite the opposite of the spiritual. The physical cosmos, in other words, "mirrors" or reverses spiritual reality; so what is truly the rim seems to us the hub. In actuality, the bent and silent Earth is at the edge of all life: "Earth is the rim, the outside edge where being fades away on the border of nonentity. A few astonishing lines from the *Paradiso* . . . stamp this on the mind forever."[45]

Man was considered a microcosm of the universe; he has a Rational Soul, Sensitive Soul, and Vegetable Soul. The Rational Soul has two faculties: Intellect (*Intellectus*) and Reason (*Ratio*). The Sensitive Soul has ten Senses or Wits; five are outward (sight, hearing, smell, taste, touch), and five are inward (memory, estimation or instinct, imagination, phantasy, common sense). The Vegetable Soul is nutrition, growth, and propagation. Intellect is the higher facility that approaches angelic intelligence. Lewis differentiates intellect and reason by comparing them to rest and motion. While intellect can see a self-evident Truth, reason must proceed sequentially to prove a Truth that is not self-evident.

Imagination retains what it perceives, whereas Phantasy separates and unites. Phantasy is higher than imagination. However, Lewis observes that no medieval author describes these faculties as poetic. In addition, in English, Imagination did not mean just retaining things perceived but also thinking about or having things in the mind.[46]

The Music of the Spheres

The Music of the Spheres is a medieval description of the universe used by Lewis and Tolkien, as well as modern Christian fantasy writers such as Madeleine L'Engle. As scholars of medieval literature, both Lewis and Tolkien would certainly be familiar with this key concept in ancient and classical philosophy. In *De Institutione Musica*, Boethius identified three kinds of music: the music of the universe, vocal, and instrumental. The music of the universe is created by the movement of heavenly bodies, the four elements, and the four seasons. According to the Pythagorean model, the sun, moon, and planets revolve in concentric circles around the Earth, each fastened to a sphere or wheel. They are aligned in such exact mathematical relationships and revolve at such constant speeds that each creates sound waves, proportionate to its speed of orbit, as it moves through space. Each planet sings one note, creating a never-ending chord. Thus the orbits were pictured as a huge lyre or violin with strings curved in circles, tuned by the hand of God and creating a symphony of sound. The Platonists believed that the music was created by the singing of the Intelligences who sat on each sphere.

When Johannes Kepler, a seventeenth-century astronomer, learned that the planets move in elliptical, not circular, paths with different speeds, he calculated the changing speeds, size, and shape of each planet to determine what tone each gave off. According to his theory, the Music of the Spheres was a continuous but ever-changing song.

People of the Middle Ages did not think space dead and silent but rather filled perpetually with sweet sound, "a vast, lighted concavity filled with music and life."[47] We on Earth cannot hear the music, they said, for two reasons: because of the Fall (sin) and because it is too familiar to us to be heard. In his poem "The Ecstasy," Lewis says there is a constant, dull, relentless rhythm beneath Nature's surface even though the "permanent background" has failed our ears.

Another medieval diagram of the universe gives us a possible source for Lewis's idea of fallen Earth as the "silent" planet in his Space Trilogy. Apollo, or God, is envisioned as enthroned in Heaven; beneath him a serpent plunges to Earth. There are eight strings, eight musical modes, and eight celestial spheres. But earth makes nine—one too many—thus destroying the perfection of the scheme. In *Survival of the Pagan Gods*, a book Lewis refers to several times in *The Discarded Image*, we learn that in 1518, Gafurio, basing this theory on Cicero, corrected this little inconsistency by declaring that Earth, being motionless, was therefore silent. So Earth's Muse (Thalia) does not take part in the Music of the Spheres. Lewis explains that the sin brought upon Thulcandra by the Bent Archon causes it to be silent; the Oyarsa no longer communicates with the other Oyeresu. As Screwtape says, noise is the Devil's only defense against the music, melodies, and silences of God's universe. Similarly, in Tolkien's mythology, Melkor introduces disharmony into Eru's grand musical themes.

When Ransom is triumphant in winning one of many arguments against the Un-man and thus in holding the Green Lady a bit longer from temptation, such revelry, dance, and splendor pour into him that, though it makes no sound, it can only be described as music: "It was like being present when the morning stars sang together." He even describes himself as an instrument that he hopes is tuned up to concert pitch. Lewis writes: "If all experienced God in the same way and returned Him an identical worship, the song of the Church triumphant would have no symphony, it would be like an orchestra in which all the instruments played the same note."[48]

The previous chapter described in detail Tolkien's creation myth in which Eru (The One) begins several musical themes that the Ainur turn into a harmonious "Great Music." It becomes "real" when Eru says, "Eä! Let these things Be!" Songs and verse also fill the pages of Tolkien's books. Hobbits are especially fond of writing songs, ranging from hymns to Elbereth to verses conveying legend and walking songs. It is the Elves who, as the most skilled musicians, can enchant with their songs. In *The Lord of the Rings*, the artistic music of the Elves dispels evil. Their songs, laughter, and clear voices containing more melodies than any mortal voice dispel the black shadow. In Lothlórien, Sam comments that he feels he is "inside a song."[49]

The idea of God creating the universe through singing is found as well in Lewis's *The Magician's Nephew*. Aslan creates Narnia by singing "the most beautiful noise Digory had ever heard." Other voices blend in harmony with it, but in "higher, cold, tingling, silvery voices" that become stars, constellations, and planets bursting into sight in the sky. Next, as the sky becomes lighter, Digory can see the many colors of a "fresh, hot and vivid earth"; then a young sun arises, laughing with joy. A soft, rippling music produces first grass, then trees. Polly notices a connection between the notes Aslan is singing and the things he is creating. After singing Narnia into being, Aslan speaks: "Narnia, Narnia, Narnia, awake. Love. Think. Speak. Be walking trees. Be talking beasts. Be divine waters."

The Great Dance

Just as the created universe was an act of and in a state of music, it was also believed to be in a perpetual dance. Like the music metaphor, the dance was used by mystics and poets such as Dante, Sir John Davies, and Milton to show the harmony, order, freedom, and measured movement of the universe. The medieval picture of the Intelligence of the *Primum Mobile* was a girl gaily dancing and playing the tambourine. Many cults also believed that any pomp on Earth reflects this dance in order to participate in it and bring about the union of God and man. Later, however, Newton and Galileo destroyed these ideas by declaring that the universe runs more like a machine.

The Dance is an appropriate metaphor for the perfect joy, harmony, and unity of all creation, where every person, animal, plant, and stone plays a vital part. Each being produces a precise note that blends into the harmony of the universe; so too each individual's path is part of the Dance of the whole. While evil beings desire to create disharmony and discordant music, a similar temptation is to dance on one's own. In *Mere Christianity*, Lewis writes, "The whole dance, or drama, or pattern of this three-Personal life is to be played out in each of us: or (putting it the other way round) each one of us has got to enter that pattern, take his place in that dance. There is no other way to the happiness for which we were made."[50] In *Perelandra*, for example, at the end of the song of the eldila, Ransom is granted a vision of this Dance. As the gods descend on St. Anne's, those present feel as if they are taking their places in the "ordered rhythm of the universe, side by side with punctual seasons and patterned atoms and the obeying Seraphim."

The Great Chain of Being

Individuals were believed to have a place both in a Dance and in a "Chain" or hierarchical ladder of beings. This Chain descended from God and to a vast number of precisely ordered angels, to man, beasts, and finally various inanimate objects. Every particle of creation was a link in the Chain, important for its own special role in God's plan, and every step in the ladder was filled (this was called "plentitude") with beings. According to the medieval model, space was inhabited by an enormous number of intermediaries between man and God who lived between the Empyrean and the moon. According to Lewis, "Medieval man looked up at a sky not only melodious, sunlit, and splendidly inhabited, but also incessantly active."[51] Traditionally, there were said to be nine classes of angels ranging from seraphim to angels.

Hierarchy and the belief in divine creatures is central to both Tolkien's and Lewis's mythologies. In Tolkien's works, beings are ordered in relation to other beings as well as within their own kind. For example, there are the "High" Men of the West, the "Middle" Men of the Twilight, and the Wild Men of Darkness. By the end of the Third Age, Men are taking the place of Elves at the top of the hierarchy.

In *The Discarded Image*, Lewis discusses fairies (Longaevi, long-livers) in ancient literature. Their size is unclear, but their other features are important. Three types of fairies are horrors, diminutive, and High Faeries. Each type had a different poetic purpose. The dark view of fairies was strongest in the sixteenth and early seventeenth centuries. Beginning with Shakespeare, they became increasingly prettified and trivialized, eventually becoming the traditional fairies of children's literature. High Fairies are portrayed with material splendor, energy, and passion. Four theories about their nature were that they are a third species distinct from angels and men, a demoted class of angels, the dead, or fallen angels (devils).

The Medieval Viewpoint

The medieval view of the universe, from which Tolkien and Lewis draw heavily, combines these ideas of music and order. The modern view of space is an example of the contrast between our perceptions and that of the medieval period: "Nothing is more deeply impressed on the cosmic imaginings of a modern than the idea that the heavenly bodies move in a pitch-black and dead-cold vacuity. It was not so in the Medieval Model."[52] The universe was finite, perfectly spherical, and harmonious. Looking at the sky gave a medieval observer the sense of looking out on a sea or forest with no horizon. Space was not pitch black, cold, or dead. Nor was it silent because the planets created harmony and sound. Thus you would look up at a "world lighted, warmed, and resonant with music."[53] Furthermore, you would feel as if you were looking *in*. Spatial and spiritual orders were opposites; that is, the physical cosmos mirrors reality. Whereas humans consider themselves the center of the universe, we are really on the rim, watching the celestial dance from the edge. Man stands at the bottom of a staircase with a top invisible with light.[54]

The tendency of our age has been a diminishing concern for objects and an increasing compulsion to dissect them. Ingrained in each of us is the idea that we arrive at the reality of something and, in fact, "possess" it by analysis. In the Middle Ages, on the other hand, men like Merlin were part of an old order in which matter and spirit were one, every operation on Nature a personal contact that involved loving, reverencing, and knowing the spiritual qualities of Nature. According to Lewis, there were also neutral intelligences in the earth that were neither good nor bad and whom men could encounter by investigating plants and minerals. Man was more in touch with these powers and spirits behind Nature, as well as the secrets, myths, and mysteries locked within it.

Now, says Lewis, the universe is divided into two halves—the natural and supernatural—and we are encouraged never to think of both in the same context. The "new astronomy" beginning in the seventeenth century reduced Nature to the mechanical and mathematical instead of the genial and animistic. After medieval man "came the modern man to whom Nature is something dead—a machine to be worked, and taken to bits." The world was thus emptied of its indwelling spirits, as well as the old mythical imagination through which man could identify with Nature and see the sun as a god rather than a collection of gases.[55] "The soul has gone out of the wood and water," Ransom laments. As Lewis illustrates so well in his books, Nature has, in effect, "hidden" herself from us because man has maltreated and manipulated her.

In *The Abolition of Man*, Lewis points out that in order to understand Nature we have reduced it to a category or an abstraction and thus lost sight of its individuality and divinity. Mark Studdock's education, for example, has made things he reads and writes about more real to him than visible things. Statistics are more real than actual people. In his writing, he uses terms such as *classes* and *populations* rather than *man* or *woman*. In contrast, Ransom realizes that nothing is a copy, model, or more or less important than anything else. He must therefore go to another planet to simply realize that Nature herself is a thing in her own right, separate from us and important for her own sake. Describing his entire encounter as "too definite for language," Ransom sees life on Perelandra as a "colored shape." He had once thought of space as a "black, cold vacuity, the utter deadness, which was supposed to separate the worlds." Yet, "pulsing with brightness as with some unbearable pain or pleasure . . . the stars seized all his attention, troubled him, excited him." The name *space* becomes a "blasphemous libel" for such an "empyrean ocean of radiance." How can one call it dead when he feels life pouring into him every minute?

To Ransom's surprise, space is full, an excess vitality of life, the womb of living creatures where heat and light take on new qualities. He even must believe in the old astrology as he feels " 'sweet influence' pouring or even stabbing into his surrendered body. . . . He felt his body and mind daily rubbed and scoured and filled with new vitality." Earth is a ball spinning not through empty space but in a "densely inhabited and intricately structured medium." This heaven is "tingling with a fullness of life for which infinity itself was not one cubic inch too large." Constantly does Ransom feel a sort of "lift and lightening" of the heart, a "soaring solemnity," a "sense, at once sober and ecstatic, of life and Power offered in unasked and unmeasured abundance."

Whereas Ransom had once thought of other planets as rocky desolations, he learns that Malacandra and Perelandra are extraordinarily beautiful. But in contrast to the fullness and vitality of space itself, the planets seem to him, as they are to the eldila, mere holes or gaps in the living Heaven. The Green Lady calls them "little lumps of the low swimming in the high." Moreover, Earth itself becomes in this perspective a mere dead, silent, cloudlike waste— simply space. Ransom's peek at Earth from the sorn's telescope is one of "the bleakest moments in all his travels." Similarly, Ransom had thought of other creatures as the traditional horrible, monstrous, abominable science fiction bogies with feelers, tentacles, horns, stingers, jaws, and bulbous eyes.

But he learns that there are two ways of viewing everything, depending on "where you are standing" and how much one knows about it. For example, looking at a hross from an earthly perspective, it becomes abominable and disgusting—a seven-foot man with a snaky body covered with thick black hair and whiskers. But from another perspective, it becomes delightful, with everything an animal ought to have: glossy coat, liquid eye, sweet breath, and white teeth. In addition to these qualities, they have, "as though Paradise had never been lost and earliest dreams were true, the charm of speech and reason." Likewise, under the influence of the Director, Jane is suddenly able for the first time to see mice as they really are—"not as creeping things but as dainty quadrupeds" or "tiny kangaroos."

Ransom, in turn, begins to see men from a Malacandran point of view. The ugly pfifltriggian portrait of him chiseled in stone, he realizes, is an idealization of humanity. With a renewed viewpoint, he sees Weston and Devine coming toward him as figures with thick, sausage-like limbs, pear-shaped bodies, square heads, heavy and narrow feet, lumped and puckered faces, and variegated flesh fringed with a dark bristly substance before he recognizes them as men. These ideas all illustrate both Lewis's and Tolkien's views of "recovery," a fresh way of viewing things, as will be discussed in detail in the final chapter.

METAPHORS FOR ART

Tolkien and Lewis draw on this rich background of literary theory and medieval models of the universe for their own metaphors for art.

Tree and Leaf

Tolkien's view of fantasy is fictionalized in his autobiographical story "Leaf by Niggle," one of the few stories unrelated to his mythology. It was written before the War and read aloud to his friends early in 1940. Tolkien describes this story as the only thing he ever wrote effortlessly, waking up with the story complete in his head and then writing it down in one sitting without much change.[56] He found this story moving whenever he reread it.[57]

Niggle is an ordinary, silly, unsuccessful painter with a long journey to make (death). He must do many things he considers a nuisance—in particular, odd jobs for his lame neighbor Parish and

others. Niggle dislikes Parish for being so needy and for his disregard
of painting, which Parish and his wife call "Niggle's Nonsense" or
"That Daubing." In turn, Niggle calls Parish "Old Earth-grubber."

Most of Niggle's paintings are too large and ambitious because he
is better at painting leaves than entire trees. He spends hours on just
one leaf by working on its shape and sheen. But he wants to paint a
whole tree in which the leaves are all the same style yet different.
One of his paintings in particular causes him problems. From a single leaf in the wind it evolves into a Tree with branches and roots.
This Tree is both curious and unique. There are birds in the
branches, as well as glimpses of a country, forest, and mountains in
the distance. Niggle has also tacked other pictures around the edge
so that the canvas is unwieldy. Despite his hope of finishing this picture before his "journey" of death, it keeps growing, and Niggle
keeps getting interrupted. Because he will not have time to complete corners, he must give just a hint of what he wants.

While Niggle believes his painting is both unsatisfactory and yet
the one beautiful picture in the world, he longs for someone to
affirm his art. In the meantime, because his garden becomes
neglected, his neighbors hint that he may get a visit from the Inspector of Houses. Here Niggle is somewhat like the deserter Tolkien describes in "On Fairy Stories." Two kinds of escape are the
flight of the deserter who wants to escape duties and the flight of
the prisoner who wants to escape his prison and experience freedom
through fantasy. Ironically, Niggle spends time on a painted tree,
while his living garden is neglected. Parish is again critical, seeing
only weeds in the garden, just as he sees nonsensical patches and
lines in the painting. What Niggle needs is help with the weeds and
praise for his painting.

Parish also convinces Niggle to stop painting in order to fetch a
doctor for his ailing wife and a builder to repair his leaking roof.
Ironically, Niggle himself becomes sick because of his journey
through soaking rain. Unable to paint and recovering in bed, he can
only imagine leaves and branches in his head. When he is finally
able to resume work, he no longer sees visions of patterns or mountains. As expected, Niggle receives a visit from the inspector, who

chastises Niggle for not using his canvas, wood, and paint to make temporary repairs to Parish's house. Houses come before pictures. Furthermore, Niggle is told to begin his journey, which most view as representing death, with his jobs unfinished.

Along his journey, Niggle makes several stops. His first stop is the Workhouse, where he begins worrying about the past—especially his failure to help Parish more. Although he receives no pleasure from life, he begins to find satisfaction in performing his tasks more efficiently.

One day he hears Voices from a Bard or Court discussing his case. They accuse him of wasting time rather than preparing for his journey and neglecting duties he considered mere interruptions. Despite the fact that he was a weak little man who had no potential, he was a painter who took pains drawing leaves for their own sake. In addition, they consider his final deed for Parish a true sacrifice. As a result, he is permitted to move on to Gentle Treatment.

As he travels by bicycle, the grass and land seem familiar. Then he sees his own Tree, only completed. "It's a gift," he says of both his art and the Tree. All the leaves are there: those he completed, those he only imagined, and those he had not even begun. In the distance are the Forest and Mountains. These are no longer just surroundings, for now as Niggle walks toward them, more and more distances appear. The Mountains in the background slowly get nearer. But they do not belong to the picture; they link to another stage or picture. Tolkien likens these trees and mountains to untold stories. While they can never be approached, they eventually become near in Paradise.[58] There are also "inconclusive regions" in the Forest that still need to be continued.

Finding another tree that he wants to work on, Niggle realizes he needs Parish to help him. Because Niggle puts in a good word for Parish, Parish is available to help him. Ironically, their roles are reversed. Niggle is now able to manage his time and complete tasks. He also is better at building and gardening, and thinks of new flowers and plants. Parish, on the other hand, spends considerable time just looking at trees and is best at implementing Niggle's visions by building and gardening.

As their work grows nearly complete, a shepherd guide offers to take them farther on their journey. Because Niggle has begun to look more often toward the Mountains, he is eager to move on. But Parish decides to wait for his wife. The guide explains that they are in Niggle's Country, which contains Niggle's Picture and Parish's Garden. Parish is amazed at how he had never appreciated Niggle's Picture. It never looked real then because it was only a glimpse; if Parish had only tried, he might have caught it. Niggle chooses to continue on uphill toward the Mountains.

The final judgment of Councillor Tompkins is that silly little Niggle's art was not practically or economically useful. His painting was "private day-dreaming" and fiddling with "pretty" leaves and flowers. He never completed anything. But Councilman Atkins admits that he had torn off a corner of one of his paintings depicting a mountain peak and spray of leaves that he never forgot. All that remains is one intact leaf that he had framed—called "Leaf By Niggle"—and placed in a museum that eventually burns down.

Niggle's region is named Niggle's Parish, a play on the name of his neighbor and a local community. In addition, the Greek meaning is "neighbor" or "sojourner." It becomes a place for holiday, refreshment, convalescence, and "the best introduction to the Mountains." Niggle's journey and Niggle's Parish are no doubt similar to Frodo's journey at the end of *The Lord of the Rings*. Tolkien explains that Frodo goes both to purgatory and a reward, and he has a time for reflection, peace, and gaining understanding.[59]

In his letters, Tolkien explains that Niggle is intended to be a real person with some biographical elements rather than an allegorical representation of one virtue or vice. His "purgatorial" story is part apologia and part confession, myth rather than allegory.[60] Similarly, the name *Parish* has no significance but was a matter of convenience for the Porter's joke about the train leaving for "Niggle's Parish in the bay."[61]

Like Niggle, Tolkien was an accomplished artist. He drew pictures of trees, including one for the cover of *Tree and Leaf*, the volume in which "Leaf by Niggle" was published. Tolkien mentions having among his papers several versions of a mythical "tree" that he drew when he felt like "pattern-designing." They contain many leaf shapes, as well as flowers of all sizes, which represent poems and legends.[62] But these elaborate colored drawings are more suited for embroidery than painting, he writes.

In addition, Tolkien calls himself a "natural niggler."[63] For example, he niggled about the incorrect spelling of *dwarfs* and other words in the Puffin edition of *The Hobbit*. Tolkien believed that his university job of teaching, grading, and attending meetings interfered with serious work. In addition, his colleagues considered his work "trivial literature."[64]

Trees are significant throughout Tolkien's life and mythology. The story itself was inspired by a poplar tree mutilated by its owner.[65] Tolkien always took the side of trees against those who hate and injure them.[66] Kilby writes that the tree in Tolkien's works is a symbol of beginnings and endings, significant people, and historical events.[67] In *The Silmarillion*, for example, the Two Trees Telperion (white) and Laurelin (gold) provide light for Valinor. The White Tree of Gondor that Aragorn replants when he becomes king is descended from the Two Trees.

"Leaf by Niggle" also was inspired by Tolkien's preoccupation with *The Lord of the Rings*, a story he wanted to write for an adult audience using a "large canvas."[68] It describes anxiety about his own "internal Tree" that he wanted to finish but feared he would never complete.[69] It kept growing out of hand by revealing "endless new vistas." He compares his own method of writing as a "branching acquisitive theme."[70] In the foreword to *The Lord of the Rings*, Tolkien says the story had roots in the past and "threw out unexpected branches." He found his own "untold stories" the most moving and thought that, like Niggle's distant trees, they could never be approached.[71] *The Lord of the Rings* is a "Frameless Picture" showing a brief period in Earth's history and surrounded by the "glimmer of limitless extensions in time and space."[72] The leaves are individual stories or even scenes and details. In writing *The Lord of the Rings*, Tolkien, like Niggle, had no idea where he was going. But because the world kept threatening, he kept getting "stuck" and did not know how to proceed.[73]

In "On Fairy Stories," Tolkien describes a student of fairy tales who believes he is just collecting leaves from the Tree of Tales. This Tree is the combination of all the literary tales written. Its branches are "intricately knotted and ramified history." He might feel as if he could never design a new leaf for the Tree.[74] Or he may feel that others have already discovered the tree patterns ranging from buds to unfolded leaves and all the colors of the seasons. But a seed can be planted in any soil. The author, affected by his experiences, uses the "soil of experience" for the germ of his story. He also writes out of the "leaf-mould" of memories.[75]

Each leaf uniquely embodies the pattern.[76] Even though trees have produced leaves for generations, a leaf may be the one embodiment, the first one that someone has recognized and experienced. Each embodiment is a new creation. Just as certain stories about a dying god repeat in mythology, so too are there repeating patterns in creation. For example, even though stories may seem to have the same plot, the atmosphere and "unclassifiable individual details" give the plot life.

Jeffrey MaCleod and Anna Smol point out that Tolkien uses the images of planting seeds and splintering lights to represent repetition or recapitulation of themes and subjects. For instance, the story of Aragorn and Arwen recapitulates the story of Beren and Luthien. Although stories may use the same pattern, they are unique. Similarly, human creations are recapitulative because they are derived from the divine Creator. Our creations are unique but fit within pre-existing patterns.

In the Introductory Note to the story, Tolkien also relates the tree and leaf symbols to sub-creation. The artist may actually help in the "effoliation" and "enrichment" of creation.[77] According to Tolkien, the word *effoliation* ties together his essay "On Fairy Stories" and "Leaf by Niggle."[78] He was fascinated by botany books, particularly related specimens. They made him think about the years of descent and the pattern and design of each living thing as recognizable and separate from its individual embodiment of the pattern.[79]

Just as Niggle continues to work on his art throughout his journey, Tolkien's poem "Mythopoeia" describes Paradise as True rather than "mirrored truth" and a place where artists will continue to "make anew." Tolkien believes there are no boundaries to a writer's work except those imposed by his own finiteness.[80]

In discussing the Truth that art should reveal, Tolkien considers it a story still in the making. He wanted to leave his mythology open to additions by other "minds and hands" in the form of other media, such as painting, music, and drama.[81] Shippey suggests that Niggle and Parish may be two aspects of Tolkien's own personality.[82] However, in "On Fairy Stories" and *The Silmarillion*, Tolkien suggests that sub-creation requires a cooperative group effort. Niggle's work requires a partnership with Parish and must move from his own private work to something that involves and benefits others.

Living Pictures

While Tolkien uses a painting and tree to depict sub-creative art, Lewis uses pictures to convey the difference between the limitations of art and the "other" world it points to. His own art began with static "mental pictures." In contrast, Lewis uses "living pictures" in his stories to represent the eternal Truth that art reflects. The secondary world created by the imagination presents the world that lies behind appearances. Because this world is even more real than the world of "fact" we see in space and time, both worlds are necessary parts of the whole Truth.

In *Pilgrim's Regress*, Wisdom tells John that the Landlord's stories are picture-writing to show people as much Truth as they can understand. An example is the legend of the Landlord's Son who became one of the tenants and was killed. This beautiful story "is a picture of the life of Spirit itself."[83] The starting point for people is a picture rather than Rules. The Landlord also sent many messages through pagan stories that awakened desire.[84] Although the Landlord sends many kinds of pictures, the message is universal and awakens desire and longing.[85] Because previous pictures were of things not in the world, the Enemy made people believe the picture was the thing they wanted. Here Lewis traces the way philosophies about art and nature have changed. For example, one result was idolizing the picture or corrupting the message.

Lewis uses the picture image in *The Magician's Nephew* to raise the issue of what is real. Digory experiences a strange "echo" during his first time in the Wood Between the Worlds: "If anyone had asked him: 'Where did you come from?' he would probably have said, 'I've always been here.' That was what it felt like—as if one had always been in that place." Polly says, "I had . . . a sort of picture in my head—of a boy and a girl, like us—living somewhere quite different—and doing all sorts of things. Perhaps it was only a dream."

In *The Voyage of the "Dawn Treader,"* on Eustace's bedroom wall is a lovely picture of a sailing ship on the sea. This picture shows the contrast between static pictures and becoming part of a story. The more Lucy stares at it, the more real and alive the scene becomes—in fact, the waves start to roll up and down, and the air smells wild and briny. Lucy, Edmund, and Eustace are even slapped in the face with salt water. As Eustace attempts to smash the picture, he finds himself standing on the frame, and then is swept into the sea and into Narnia.

Living pictures, on the other hand, represent the ideal story. In one of the most memorable passages in all of the Chronicles, Lucy, in reading the Magician's Magic Book, comes across a "spell for the refreshment of the spirit." Lucy finds that she is living in the story as if it was real and all the pictures were real, too. It is about a cup, a sword, a tree, and a green hill, and is the loveliest story she has ever read. But she can neither read it again nor really remember it. Ever since that time, though, Lucy defines a good story as one that reminds her of this forgotten story. Aslan, who is said to be "at the back of all the stories," promises her that he will tell that story to her for years and years. The children can now begin the Great Story.

Similarly, in *Till We Have Faces*, the Fox leads Orual to a room quite different from the dark cave in which she had presented her case against the gods. The cool bright chamber contains three walls and a fourth containing vine-covered pillars and arches. The walls are painted with stories that turn out to be living pictures. Orual finds that she is living in the story as if it was real. Unlike her dead book—her case against the gods—the living pictures used to present the gods' case show their mercy in allowing Psyche to finish the tasks for her, as well as how to escape from Ungit forever.

The Star: *Smith of Wootton Major* and *Farmer Giles of Ham*

In another shorter work, *Smith of Wootton Major* (1967) (originally called "The Great Cake"), Tolkien uses several metaphors to depict the gift of fantasy and nature of Faery. Tolkien was to write an introduction to George MacDonald's "The Golden Key." As he began explaining the meaning of "fairy" by writing "This could be put into a short story like this," the story took off on its own.[86] In a letter to Clyde Kilby, Tolkien writes that he disliked MacDonald and allegory. Some believe that the story is about Tolkien's anxiety over old age and a farewell to his art.[87] Tolkien also describes *Smith of Wootton Major* as "a little counterblast to Lewis."[88]

The setting is an imaginary countryside; Wootton Major is "not very far away," "not very long ago," and "not very large." It is known for its crafts but most famous for its cooking. The Village Council owns a large Kitchen run by a Master Cook. The most beautiful building, the Great Hall, is no longer as decorated as it had once been. The town's most popular festival, called The Feast of Good Children, is held every twenty-four years, and only twenty-four children are invited. The Master Cook is expected to make a Great Cake that is unique, new, and surprising.

Wootton Major has had commercial success with their crafts because of their contact with Faery. Although Faery exists independently from the town, they still have a relationship, which is vital to keeping the village from declining. Here Tolkien draws on the Irish and Welsh traditions of nonhuman creatures with supernatural power living in the countryside in a fairy mound or underworld.[89] He also shows that Faery is real and exists independently of human imagination.

The Elves send to Wootton Major the King of Faery (Alf) to be an apprentice. After the Master Cook goes away on a holiday, he returns greatly changed and brings back Alf. They also send a small silver star as a token of those the Elves guide and protect. In Tolkien's Elvish language, the words *Elf* and *star* are both derived from the word *EL*.[90]

Three years later, the Cook leaves for good and puts Alf in charge. However, the village appoints the solid but sly Nokes as Master Cook. Nokes decides that the Great Cake should be sweet, rich, covered in sugar icing, and topped with a Fairy Queen dressed in white with a wand in her hand. While he assumes that children's taste requires fairies and sweets, he is unsure what goes inside a cake. Old recipes don't help him because they mention spices he does not have. However, inside a black box he discovers the tarnished star to put inside the cake. Alf warns him it is "fay," from Faery. Nokes mockingly tells him, "You'll grow up some day." Nokes is thus the example of the skeptic or unbeliever who mocks the serious world of fairy.

Although the children find the cake "pretty" and "fairylike," Alf is understandably displeased. There is just enough cake, and one of the boys named Smith unknowingly swallows the star. On his tenth birthday, he awakens to the sound of birds singing. Reminded of Faery, he begins to sing strange words. The star falls out of his mouth and into his hand. He claps his hand to his forehead, where the star remains for years. His singing and words remain lovely, and he is known as an excellent craftsman. Not only does he make practical and useful objects but also beautiful and delightful things. However, he is best known for his ability to create light and delicate but strong objects from iron.

Smith becomes familiar with the perilous regions of Faery and is welcomed there as "Starbrow." He is also guarded from both Lesser and Greater Evils. The marvels of Faery are both beautiful and dangerous, and powerful weapons are needed to challenge Evils. Faery is described as containing woods, fairy valleys, and bright waters that mirror the peaks of far mountains at dawn. At the edges of Faery is a sea bearing ships returning from battles. Smith spends time looking at one tree or flower and sees beautiful and terrifying things that he cannot remember but that dwell deep in his heart. In addition, he remembers other "wonders and mysteries" things that he often ponders.

But he begins to think more and more about the mountains. During his wanderings, he comes upon the King's Tree rising into the sky and containing countless leaves, flowers, and fruits, each unique. The light is compared to the sun at noon. Although he seeks the tree thereafter, he never sees it again. His desire to go deep into the land remains with him. Eventually, he finds his way to the Inner Mountains and into the Vale of Evermorn. There he finds the greenest of green and lucid air. He dances with the Elves, including the Queen of Faery herself, experiencing speed, power, and joy. In his hair is a flower that he brings back home. This Living Flower never dies and emits a light that never dims. In casting shadows on the wall, it makes Smith's shadow huge. His son, who had never spoken before, says it makes his father look like a "giant." This shadow, we learn later, is the Truth. They keep the flower as a family treasure in a locked casket that has the power to close on its own.

Smith eventually receives a summons from the Queen of Faery, who can communicate with him without words. She tells him to not be ashamed of the dancing figure on the Great Cake because this is better than no memory of Faery. Some will have just a glimpse; others will have an awaking. Because he has desired to see her, his wish has been granted. He is also instructed to tell the King, "The time has come. Let him choose." Sadly, it is time for him to leave Faery forever and select his successor. The Queen's touch makes him feel like he is in the World and in Faery simultaneously and yet outside them both.

On his way home, he conveys the Queen's message to a stranger, Alf the apprentice, who has not aged. Smith learns that his father, Rider, had brought the star from Faery and placed it in the black box. Alf tells Smith it is now time to relinquish the star. One point of the tale, then, is passing "power and vision to the next generation." [91]

Alf plans to bake another great Cake and place the star inside it. The once plain box is now decorated with silver scrolls, and inside are fresh spices. When Smith removes the star from his forehead, it produces a stab of pain and appears as a blur of light. Because he gives up the star freely, Smith is permitted to pick the child to whom it will go: Nokes's great-grandson Tim. The child, like he was, is not an obvious choice. Alf reveals that he had already chosen Tim as well. However, the boy will not know because that is the way with gifts.

Although Smith will be going on no more journeys to Faery, he will now have time to teach his son Ned more than just working with iron. Smith shows his son a tiny silver flower of bells from Faery that he plans to give as a gift to a two-year-old to play with. Ned says the scent reminds him of something he has forgotten.

Now in his late eighties, Nokes still wonders what became of the star. He refuses to believe Alf when he reveals that Smith received it, just as he refused to believe the star was from Faery. Alf reveals that he is the King of Faery. But Nokes considers it just a bad dream and Alf too artful and nimble. Nokes still has no respect for Faery. Alf then appoints Harper to be Master Cook and leaves. Smith and Harper paint and gild the Great Hall, restoring it to its old glory.

Faery represents sub-creative imagination, unpossessive love, and respect for animate and inanimate things.[92] This aspect of the story is not allegory, and it is not about religion. However, Tolkien admits that the human elements in the story could be considered allegory. The Great Hall and Master Cook represent the village church and the parson's losing touch with the arts and having diminished functions.[93]

In a contrasting short work, *Farmer Giles of Ham* (1949), Tolkien mocks the typical elements and tone of fairy tales. This story has an unlikely hero, no battles, and uses satire to parody the traditional heroic epic. Tolkien wrote the story lightheartedly, so the anachronisms were intentional.[94] Even the preface is a satire, as Tolkien mocks scholars like those he criticizes in his essay on *Beowulf*.

Tolkien places the story in the valley of the Thames before the time of King Arthur, so unlike most of his works, the location and time are more specific. Red-bearded Giles is described as slow and unconcerned about the "Wide World." His dog Garm can speak in order to bully, brag, or wheedle. After Giles wounds a dull-witted giant with a gun called a blunderbuss, he becomes the unlikely Hero of the Countryside. Tolkien's definition of "blunderbuss" is taken from the *Oxford English Dictionary*, which Tolkien helped work on, and the Four Wise Clerks who provide it are a reference to the four editors. The king sends Giles a letter of commendation, as well as a belt and sword called Tailbiter that had once belonged to the greatest dragon-slayer of the realm.

Dragons have not appeared for a while in this kingdom, and young dragons consider knights to be mythical or rare. The giant reports that there are no more knights, only stinging flies. Thus the dragon Chrysophylax Dives, who has a wicked but uncourageous heart, sets off for the Middle Kingdom. The knights, however, do nothing other than waste time talking about hats and find various excuses not to hunt it. Here Tolkien satirizes knighthood. One knight ironically calls knights "mythical." The people thus call on Giles, arguing that courage rather than official knighthood is all that is required. After running out of his own excuses, Giles confronts the dragon, eventually chasing it into the center of town. The exhausted creature agrees to make remunerations for all his damage and vows never to disturb their land again.

However, having no conscience, the dragon fails to return. The king consequently orders Giles, servants, and knights on a quest to find the dragon to punish him for lying. When they come upon Chrysophylax, the men scatter or are killed. Giles, however, argues for a considerable time with him. He makes a deal with the dragon to let him keep back a small portion of the treasure in return for keeping most of it himself and having the dragon carry it back. The remaining servants enter Giles's service. Disrespectful of the King's authority, Giles refuses to give him any of the treasure. Giles then becomes so notorious that he becomes King and establishes a new order of knighthood. Having also gained the dragon's esteem, Giles releases Chrysophylax. The creature regains some self-worth by devouring a dragon and telling off the giant who lied.

This story contrasts the serious tone of *Smith* and "On Fairy Stories." Tolkien does, however, illustrate characteristics of heroic fantasy by showing the opposite. For example, knights are useless in slaying dragons. As the narrator informs us, an unlikely hero can stand up to threats of giants, dragons, and kings through luck and by using his wits. Tolkien also uses many elements found in his fantasy works, such as the magical sword, cunning dragon, and reluctant hero. Critics have noted numerous references to the many genres that influenced Tolkien, as well as classics ranging from *Beowulf* to nursery tales. Shippey even proposes that the short novel is an allegory about creativity versus dull academic scholarship, just as *Smith* may satirize philological versus literary approaches to the study of English.

Mountains

In both "Leaf by Niggle" and *Smith of Wootton Major*, Tolkien mentions distant mountains. For instance, in "Leaf by Niggle," glimpses of the mountains can be seen in Niggle's painting. In creating his own mythology, Tolkien realized that he must tell a story, but it was the untold stories that moved him the most. He compares these untold stories to mountains seen from far away. In several of his stories, Tolkien mentions glimpses of far-off mountains to symbolize momentary visions of the ideal world.

After he goes on his journey, Niggle sees his Tree completed. In the distance are the Mountains that get nearer as they are approached and that link to another stage or picture. Niggle longs for the Mountains. Thus the end of the story describes him moving uphill toward them, with the narrator unsure of what became of him. The area where Niggle and Parish work, called Niggle's Parish, is "the best introduction to the Mountains."

Similarly, in *Smith of Wootton Major*, Smith longs for the mountains in Faery. Faery contains woods, valleys, and waters that mirror the peaks of far mountains at dawn. The Queen of Faery tells Smith that the image of the Dancing Fairy on the Great Cake was a "glimpse" of this world.

Both Tolkien and Lewis use the word *glimpse* to describe the writer's brief insights in this imperfect world into the permanent world. As will be discussed later, Tolkien believed one of the highest functions of fairy stories is the "eucatastrophe" (good catastrophe), which is a "sudden glimpse" of reality or Truth. Lewis also uses the word *glimpse* to describe our feeble attempts to see God and the ideal, but he uses glass or mirror images to represent blurry glimpses of God or of the ideal in a looking glass.

A thread throughout all of Lewis's life was the search for "Joy." It began as a series of "aesthetic" experiences scattered through his younger years. For example, the low line of the Castlereagh Hills that he could see from his nursery window taught Lewis longing or "Sehnsucht."[95] Thus in Narnia, the things we desire are associated with the distant mountains of Aslan's Country. In "Myth Became Fact," Lewis describes myth as the mountain from which streams "arise which become truths down here in the valley" of separation.[96]

Light

Light is another metaphor that both Tolkien and Lewis use in their fiction to depict the divine light that comes from God to man. Tolkien refers to intimations of God as splintered fragments of light; the misuse of light can also be compared to the Rings of Power. Lewis sees Christ as the light of the world that illumines the mind.

Light in Tolkien

Tolkien writes to his son Christopher that when he was taking the Sacrament, he thought he saw the Light of God with a mote suspended in it "glittering white because of the individual ray from the Light which both held and lit it."[97] He uses the same imagery in "On Fairy Stories" by comparing God to a single White light that is splintered into many hues and becomes the refracted light of man as sub-creator.[98]

Similarly, in *The Silmarillion*, Eru's original Flame Imperishable splinters and fragments throughout history. Despite being farther from its source, the light can be crafted numerous times into new things. Yavanna, the goddess of growing things, asks Aulë to create two mighty lamps for Middle-earth: Illuin and Ormal. Varda, the Queen of the Valar and goddess of light, fills the lamps set on pillars. But Melkor destroys the pillars, breaking the lamps and spilling their flames on the earth. The first light is put out and cannot be brought back. Then Yavanna calls forth a new light in the form of two Trees: gold Laurelin and silver Telperion. Like Eru, she creates the trees by singing. Tolkien calls the Light of Valinor the light of art undivorced from reason and that sees things scientifically and imaginatively or sub-creatively and calls them "good."[99]

Fëanor, son of Finwë King of the Noldor, is the Elves' chief artificer. He is the student of Mahtan, who learned from the Vala Aulë. Not only is he a master craftsman, but he also invents the Tengwar script and creates the palatíri. The pinnacle of his achievement, though, is creating the three Silmarils ("radiance of pure light"), or Great Jewels, by capturing the light of the two Trees of Valinor in them. Tolkien does not explain how he creates them, but neither the Valar nor Fëanor can copy them.

This act preserves the last vestige of the divine on Middle-earth. It also symbolizes the sub-creative function of the Elves.[100] This becomes the most renowned work of the Elves, but Fëanor begins to greedily love them and refuses to share his creative works. Light illuminates and makes visible; it is not to be possessed. This possessive attitude eventually leads to the fall of the Elves.

After Melkor is released from prison, he too desires the Silmarils. Melkor attacks Valinor and with the aid of the spider-creature Ungoliant destroys the two trees of light. He also kills Fëanor's father and steals the Silmarils, placing them in his iron Crown. Eventually, one ends up in the sea, one in Earth's deeps, and one, Eärendil, becomes a star. Fëanor vows that he will not rest until he retrieves the Silmarils. His sons and many Noldor leave Valinor to go to Middle-earth and are thus banned from returning. Wars and tragedies follow, resulting in the Elves' sorrow.

Before the Trees die, Yavanna obtains a flower of silver from Telperion and a single gold fruit from Laurelin. From these, the Valar create a sun and moon for Middle-earth, because the second Children of Iluvatar are about to awaken there. Tolkien writes that the lights of the Sun and Moon are derived from the Trees after they are "sullied" by Evil.[101] The Sun is thus symbolic of the fallen world and imperfect vision.[102] Anyone on Middle-earth who looks at the sun and moon sees the ancient light of the Two Trees.

The story of the Silmarils is also told in the tale of Beren and Lúthien. Tolkien referred to himself as Beren and his wife Edith as Lúthien.[103] It was also one of the first stories Tolkien shared with Lewis, who was impressed by the realistic background and mythic quality. It tells of the marriage of an Elf and a mortal, the recovery of a Silmaril, and the lust for it that leads the Elves to disaster.[104] Lúthien is the daughter of the Elven King Thingol and the Maia spirit Melian of the Valar. Thingol, Melian, and Lúthien live in Doriath, home of Menegroth or the Thousand Caves. It exemplifies the finest craftsmanship of the Elves in the Eldar Days. In this subterranean hall are rocks that look like living stone. On the walls and pillars are carved beasts, birds, and trees. The halls are also decorated with tapestries depicting the Valars' deeds.

Considered the fairest and most beautiful of the Children of Ilúvatar, Lúthien has a "shining light" in her face and with her song holds a power over nature. In Lúthien, then, are the two ideals of light and music. Beren, Lúthien's mortal lover, and King Finrod Felagund, the nephew of Feanor, fight with Sauron in songs of power. Beren and Finrod are taken prisoner. But Lúthien sings a song that defeats Sauron and frees the prisoners. The two journey on to confront Morgoth, who wears the stolen Silmarils in his Iron Crown. Lúthien sings a song that is so lovely and powerful that he is blinded. The Silmarils suddenly blaze with a white flame that so weakens Morgoth that they escape with one Silmaril from the Iron Crown.

Earendil the Mariner and father of Elrond eventually gets possession of the Silmaril. With this light, he travels back to the lost West and Valinor. Listening to his pleas, the gods take pity on the Elves. The Valar then march to Middle-earth, ending Morgoth's reign. Earendil and his Silmaril are transfigured into the Star of Hope, a herald star that gives men hope.[105]

Men seek the light—their hearts are turned westward because they believe they will find light there.[106] Similarly, the light of a small twinkling star provides hope to Sam in the forsaken land of

Mordor. It is like a clear, cold shaft piercing him with the realization that the Shadow will pass; "there was light and high beauty for ever beyond its reach."[107]

The story of the Silmarils continues in *The Lord of the Rings*. Before they enter Mordor, Sam realizes that they are in the same story as Beren and Lúthien, because light from the Two Trees of Valinor is in the small Phial of Galadriel that Frodo carries.

Created Objects as Gifts or Possessions

The Silmarils can be compared to the Rings of Power. First, they demonstrate that the creator's essence can go into that which is created. Yavanna, Fëanor, and Sauron all create important objects that drain the creator's powers and cannot be duplicated. In addition, these objects illustrate the two end results of creation: to produce gifts for the enjoyment of others or to hoard art like a treasure and use it to dominate others.

For example, Yavanna puts her thought of things into making the Two Trees. When Ungoliant devours their light, Yavanna says that within Eä, she can never create them again.[108] Yavanna also predicts that the dwarves will not love what she loves. They love the things they create with their own hands rather than living things. Their view of Earth as the source of gems and minerals is utilitarian. Similarly, part of Fëanor's essence goes into making the Silmarils. He creates them hoping to make something permanent and fairer than anything the Eldar have made. However, he considers them his possession rather than objects of beauty to be shared. At first his heart is "fast bound" to them. Then he begins to be greedy, begrudging others even the sight of them. If he must break his jewels, then his heart will break, and he will be slain.[109]

Other objects receive the creator's power. Sauron forges One Ring as a tool of power to be the most powerful of the Rings, providing him with mastery over the others. It is inscribed with artificial Tengwar script, or Black Speech. But he too must put his own power and will within the Ring, thus making him dependent on it and giving it a power and will of its own. In Volume 10 of *The History of Middle*

Earth, Tolkien writes that just as Sauron focused all his power in the One Ring, Morgoth disseminated his power into Arda's matter, making all of Middle-earth Morgoth's Ring.[110]

Unlike the Silmarils of light, the Ring is gold that cannot be destroyed even by dragon fire—except by throwing it into the fires of Mount Doom where it was forged. Gandalf notes that Sauron concentrates so much on power that the thought does not enter his heart that the Ring could be taken to Mordor for destruction. If the One Ring is unmade, Sauron will be prevented from recovering his former power. In contrast to the "creation" theme in *The Silmarillion,* *The Lord of the Rings* describes an "anti-quest" with the goal of destroying rather than finding, unmaking rather than making.

The Ring is never shown to be evil; rather, its power is a temptation. The Ring bearer dominates others' wills and increases the wearer's innate talents, also extending life but making it a burden. In contrast to the illuminating light of the Silmarils, the Ring dims the wearer's sight of physical things and makes him invisible to physical beings. Tolkien describes the Ring as a mythical way of representing the idea that potency or potentiality must be external so that it can pass from one's control and then produce results.[111] This idea also parallels Tolkien's view of art itself; the artist must release it freely to others.

The ability to create is a gift that can be used well or abused, just as the beauty of the created object can inspire either love or greed. The purpose of making is to "be" and to give pleasure to those who observe and participate in it. The object of art, in turn, is a gift from the artist to the audience, who have the freedom to use it as they wish. But the sub-creator's right to freedom can be used wickedly and create great harm.[112] When misused, the object is created for personal use and power and hoarded, just as a dragon hoards its treasures. The hoarder does not appreciate, share, or care for the hoard. In *The Hobbit,* Thorin the dwarf criticizes dragons for stealing and plundering; they don't know the difference between a good or bad work and cannot make anything for themselves. Smaug is so enraged when his two-handled cup is missing from his hoard that he is compared to rich people who have more than they can enjoy and then lose something they have owned but have never even used or wanted.

Artistic creation is never selfish but delights in the world for its own sake and desires to enhance it and help it fulfill its potential. Aulë, for example, delights in the act of making and the things he makes rather than possessing or mastering them. It is said that he "gives and hoards not." The Elves too appreciate the physical world for its own sake as "other" rather than a source of power. Matthew Dickerson and Jonathan Evans argue that Tolkien's theory of creation is tied to the concept of stewardship. Being created in the image of God requires a belief in the importance of the physical world and the importance of caring for and respecting God's creation. The gift of creativity should also be cared for, respected, and used well. Similarly, Christopher Brawley believes that writers like Tolkien and Lewis shift from the anthropocentric to an ecocentric or biocentric paradigm by renewing a right relationship with Earth and nature.[113]

Tolkien's view of power is also related to naming. As Tolkien writes in "Mythopoeia," a tree is not a tree until it is named. Naming brings things into existence, as seen in both Tolkien's and Lewis's description of creation. Furthermore, according to ancient tradition, the name of a thing expresses or contains its true nature. Bilbo, for example, mistakenly reveals his name to Gollum. Therefore, knowing the true name of a person or thing gives power. In turn, refusing to name something is a refusal to use power.

Light in Lewis

Like Tolkien, Lewis uses the light analogy to describe man's imperfect works reflecting God's Truth.

In several of his essays, Lewis discusses the fact that events and physical sensations must originate somewhere. Nature is lit up by a light beyond, indicating that "Someone is speaking who knows more about her than" we can from inside her.[114] Although "by light we can see things" but are unable to see it, we are still conscious of light. Lewis says that sunlight in the woods can show things about the sun that you cannot get from books on astronomy: "These pure and spontaneous pleasures are 'patches of Godlight' in the woods of our experience."[115] Light, then, is the pointer to Concrete Reality, and the visible world points to the invisible world: "Nature is only the image, the symbol; but it is the symbol Scripture invites me to use. We are summoned to pass in through Nature, beyond her, into that splendour which she fitfully reflects."[116]

Lewis was influenced by Samuel Alexander's *Space, Time, and Deity* (1920), which presents the theory of Enjoyment and Contemplation: One cannot act and contemplate an act at the same time.[117] He distinguishes three things: the Unconscious, the Enjoyed, and the Contemplated. Mental pictures are what thought leaves behind when interrupted. Lewis realized that hoping to find the Joy he longed for his whole life couldn't be achieved. Rather, everything is just a track left by Joy's passage. Thus images are inadequate sensations mistaken for Joy itself.[118]

Similarly, while God is Light and pervades everything that exists, we cannot see the Source Itself, only the manifestations, especially Christ, the incarnated Light. Man and nature are imperfect reflections and broken images. We see the true nature of reality through a veil and shadows and express it through abstract symbols. Lewis uses this analogy to illustrate the idea that "statements about God are extrapolations from the knowledge of other things which the divine illumination enables us to know."[119] He uses the analogy of a beam of light coming through a hole in a toolshed. There is a difference between looking along and looking at the beam. Neither experience is better than the other. Instead, we must look both *along* and *at* everything.[120] While we might prefer "an unrefracted light giving us ultimate truth in systematic form," God did what was best.[121] In *Pilgrim's Regress*, Vertue echoes Tolkien's imagery by singing,

How should man live save as glass
To let the white light without flame, the Father, pass
Unstained: or else—opaque, molten to thy desire,
Venus infernal starving in the strength of fire![122]

In many of his novels, Lewis almost always associates God and Heaven with the biblical metaphor of light. For example, in *The*

Last Battle, the children move "further up and further in" to Aslan's Country. They scale a waterfall that is compared to "climbing up light itself."

In *Out of the Silent Planet*, Ransom realizes that the planets are mere holes or gaps in the heavens because space is full of life. He considers the possibility that "visible light is also a hole or gap, a mere diminution of something else. Something that is to bright unchanging heaven as heaven is to the dark, heavy earth." For God himself is a more perfect light than we know on Earth, the "intolerable light of utter actuality."

At the end of *Perelandra*, as all the eldila and creatures gather around the King and Green Lady, Ransom notices that everything is bathed in a pure daylight that has no particular source. After that experience, he understands what is meant by light resting on something holy but not emanating from it. The Great Dance is described as being woven out of cords or bands of light; each thing "is the end and the final cause of all creation and the mirror in which the beam of His brightness comes to rest and so returns to Him."

Throughout the Space Trilogy, Lewis also uses the limitations of our physical sight to illustrate the limitations of our spiritual vision and different gradations of our spiritual blindness as a result of the Fall in Eden. A perfect example is the eldila, whom Ransom finds hard to see because light goes right through them. He is told that we cannot see light because light is "on the edge" for us. Just as we cannot see some physical realities, the impaired nature of our spiritual vision blinds us to spiritual reality. Light is thus an appropriate metaphor for exemplifying that we cannot know the whole of reality or go "behind" events. Light is only a pointer to something else: Light Itself, or Maleldil. Although we cannot see the source of light, we are nevertheless conscious of it, and it enables us to see things.

In *Till We Have Faces*, Orual's veil symbolizes the inner blindness that keeps her from seeing the clarity of the proof the gods give her. As a result, Orual cannot see the light of the gods but rather associates them with darkness, riddles, and uncertainty.

Light and blindness serve as metaphors for the problem of the nature of reality that Lewis and Barfield debated in the Great War.

Reality is not simply that which can be observed. Lewis wrote the story "The Man Born Blind" in the 1920s when he and Barfield were deep in the Great War debate over appearance and reality. Tolkien, who emphasizes the contrast between light and darkness, was familiar with the story, although it contained differences from the final version.[123] In this story, Robin, a man who has recently gained his sight, wants to see the light people have always told him about. After continual questioning and confusion, Robin becomes convinced that no one really knows what light is. Instead, he is only aware of the effects of light: heat, colors, and shadows.

When one day he takes his first walk alone, he comes upon a painter who tells Robin he is trying to "catch the light." He explains that you can see solid light that you can drink or bathe in. Pointing to a vapor spiraling up from the bottom of a stone quarry, he shouts, "There's light for you if you like it." Robin vanishes, and then there is a sound of a body falling. Robins wants so much to become part of the light that he jumps into it. He has mistaken the effects of light for light itself.

Here Lewis also uses light as a symbol for a reality we have lost but which was very much visible in the past. Robin becomes convinced that there are gradations of blindness: There are those who had actually seen the Light itself, those who heard these people tell about it, and finally those who heard rumors about it or disbelieved it. Lewis got this idea from H. G. Wells's "Country of the Blind," thus illustrating our own loss in belief that men actually walked and talked with God: "During centuries a gradual atrophy of sight must have spread through the whole race."[124] Wells himself writes that later generations not only had semantic problems but even questioned the verity of the stories and replaced them with their own ideas.[125] Robin experiences semantic problems throughout the story.

We are likewise so removed from the experience of Light itself that our words like *light* are abstractions and insignificant symbols on paper. In his poem "The Country of the Blind," Lewis writes that we talk of light "as a symbol of / Abstract thoughts." Lewis also illustrates the way we have lost even the desire to tell about the light.

The painter Robin meets is in danger of becoming like the painter in *The Great Divorce* who paints only for the sake of painting. In this book, Lewis uses the analogy of a painting to represent an imitation of reality. The Spirit tells the Ghost that he painted on Earth because he saw glimpses of Heaven in the landscape. His painting was successful because others could also see the glimpses. "But here you are having the thing itself. It is from here that the messages came." His painting is not really necessary because they can now see the country itself. He will not be able to continue painting if he is interested in the country only for the sake of painting—"paint for its own sake." When the Ghost first began painting, his interests were different. The Spirit says, "Light itself was your first love: you loved paint only as a means to telling about light."

Reflection

Lewis's use of the light metaphor is tied to another—that of mirror or reflection of reality.

Lewis defines *creation* as preconceiving something in the mind and then, without any preexisting material, causing it to be; after its creation, the created object is something other than the "Cause."[126] However, only God can create the basic elements.[127] God also created history as a creative act in which each soul and each particle matters. Events are like a work of art in which each makes a contribution and "is both an end and a means."[128]

As free and unique individuals, each of us is "a Divine work of art, something that God is making, and therefore something with which He will not be satisfied until it has a certain character."[129] For example, in *Perelandra*, Ransom describes the King as God's "live image, like Him within and without, made by His own bare hands out of the depths of divine artistry, His masterpiece of self-portraiture coming forth from His workshop to delight all worlds." In contrast, the Un-man twists the use of art by tempting the Green Lady to invent stories or poems about things that "might be." He wants her to imagine herself seizing a grand role in the world's drama and placing herself at center stage.

That Hideous Strength continues the same theme as Jane wonders if "one were a thing after all—a thing designed and invented by Someone Else and valued for qualities quite different from what one had decided to regard as one's true self?" In Maleldil's presence, she feels herself a person, "yet also a thing, a made thing, made to please Another and in Him to please all others, a thing being made at this very moment, without its choice, in a shape it had never dreamed up."

Divine virtue passes down to us like rungs on a ladder, and the "mode in which each lower rung receives it is, quite frankly, imitation."[130] The New Testament clearly uses the word *originality* as only God's prerogative, and even life is "an art of imitation." It "leaves no room for 'creativeness.'" "There is not a *vestige* of real creativity *de novo* in us."[131] For example, we cannot imagine a new color or sense. For every other being, this ability is comparable to reflecting as in a mirror.[132] The New Testament therefore does not allow the idea of creativity or originality for mankind but rather the opposite; originality is only God's privilege.

Because the New Testament uses words like *mirror* and *imitation* to describe itself, can literature, which derives from real life, aim at being creative, original, or spontaneous?[133] For Lewis, literature is not genius or self-expression. Because everything originates with God, all things, including imaginative inventions, must reflect heavenly Truth.[134] "Reflect" is important because the "lower life of the imagination" is merely an image rather than a beginning of or step toward the higher life of the spirit. Only God can cause it to be such.[135] Our duty and joy should be found as simply "reflecting like a mirror."

The Christian is to Christ as a mirror is to an object.[136] Our destiny is "becoming clean mirrors filled with the image of a face that is not ours." Lewis likens the process to a Platonic doctrine of a "transcendent Form partly imitable on earth."[137] We are "mirrors whose brightness, if we are bright, is wholly derived from the sun that shines upon us."[138] In *The Great Divorce*, Heaven is described as reality itself. His disciples are reflections of His Light: "The Glory flows into everyone and back from everyone: like light and mirrors,

But the light's the thing." Similarly, Lewis describes the Great Dance Ransom witnesses on Perelandra as woven out of cords or bands of light: "Each thing . . . is the end and final cause of all creation and the mirror in which the beam of His brightness comes to rest and so returns to Him."

In Heaven, writes Lewis, Christians will turn away from the "portraits to the Original" and put on God's glory: "We are to shine as the sun, we are to be given the Morning Star."[139] A striking illustration of this principle occurs at the end of *Till We Have Faces*, when Orual finally becomes Psyche. She looks down and sees two reflections in the water: "both Psyches, both beautiful . . . beyond all imagining." Orual and Psyche are alike but still their unique selves, as well as reflections of the god, the only "beauty there is."

Until that time, each man must live "as a glass / To let the white light without / flame, the Father, pass / Unstained."[140] Our perceptions of God are dependent upon the condition of the glass or mirror through which we reflect God. "Just as sunlight, though it has no favorites, cannot be reflected in a dusty mirror as clearly as a clean one . . . the instrument through which you see God is your whole self. And if a man's self is not kept clean and bright, his glimpse of God will be blurred—like the Moon seen through a dirty telescope."[141]

An artist should thus never believe that he can bring "into existence beauty or wisdom" that did not exist but rather something embodying "some reflection of eternal beauty or wisdom."[142] Christian criticism therefore has an affinity with the "Platonic doctrine of a transcendent Form partly imitable on earth; and remoter affinities" with the Aristotelian doctrine of *mimesis* and the "Augustan doctrine about the imitation of Nature and the Ancients."[143]

Our minds can imagine: We can create mental pictures of objects, humans, and events. But we can create nothing new—only recombine our material provided through "sense data."[144] Thus poets, musicians, and inventors never "make," only build from, rearrange, and recombine elements and materials that already exist from the Creator. Lewis compares writing a book to being less like creation than planting a garden or begetting a child.[145] Everything we know about the act of creation is derived from what we can gather about the relationship of creatures to their Creator. Humans can only be truly creative when their will is God's. "When we act from ourselves alone—that is from god *in* ourselves—we are collaborators in, or live instruments of, creation."[146] This act negates Adam's "uncreative spell that he put on mankind."

While imagination was frowned upon in Reformed theology, Lewis follows the Anglican tradition that held a positive view of imagination similar to that of the Romantic poets. He consequently believes that imagination can be an oracle of Truth but was corrupted due to the Fall. Nevertheless, God uses imagination and mental pictures to communicate. The artist's goal is not to describe his imagination but to arouse the readers' imaginations—"not to make definite pictures, but to find again in our own depth the Paradisal light of which all explicit images are only the momentary reflection."[147] We can only imagine for ourselves. If we describe what we imagine, we can cause others to create their own mental pictures. These images may only be roughly similar to our own, however.

Dorothy Sayers, who knew Lewis and influenced his ideas, has similar views of creation. In *The Mind of the Maker*, Sayers draws an extended comparison between God as Creator and the writing of books. Sayers argues that instead of the words *copy* and *imitation*, we should substitute the words *image* or *image forth*, because an image expresses something unimaginable. While God created out of nothing, we build and rearrange in new forms. Yet the artist is not limited by matter: "The components of the material world are fixed; those of the world of imagination increase by a continuous and irreversible process, without any destruction or rearrangement of what went before." This act is the nearest we can come to "creation out of nothing," and "we conceive of the act of absolute creation as being an act analogous to that of the creative artist."[148] Our minds and the Maker's Mind use the same pattern, and their works are made in their own image. But while God made the world from nothing, man cannot create by making something from nothing: "We can only rearrange the unalterable and indestructible units of matter in the universe" and put them together in new forms and patterns.[149]

TOLKIEN, LEWIS, AND PLATO

In his correspondence with Owen Barfield, Lewis sketches a picture as a sort of analogy to what he conceives to be man's relationship to reality. Lewis shows a man tied to a post surrounded mainly from the back by clouds. The man is looking into a mirror, which reflects a house, a road, and the man himself walking down the road. The clouds, Lewis says, represent what he calls reality. The man is tied to the post so that he cannot turn around and see the clouds; he represents the finite personality. The mirror shows as much reality "and such disguise of it" as can be seen from his position and includes the man himself as an empirical object. The mirror is surrounded by a steel frame, which represents the "finitude and deadness of every mere object." Because the man can only study the mirror with his eyes ("equal implicit cognition"), he must reach back as far as he can with his hands in order to get a touch of the real. In another sketch, a man is trying unsuccessfully to depart from traditional academic knowledge and get new images from the mirror.[150] Lewis identifies his mistake as assuming that the reflection in the mirror was Reality, Light itself.

In *The Last Battle*, Lewis again uses the mirror analogy to explain the power of myth to get at that Reality. Imagine a room with a window that looks out on a sea or green valley with mountains in the distance. Opposite that wall is a looking glass. If you look away from the window, you may suddenly catch a glimpse of the scene in the mirror: "And the sea in the mirror, or the valley in the mirror, were in one sense just the same as the real ones, yet at the same time they were somehow different—deeper, more wonderful." Thus if you are tired of the real landscape, look at it in a mirror. "By putting bread, gold, horse, apple, or the very roads into a myth, we do not retreat from reality: we rediscover it."[151] We all "long to go through the looking glass, to reach fairy land."[152]

Lewis's view of reality, involving man's separation from his heavenly potential, can be described as Platonic. Briefly, Plato believed that the real, stable, permanent part of the universe exists in a supernatural, supersensible "heaven" as Ideas or Forms. The physical world is only the realm of appearances rather than solid reality—illusory, transitory. In this way, it is only a shadow or copy of the "real" world. However, Lewis does consider Plato wrong in believing concrete flesh is bad.[153] In *The Discarded Image*, Lewis explains that Platonism taught that the invisible world is made from an invisible pattern. It was also believed that we lived before we became incarnate on earth—i.e., the preexistence of the individual soul.[154] Lewis then identifies the differences between the creation as described in Christianity and Neo-Platonic theories such as those of Macrobius. God creates Mind (*Mens*) out of Himself. When Mind contemplates her Creator, she preserves her author's likeness. But when she looks behind herself, she creates out of herself the Soul (*Anima*). The creation of nature is thus a series of diminutions.[155] These different views of creation are important because Tolkien and Lewis share contrasting views.

For example, the description of creation in *The Silmarillion* has parallels to Neo-Platonism. Plotinus is credited with establishing Neo-Platonism in the third century based on Plato's teachings. According to Neo-Platonism, the ultimate deity is called "The One." Creation is a series of emanations from this perfect One. From The One also emanates the Divine Mind or Logos containing all the forms of individuals. Below this is the World Soul, which links the intellectual and material worlds. The world is the result of a chain of emergence through emanations that flow from The One. While The One is pure spirit, the emanations radiate outward and downward, becoming more material. Each level of emanation (hypotasis) causes the next lower one, and each becomes more physical. In addition, each image contains an image of the preceding one, but each is inferior to the previous. This process is similar to a stone dropping in water, with waves radiating outward and becoming weaker.

Creation and emanation are two contrasting views of the same effect. Creation, according to Christianity with Platonic influences, differentiates between the Creator and creation. God creates from nothing, and the created is imperfect. In contrast, in emanation theory, the perfect One emanates concrete plurality. It is not the

Creator who creates imperfection, but rather, imperfection emerges as a result of separation from perfection. Tolkien's view that nothing is evil in the beginning is similar to this concept.

Some critics see similarities between Tolkien and other philosophers. Ralph Wood, for example, describes Tolkien as an advocate of Aristotelian metaphysics. For Tolkien, transcendent reality is found in the depths of this world. That is why his secondary world is portrayed as real, with its own laws. Tolkien did not accept the Platonic or Neo-Platonic idea that the spiritual world is superior to the physical. Tolkien's views have also been compared to those of Saint Augustine of Hippo, who used the terms *phantasia* and *fantasma* to describe types of fantasy. Phantasia (fantasies) are mental images of objects. Fantasma (phantasms) are the result of memory and thus the link between memory and imagination. Houghton notes parallels between Tolkien's account of creation and St. Augustine's, in which God creates angels, a divine plan about what will be created, then the physical world that the Holy Spirit gradually develops.

Lewis's views, on the other hand, were clearly influenced by Platonism. In his fiction, Lewis depicts this world as a shadow of reality. In *Perelandra*, for example, Mars tells Ransom, "You see only an appearance, small one. You have never seen more than an appearance of anything." He sadly realizes, "I have lived all my life among shadows and broken images." He begins to believe in Weston's philosophy that the beauty and innocence of this new planet and all the affection he had ever known on Earth are but a dream, illusion, "outward show": "Reality lived—the meaningless, the un-made, the omnipotent idiocy to which all spirits were irrelevant and before which all efforts were vain."

In *The Silver Chair*, the Green Witch flings a green powder into the air and strums a mandolin, making thinking difficult. Her enchantment begins to convince everyone that their world is but a dream and her lamp the real sun: "You can put nothing into your make-believe without copying it from the real world, this world of mine, which is the only world." To contrast attempts by evil beings like the witch to confuse dream and reality, Lewis also uses dreams to provide hints of a better world. According to the narrator in *The*

Lion, the Witch and the Wardrobe, sometimes in a dream someone says something that seems to have "a lovely meaning, too lovely to put into words, which makes the dream so beautiful that you remember it all your life and are always wishing you could get into that dream again." A similar experience occurs in *The Voyage of the "Dawn Treader"* when Lucy reads the Magician's Magic Book and comes across a "spell for the refreshment of the spirit." Although she can neither reread nor really remember it, Lucy defines a good story as one that reminds her of it.

Lewis's Platonism is most obvious in *The Last Battle*, when Aslan's followers go to His country. The children notice that things are "like" but "not like" things in Narnia. Professor Kirke explains, "It was only a shadow or copy of the real Narnia . . . just as our own world, England and all, is only a shadow or copy of something in Aslan's real world." It is as different as things are from shadows or being awake is different from a dream. "It's all in Plato." Walter Hooper suggests that this is a reference to Plato's *Republic* and *Phaedo* in which he describes the "immortality and unchanging reality of changing forms."[156] The children find the real Narnia and real England, of which the others were only a shadow or copy. In fact, Aslan calls England the "Shadow-Lands."

Aslan's Country is like the Old Narnia but "more like the real thing." The difference is like a reflection of a landscape in a mirror, where the reflection is real but "somehow different—deeper, more wonderful more like places in a story." The Platonic ideal is a solid, concrete reality where "every leaf stood out so sharp that you'd think you could cut your finger on it." In *The Great Divorce*, Lewis likewise notes that in comparison to the ghostly earthlings stumbling on Heaven's soil, things in Heaven are much "solider," even harder, in comparison—you can cut your finger on the grass. Life is weak and flimsy compared to the solid reality it reflects.

Lewis thus reverses the shadowy Platonic conception of Heaven. We tend to associate God and Heaven with the "sky" and "spiritual," forgetting that our language is only symbolic and incapable of describing or understanding them. Consequently, says Lewis, God has become to many "like a gas diffused in space" or a "mist streaming upward"—vaporous, vague, indefinable, shadowy. We also have a "vague dream of Platonic paradises and gardens of the Hesperides" that represent the heaven we long for. Although we associate spirit with ghosts and shadows, instead, spirit should be presented as "*heavier* than matter."[157]

Critics differ about the effect of Lewis's Platonism on his fiction. Anna Blanch believes that Lewis's Platonism affects how we read the Chronicles. An allegory leads the reader *out* of the book to a conception, but in the Chronicles, a reader does the reverse and moves *into* the book to an image that enriches the concept. The reader then moves from the book to the real world and to God.[158] Dennis Quinn, on the other hand, attacks Lewis on the grounds that Platonism "diminishes the reality of the sensible world and substitutes for it a world that exists only in the mind."[159] In discussing *The Faerie Queen*, for example, Lewis points out that the Neo-Platonism allowed the artist to imitate the reality in his own mind rather than external Nature, thus scorning faithfulness to fact and glamorizing the spiritual world at the expense of the real. The Narnia tales, Quinn argues, deny the reality of the created universe or imply that our world lacks wonders or marvels.[160]

Gunnar Urang observes that owing to the strong Platonic influences, Lewis emphasizes the relationship of God as Creator to his creation, particularly "otherness": "transcendence over immanence, eternity over time, objectivity over subjectivity, and the supernatural over the natural."[161] His exaltation of transcendence and the supernatural affects the symbols, images, and analogies he uses. It also results in his use of the dream framework, other planets, and encounters with superhuman creatures who convey "otherness."[162] This emphasis explains some of the techniques used in his fiction such as the "deceptive surface" (quest or space journey) and the "tendentious narrative technique." In the latter, a skeptical reader is encouraged to identify with an unbeliever so that as the novel proceeds, he and the character both move toward belief.[163]

While Tolkien believes that the happy ending comes in the hereafter, fantasy gives a brief glimpse of "Joy beyond the walls of the world."[164] In *Smith of Wootton Major*, when Smith swallows the

Faery star and then experiences its effects on his tenth birthday, he suddenly feels that he is remembering what he once knew. It reminds him of Faery, even though he has never been there. He sings a song with strange words that he automatically knows by heart. Later, when his son Ned hears the chimes from a trinket Smith has brought back from Faery, the boy says the bells have a scent that reminds him of something he has forgotten.

Lewis uses a stable door in *The Last Battle* and in several of his other writings as a symbol for the entrance to that Platonic reality that we have always longed for because we have vague Words-worthian recollections of a past glory. "We long to be inside of some door which we have always seen from the outside. . . . to be at last summoned inside would be both glory and honour beyond all our merits and also the healing of that old ache." Someday, says Lewis, we shall again be permitted to "get in . . . pass in through Nature, beyond her, into that splendour which she fitfully reflects."[165]

For both Tolkien and Lewis, fantasy provides us glimpses of both a past and future Joy and a reality beyond earthly limits. The next chapter describes the methods they used to portray their secondary worlds.

5

Achieving Other Worlds

Tolkien's and Lewis's views about the purpose of fantasy affect the way they depict their created worlds. This chapter presents their views about the characteristics of secondary world fantasy, as well as the techniques each writer uses to develop and describe his worlds.

SECONDARY WORLD FANTASY

There are numerous definitions of fantasy literature, but in general, critics define it as creating a world that contains elements that are not part of our own world. This world may be a parallel world, Earth in the past or future, or a world in another universe. Both Tolkien and Lewis use the term *romance* to describe the fiction that they love. What they meant by romance is the hint of another world; one must "hear the horns of elfland."[1]

Lewis defines seven types of "romantic" literature, although some works may fall into more than one category.[2]

- Stories about dangerous adventures
- Marvelous literature about magicians, ghosts, fairies, witches, dragons, nymphs, and dwarves
- Art dealing with "titanic" characters, extreme emotion, and codes of honor
- Romanticism dealing with the abnormal and macabre
- Works of egoism and subjectivism
- Revolts against civilization and conventions, including primitivism (backward-looking) and revolution (forward-looking)
- Works with sensibility to natural objects

Tolkien describes his own works as "heroic romance, an older type of literature."[3] This type of prose and narrative verse popular in medieval Europe was often based on legends and fairy tales. Fantastic stories set in a distant time or place usually contain a hero who goes on a quest. Lewis preferred the second category, marvelous literature.

Both writers describe characteristics of successful fantasy. To attract both young and adult readers, a fantasy work must first of all be a good story—a straightforward adventure.[4] Tolkien's primary goal, for example, was to succeed in writing a good story with an attractive atmosphere and background. Action must be compelling, believable, pleasing, exciting, moving, and relevant.[5] However, this goal is unachievable unless the topic is worthwhile and relevant to the human condition.[6] Like all good literature, the story must be interesting and pleasurable rather than exist solely to present Truth or philosophy, because it should not be used as a means to an end. Thus the author shouldn't try to "bring in" Christian "bits."[7] Good stories also add to life by giving us new sensations and enlarging our conception of possible experiences.[8] Lewis writes, "Of every idea and every method the Christian writer will ask not 'Is it mine?' but 'Is it good.'"[9]

For Tolkien, a key element of fantasy is making and glimpsing other worlds. Instead of *magic*, Tolkien prefers the term *enchantment*—the creation of a secondary world into which both "designer" and "spectator" can enter. In "On Fairy Stories," Tolkien writes that creative desire seeks "partners in making."

Although Tolkien wrote his book as an experiment in "inducing 'Secondary Belief,'" he maintains that the sub-creator draws on reality.[10] Traditionally, the word *fantasy* has been associated with the unreal and imaginary. In "On Fairy Stories," Tolkien writes that "Creative Fantasy" recognizes fact but isn't a slave to it. While fantasy is free "from the domination of observed 'fact,'" it also recognizes "that things are so as in our world." It is made from the primary world of simple, fundamental things and rearranges primary matter in secondary patterns.[11] In fact, writing fantasy is a rational activity: the clearer the reason, the better the fantasy produced.[12] Fairy stories depend on the real world's sharp outlines rather than blurring them.[13]

Fantasy therefore cannot use any device that suggests it is an illusion. Although it begins with "arresting strangeness," it is not dreaming or hallucination. Robert Scholes writes, "No man has succeeded in imagining a world free of connection to our experiential world, with characters and situations that cannot be seen as mere inversions or distortions of that all too recognizable cosmos."[14] The beginning and ending of fairy tales ("once upon a time" and "they lived happily ever after") are artificial devices like picture frames. They do not deceive anyone. The beginning and end focus the observer on just one part of the country and influence the picture.[15]

Art creates a new secondary world in the mind that should have an inner consistency of reality.[16] For example, anyone can say "green sun." But an effective writer will make a secondary world where a green sun will be credible, commanding secondary belief. Tolkien describes this skill as an "elvish craft." The idea of a green sun comes from H. G. Wells's story "The Plattner Story."[17] While we are familiar with both "green" and "sun," Tolkien is combining known things in new ways. By defining the secondary world as sub-creation with an inner consistency of reality, Tolkien makes it a reality apart from our own. Tolkien believes this consistency is difficult to create. The moment a reader begins to disbelieve, the spell is broken, and the art fails.[18] The reader is thrust back in the primary world looking from the outside to the secondary world. Suspending disbelief is different from believing; it is like playing make-believe. There is an important distinction, though, between primary belief—faith in the Gospels—and secondary belief, which is required for fiction.

Tolkien's views challenge Coleridge's statement that the writer should create a "willing suspension of disbelief" in the reader. Coleridge describes his role in collaborating with Wordsworth on Lyrical Ballads: "It was agreed, that my endeavours should be directed to persons and characters supernatural, or at least romantic, yet so as to transfer from our inward nature a human interest and a semblance of truth sufficient to procure for these shadows of imagination that willing suspension of disbelief for the moment, which constitutes poetic faith."[19] For Tolkien, on the other hand, successful fantasy does not make the reader conscious of it. Entering the secondary world is like playing a cricket game. The enthusiast is in an enchanted state, playing for no external motivation. But a person simply watching is on a lower level.

Lewis gives advice on how to write about other worlds. Unsuccessful or lesser forms of science fiction and fantasy include wish fulfillment or using the "other world" simply as a backdrop for action. The secondary world must not be the setting for a story that could have been told in another way. A writer shouldn't send readers to faerie only to present what we already have here on earth. Rather, the purpose of the secondary world is to create wonder, serve as a metaphor for our world, and catch the reader unaware. It must be different enough from our world to make it worth going to faerie for, and something must happen once the reader gets there. Finally, the writer must not break the spell and bring the reader back to earth with a bump.[20]

It is also important to establish the reality of the supernatural. In fantasy, details of setting and atmosphere are especially important because they have several functions, including spiritual significance. The setting is often in peril by evil beings. The physical journey through the landscape also usually parallels the character's inner journey. Setting can also provide religious images. For example, some see the vertical Malacandran landscape as an image of spiritual aspiration. Similarly, the floating islands versus the Fixed Land of

Perelandra suggest the difference between obedience and conformity or adherence to rules without conviction. Sensory impressions become metaphoric and show or suggest rather than explain ideas. Water, for instance, is often a baptismal or cleansing symbol; dark forests, fog, ice, and snow are associated with evil. Setting, then, functions as more than just a backdrop because it is a "spiritual landscape in which even the least element might carry a moral meaning."[21]

A key quality of the other world is believability. Like Tolkien, Lewis states that the secondary world should be presented as true with an inner consistency so the spell is not broken. Adequate history and background must be included, or the work will fail to convince. Dorothy Sayers suggests, "If you want the reader not only to follow but to accept and believe a tale of marvels, you can do it best by the accumulation of precise and even prosaic detail," which she calls the "trick of particularity."[22] Not only can description and other details make the world believable, but the characters must also be transported in and out effectively. Details that encourage believability include geography, maps, history, literature, and invented names. Tolkien was the master of these elements.

TOLKIEN'S SECONDARY WORLDS

Few writers create detailed secondary worlds with the completeness of Tolkien's books. According to Tolkien, he wrote slowly and carefully, considering every one of the 600,000 words he wrote; he "laboriously pondered" the placement, size, style, and contribution of all the "features, incidents, and chapters." He wrote each part many times.[23] Practically every reference was recorded with the exception of Queen Berúthiel's cats and the names of two wizards.[24] Christopher Tolkien completed his father's manuscripts *Unfinished Tales* (1980) and the twelve-volume *The History of Middle-earth* (1983–1996). These show in meticulous detail the process Tolkien used to compose and revise his books, and they provide valuable insight into his works. He would write stories on loose pieces of paper and place them in notebooks, along with revisions. In addition, he would write in ink over pencil drafts or make outlines on scraps or in notebooks.[25]

The six extensive appendixes to *The Lord of the Rings* contain even more history, ethnography, and linguistic information. They include extensive lists of kings, dates of events, family trees, calendars, and information about writing, spelling, word pronunciation, scripts, runes, and languages. He calculated times, distances, dates, and phases of the moon; created history and literature; and, of course, invented hundreds of names. He also created facsimiles of three pages from the *Book of Mazarbul* that look burned, tattered, and blood-stained. His letters reveal how the maps alone required that he and Christopher spend countless hours of work and sleepless nights to prepare the work for publication.[26] Tolkien writes that he wisely began *The Lord of the Rings* with a map and fitted the story to it.[27] The maps were essential, he felt, to the books' readers. These maps both aid consistency and help integrate the plot with the geography.

Even more important, the details, maps, and appendixes give the book historical reality. The realism, according to Tolkien, explains why *The Lord of the Rings* "feels" like history, was published, and has been enjoyed by different types of readers.[28] The three-dimensional historical air of the setting was successful, as shown by letters from people who treated it like a report of real times and places and wanted more information about details like the music, ceramics and metallurgy, botany, and history.[29] Based on letters from fans, Tolkien concluded that his books gave readers so much pleasure that they demanded more.[30] When he received a letter asking about hobbit birthday gift-giving, he was able to fill three pages with details. This is just one example of the reality and depth of the smallest details for Tolkien himself. On the other hand, he wrote to other fans that he did not have all the answers and that much of the book puzzled him.[31] Nevertheless, Shippey believes that Tolkien did not think he was making up his worlds but reconstructing a world that once existed in collective consciousness.[32] He wanted people "to get inside this story and take it (in a sense) as actual history." Thus he describes his hobbit saga as *vera historia* (true history).[33]

Lewis describes *The Lord of the Rings* as a "radical instance" of sub-creation and a unique "sense of reality unaided" in which Tolkien minimizes his debt to the actual universe.[34] For example, Tolkien avoids historical or literary references that would draw readers from his secondary world. He invents "theology, myth, geography, history, palaeography, languages, and orders of beings."[35] One of Tolkien's greatest achievements, he felt, is the profound sense of history. Lewis also describes Tom Bombadil and the Ents as characters "brimming with life" and the "utmost reach of invention" that do not seem to belong even to Tolkien himself.[36] No one character exists just for the plot; each was worth creating. Lewis considers *The Hobbit* to be so descriptive that the world the reader enters does not seem made up.[37]

Lewis mentions the surprising realism, including the similarity of the war to that of their generation. On the other hand, Tolkien himself believed he erred in explaining too many details about the setting and history—especially in Part I—and that many things are unexplained.[38] A major flaw is the distant views of even more history and legends. Yet Lewis attributes the very attraction of *The Lord of the Rings* to glimpses of history in the background. Tolkien compares it to viewing a far-off island or towers of a distant city. If one goes there, he destroys the magic unless he sees "new unattainable vistas."[39] Tolkien's mythology consists of mythical histories, and behind these stories are even more histories and untold stories. As discussed in the previous chapter, this idea is fictionalized in "Leaf by Niggle."

In the foreword to *The Lord of the Rings*, Tolkien agrees with the criticism that the book is too short. For example, the economics, science, artifacts, religion, and philosophy are sketchy.[40] However, it is better not to state everything, he cautions, because it is more realistic. For example, one reader asked if Shadowfax went with Gandalf to the Western Land. In real historical accounts, facts are omitted, and some details have to be filled in from the evidence.[41] His problem in writing *The Lord of the Rings* was the need to make readers familiar with the stories behind the mythology without telling long legends and digressing.[42] The majority of the history and related stories and poems are found in *The Silmarillion*, which was not published along with *The Lord of the Rings* as Tolkien wanted.

Tolkien claims that he presents Middle-earth as a secondary world with no references to our world.[43] He describes orcs as a "real creation" based on goblins.[44] But only an author's guardian angel or God can really determine the relationship between a work and personal facts.[45] Yet he does point out elements influenced by actual settings. For instance, the kernel of his mythology (the tale of Beren and Lúthien) was inspired by his wife Edith and a small woodland glade filled with hemlocks.[46]

While Tolkien does create a highly developed secondary world, it is based on our real world. Like everyone else, writes Tolkien, he used real life as his models.[47] As Lewis says, while Tolkien reduced the "direct debt" to the actual universe, "there are . . . subtler kinds of debt."[48] The shire is based on rural England, for example.[49] Tolkien compares himself to a hobbit because he likes gardens and trees, pipes, plain food, and simple humor.[50] However, he also says he never belonged to or wanted to be inside his invented history.[51]

According to Tolkien, some believe the Scouring of the Shire reflects the situation in England when he was writing the book. The devastation of the Shire did have some basis in his childhood experience, as his country was "shabbily destroyed."[52] Northern France after the Battle of the Somme somewhat influenced his description of the Dead Marshes northwest of the Morannon, the principal entrance to Mordor.[53] It was influenced more by William Morris's Huns and Romans, however.

Middle-earth is not a "never-never land" or imaginary world with no relation to ours. Rather, he calls it an "objectively real world" that contrasts imaginary fairyland worlds or unseen worlds like Heaven and Hell. The setting is Mother-earth in an imaginary time.[54] He preferred using Earth as his setting rather than using other planets, although some readers believe Middle-earth is another planet. Because Middle-earth has the same constellations, seasons, calendar, and vegetation as Earth, Tolkien clearly portrays it as our world rather than another planet. He did not invent the term

Middle-earth; rather, it is a modernization of an old word (*oikoumene*) for the inhabited world of men.[55] It means our world's habitable land surrounded by ocean.[56] Near the end of his life, Tolkien became concerned about the early history in his mythology concerning cosmology: the sun and moon and Arda (Earth). In his original version, Arda begins as a flat world but becomes round as a result of the Fall. According to Christopher Tolkien, his father believed the sub-creator should not violate science.[57]

For further realism, Tolkien describes himself as editor, compiler, and translator of a collection of journals called the *Red Book of Westmarch*. This large, plain book with red covers is filled with many leaves and has seven different titles in the front. The book is portrayed as being the memoirs of multiple authors, as well as real historical accounts. In *The Lord of the Rings*, we learn that Bilbo was the author of *The Hobbit*. Bilbo began the book and then passed it on to Frodo, who, in turn, leaves it with Sam. The last blank pages are reserved for him. Sam is to continue to complete and organize it. It contains their adventures (*The Hobbit* and *The Lord of the Rings*), as well as poems, histories, genealogies, commentaries, translations, manuscripts, oral tales, etc. While the original book wasn't preserved, numerous copies were made. In the preface to "The Adventures of Tom Bombadil," Tolkien writes that the poetry selections are taken from older pieces from *The Red Book*. For several pages, Tolkien describes in great detail the background of the poems. He also identifies which authors (Bilbo, Frodo, Sam) wrote which numbered fragments. Tolkien uses a similar device in *The Silmarillion* and other older tales. An eleventh-century Englishman named Ælfwine ("Elf-friend") collects and records the Elves' history and creates a collection of tales.

Charles Noad believes that this approach to writing lies in Tolkien's concern with real texts, as he translated *Beowulf*, *Gawain*, and *The Pearl*. Tolkien wanted to "produce the distinctive texts that contain those narratives and chronicles, texts that are in themselves historical artefacts," and thus that may be why he never completed *The Silmarillion*.[58] *The Hobbit* and *The Lord of the Rings*, on the other hand, are narratives.

Tolkien titled one of his essays "Beowulf: The Monsters and the Critics." Jane Chance believes that throughout Tolkien's essays and fiction he takes on these same two roles: the monster (critic and scholar) versus the artistic hero. "Tolkien displays a fictional self, a persona, divided by two different interests, art and philology (or literary criticism), which tug him first one way, then another."[59] These become evident in the mock prefaces to *The Adventures of Tom Bombadil, Farmer Giles of Ham,* and *The Lord of the Rings.* For example, he presents himself as a historian in the prologue and appendixes of *The Lord of the Rings.* At the same time, Tolkien's artistic voice denies that the book is allegory.

In *The Road to Middle Earth,* Shippey calls Tolkien's method "asterisk reality." The phrase comes from a philological method of marking reconstructed words with an asterisk (*) to show that a word is inferred and does not appear in any document. This method is used to reconstruct languages that are no longer spoken and do not exist in written records. Tolkien used a similar method of reconstructing ancient mythologies from numerous sources that are not in any historical record.

Mary Bowman observes that this historicity in the stories leads characters to think of themselves as characters in songs and tales not yet written and to imagine reader responses to those tales. They also take existing tales and apply them to their own situations. Bilbo, for example, wonders if he will be able to complete his book, hoping to end it "He lived happily ever afterwards to the end of his days." He believes books should have a good ending and that characters should live together happily ever after. But as the story progresses, more chapters must be added and the ending altered. Their own adventures are continuations of stories from the past. Stories must always be continued; tales do not end despite the fact the characters come and go when their part is completed.

Tolkien uses two narrative techniques: He exploits the distance between reader and characters and yet also shapes the reader's experience so it is like the characters'. The interlaced structure of his narration does most to separate readers and characters. This effect is created by the gap between what characters and readers realize. At other times, however, readers experience events similarly to characters. As a result, Tolkien creates a secondary world that readers "get inside" and take as actual history. But when he breaks the spell and reminds us that we are not characters, he communicates with readers outside the secondary world. Tolkien describes a similar effect in *Smith of Wootton Major*, when Smith is told by the Queen of Faery that he has been granted the desire of his heart to see her. But he must leave Faery forever. As a stillness comes over him, he is both in the World and Faery simultaneously but also outside them and surveying them; he is in sorrow and peace.

LEWIS'S SECONDARY WORLDS

Narnia

Although the Chronicles are modeled after fairy tales rather than science fiction, Lewis does provide details about the creation of Narnia, its history, and geography. Narnia is a "parallel" world to ours, appropriate to Lewis's views about the spiritual world. The other world often represents the real but invisible spiritual world that a character must learn exists even when he is not present or to which he will return after death. In *The Lion, the Witch and the Wardrobe*, Peter argues that if things are real, then they must be there all the time. Professor Kirke replies, "Are they?" He thus hints at the possibility of other worlds and the need for faith rather than sight. The question is whether Lewis's stories are as realistic as Tolkien's, or whether he wants us to believe more in the reality of the supernatural. Walter Hooper tells of a boy in Oxford, for instance, whose parents found him trying to get into Narnia by chopping away at the back of their wardrobe and into the bricks of their house.

Characters must also get in and out of the secondary world effectively and credibly. The idea of a parallel world reached only by magic is a favorite device in fantasy, and it is through magic that the children of our world get to Narnia. They enter this "parallel reality" through a variety of means: yellow rings, the wardrobe, a magic horn, a picture, and a train accident. Whenever they enter and exit Narnia, they find that time on Earth has passed differently each time. The children can never visit Narnia a second time by the same route. In fact, they can't try to get there at all. Instead, Aslan calls them in his own way and time, and it happens when they aren't expecting it. The children are usually called to Narnia when someone "in a pinch" needs them, although they are assured that there are many years of peace in Narnia. The only way to Aslan's Country from all worlds is across a river bridged by Aslan himself.

By gathering information from the seven Narnia tales, we get a fairly comprehensive idea of the geography of Narnia and the surrounding countries. Lewis mapped his own rough conception of Narnian topography, and from this sketch Pauline Baynes later drew a more detailed map for Lewis. Narnia itself seems to resemble Lewis's favorite parts of the English and Irish countrysides. After Lewis wrote the seven stories, he drew up an outline of Narnia's history. There are 2,555 Narnian years between its creation and destruction, corresponding to fifty-two Earth years. During the history of Narnia, there was an "Old Narnia" and a "New Narnia."

The Space Trilogy

According to Lewis, *Out of the Silent Planet* has no factual basis but is a critique of our own age.[60] The Myth of Deep Heaven is actually a true story—the story of Earth's past and future, the choices we will make, and what side each of us will be on in a present and ever-worsening battle. The narrator's intrusions contribute to the somewhat didactic quality of the books, however. In *Out of the Silent Planet*, the narrator relates Lewis's story as true.[61] To make the novel more "believable," Lewis then becomes the narrator in the final chapter to tell how the story was really written. He claims that he knew Ransom for several years, though they had not met, and corresponded with him on literary and philological subjects. When Lewis, quite by coincidence, wrote Ransom a letter asking whether he knew what an "Oyarsa" is, Ransom was naturally triggered into telling his amazing tale. Certain that the world would not believe them but that the dangers facing Earth are gravely cosmic and eternal, they decide they cannot be silent. Ransom decides that they should "publish in the form of fiction what would certainly not be listened to as fact" because it would reach a wider audience sooner. If they can change even one percent of their readers' conception of Space to Heaven, "we should have made a beginning."

It is important that at least some readers become familiar with certain ideas. Thus Ransom tacks on a postscript to their account, providing even more details about Malacandra. He even chastises Lewis for omitting from his fictionalized version the fact that the reason they suffered so from excess light just before their landing on Malacandra is that their shutter jammed. Ransom feels sure readers would notice and wonder about that small detail. This technique must have convinced many readers, as Lewis was surprised that someone asked him if the book were true; he assumed people just don't understand what "fiction" is.[62] The letter at the end of the book, which is also pure fiction, was a way to prepare for a sequel; it mentions the need for not only space travel but also time travel—perhaps a hint of the books Lewis and Tolkien agreed to write.

Perelandra is cleverly told within a slightly different framework to add credibility. Lewis tells how with great misgivings he prepared Ransom for a second journey, nailed him into a white coffin used to transport him to space, and how Ransom returned over a year later. He then relates the story as Ransom told it to him but manages to maintain suspense, even though we know Ransom made it through safely. The narrator is afraid of being "drawn in" and blurring the distinction between natural and supernatural. In fact, he fears he is having a breakdown.

That Hideous Strength, unlike the first two stories, is related by a more impersonal narrator who simply tells us he was born in Cambridge, was Oxford-bred, and actually visited Bragdon Wood himself. In order to give a wider perspective and objectively tell details about the Studdocks, Lewis focuses much less on Ransom.

One of the main difficulties with *That Hideous Strength* has always been the debate about what kind of novel it actually is. In the preface to the book, Lewis calls it a "fairy-tale" for grown-ups because in the fairy tale tradition, he uses humdrum scenes and persons. But, he adds, most readers today don't notice the fairy-tale method because cottages, castles, wood-cutters, and petty kings have become things of the past. When asked if it is perhaps an epic, Lewis replied that the book is rather a "romance" because it does not have enough roots in legend and tradition.[63] At any rate, the book is a complex mixture of elements, ranging from Arthurian legend and magic and derived mainly from Charles Williams, the Grail legend, Swiftian satire of man, Owen Barfield's views of language and man's relation to the universe, the Tower of Babel and other biblical stories, and, of course, an entire range of ideas that Lewis is attacking.

Just as Lewis's attempts to make his books realistic fall short of Tolkien's, so too the details of his secondary worlds are less developed. No doubt the concepts of the novels were the primary focus, with enough realism added for credibility, often for symbolic purposes. In *Out of the Silent Planet*, Lewis uses the tradition of the Mars landscape as a reddish-yellow disk blotched with greenish blue and capped with white at the poles. But its colors are subdued because Malacandra is now dying. Mars has always been believed to be a warlike planet, older than Earth, with flat highlands, dust storms, red vegetation, and desiccation. Lewis keeps much of this tradition in his own description of Malacandra. In "On Science Fiction," Lewis says when he put canals on Mars, he already knew this idea had been dissipated by telescopes, but they were part of the traditional myth in the public mind.

Lewis does describe the landscape in some detail. The effect is to change Ransom's views about Earth and provide glimpses of "myth become fact" in another world. For example, an abundance of edible weeds resilient as rubber creates a pale pink ground. There are two types of ground: handramits and harandras. The handramits, engineered when the high ground was smitten by the Bent Oyarsa of Earth and thus made uninhabitable, are geometrically shaped—some parallel, some intersecting, some triangular. Appearing as purple lines or "canals" from above, they are really engineered canyons of lowland where the warmth and air are located. Between the handramits is flat, airless, lifeless waste, created mainly by the old forests of Malacandra. Once alive with birds, they are now petrified masses of pale, rose-tinted stone "cauliflowers" the size of cathedrals. The har-andras, or high ground, are a world of naked, faintly green rock interspersed with patches of red. There the air is thinner and colder, the light brighter and sky darker than below. Mountains are greenish white and shaped like pylons with haphazard grouping and irregular shapes, such as points, knobs, or rough platforms.

To the north and east are the sand deserts of Malacandra, which appear as yellow and ochre. Windstorms raise the sand in a dull, red, cloudlike mass to heights of over seventeen feet. West are the forest lowlands, where the pfifltriggi live and which on Earth appear as the dark patches of Mars. But these are actually the old, greenish blue oceans of the planet. Overall, the landscape thus appears as a pastel, water-color picture of purplish and whitish green fringed by rose-colored, cloudlike masses. Gorges appear as purple, blue, yellow, and pinkish white created by the mixture of woodland and water.

But perhaps the most striking thing about Malacandra—as if all this were not unusual enough—is the fact that everything is perpendicular: narrow and pointed at the top, small at the base, elongated from the natural effect of lesser gravity. Ransom sees this "rush to the sky" or "skyward impulse" as symbolic of an aspiration toward God. Once home, he also finds it hard to forget the perpetual singing and the special smells of the planet—an aromatic, spicy, cold, thin tingle at the back of the nose. Lewis thus uses the landscape symbolically.

Venus has always been considered younger and warmer than Earth. It is pictured as watery, with tall mountains and thick, vapor-ous clouds that serve as a barrier between it and the heavens. Again, Perelandra combines these traditional qualities with others so unusual that Ransom finds something there "that might overload a human brain." The sky seems distant and golden because of the cloud cover so thick that it reflects light, producing a riot of colors in the atmosphere and an impenetrable darkness at night. Unlike Malacandra's pastel world, the colors of Perelandra are heraldic. Tepid and "delicately gorgeous" gold, green, and blue waves rise like columns.

On the waters float multicolored (flame, ultramarine, orange, gamboge, violet) islands of heather-like vegetable matter. Due to the action of the waves, these islands change shape constantly, creating perpetually new landscapes of hills, valleys, forests, and feathery vegetation tall as gooseberries and the color of sea anemones. The "globe trees," which provide Ransom such a special unearthly pleasure, have gray and purple tubular trunks with yellow globes of fruit perched amid splashes of oranges, silvers, and blues.

While the floating islands fill just part of the oceans, sometimes separate, sometimes forming one huge aggregate of matter, there is also a "Fixed Land" on which the King and Queen are forbidden to spend the night. This is a mountainous island with a smooth coast, valleys, and mountainy pillars or crags rising in green columns of bluish turf. At first Ransom rejoices in the stability of the land, the trees so much like those of Earth, and the silent, cool, dark atmosphere. Yet after just one restless and uncomfortable night, he again longs for the floating islands and their more pleasurable fruits and fragrant breezes. On his chase with the Un-man over the seemingly endless expanses of water, Ransom realizes how little of the planet has been seen by him or anyone else, and how many creatures exist not solely for man's benefit. Suddenly, he and the Un-man are swept through a hole in a cliff into a cavern of total darkness. Within the layer upon layer of caves he discovers a subterranean fire and insect-like inhabitants with their own ancient halls and chambers, government, and forms of worship. At first horrible to Ransom, one of these creatures becomes to him "a mantled form, huge and still and slender . . . with insufferable majesty," and he again feels like an intruder.

When Ransom emerges from this cave of ice, he finds himself on another "fixed land." Though it is blanketed off and on in mists, he can catch occasional glimpses of vast, flower-dotted mountain slopes. He contentedly climbs ever upward toward the Holy Mountain where the coronation ceremony for the King and Queen takes place. Under ripple-trees (two-and-a-half-foot trees with blue streamers) graze tiny mountain "mice" the size of bumblebees. At last he comes upon dazzling translucent crystal cliffs, their peaks immersed in red flowers. The rose-red valley at their center contains a small pool edged with lilies. This is the paradisal fixed land where the throne of the King and Queen will be and for which the other Fixed Land, by their obedience, prepared them. This is Lewis's portrait of what will happen when we, too, are given the Morning Star.

STYLE

Because Tolkien and Lewis differed in their religious purposes, their writing styles differ. Richard Purtill believes that Tolkien and Lewis use language differently. Tolkien uses language to "weave enchantments," whereas Lewis uses language to convince, enlighten, and present strange scenes and beings. Tolkien is the Poet, while Lewis is the Teacher. Tolkien works through emotions, while Lewis works through intellect. Tolkien uses language as an end in itself, while Lewis uses it to express ideas and images.[64] Tolkien's secondary world exists on its own, whereas Lewis's world exists to teach a lesson.

Tolkien describes *The Hobbit* as the story of a simple, ordinary hobbit placed in a high setting who is not artistic or heroic. It then develops from a fairy tale to the high and noble.[65] Tolkien believes a writer should extend the reach of his audience's vocabulary. Writing "down" to the audience and using flat "Bible-in-basic-English" has resulted in children and young people's having no respect or love for words, as well as limited vocabularies.[66]

However, the method of narration is clearly directed at children. The narrator addresses "you" the reader, sometimes intruding into the story and thus destroying the sense that this is a separate secondary world. In addition, not only does he know what characters are thinking and what will happen in the future, but he also comments on the significance of events and poor decisions characters make. These interpretive and judgmental comments make the account seem less historical. Background paragraphs about each race are interjected as characters are introduced to the plot. Onomatopoeia is also used to appeal to children hearing the story read aloud. As described earlier, Tolkien's narrative voice in *The Lord of the Rings* contrasts the one he used in *The Hobbit*. The narrator is impartial and less opinionated, addressing the reader less and reporting more.

Tolkien describes the tone of *The Silmarillion* as "high-mythical," elvish, and heroic.[67] In contrast, the style of *The Lord of the Rings* is a mix of poetry and high prose style with the colloquialism and vulgarity of the hobbits.[68] The poems and songs throughout *The Lord of the Rings* commemorate the heroic past and preserve Middle-earth's history. Tolkien uses what has been called an "archaic" style at times. However, he counters this criticism by pointing out that heroic scenes do not take place in a modern setting, so using a modern style is inappropriate. In addition, an ancient style is more concise and vivid.[69] David Downing describes Tolkien's style as a "pre-industrial" and "deliberate folk-tale style" because of his use of simple monosyllables and imagery. He uses simple Anglo-Saxon words and Saxonisms, such as "fell" and "leechcraft."[70]

Because he believes the reader should be free to picture scenes, Tolkien avoids specific description and, in general, uses simple words. For example, in Lothlórien, the fairest of all elvish dwellings, Frodo's eyes are uncovered and he catches his breath. But Tolkien's description of the landscape is restrained. The grass is "studded with small golden flowers shaped like stars." The sky is blue; the sun casts "long green shadows beneath the trees." There is no "blemish or sickness or deformity" to be seen.

Tolkien advocates allowing readers to "see" a scene and then provide their own interpretation. For example, just as he believes illustrations are of little value to fairy stories, so too literature is universal and "works from mind to mind." Each reader pictures an object in his own imagination.[71] One power of faerie is giving form to the visions of fantasy.[72] Thus by using adjectives, the writer becomes an enchanter, creating a new form and turning "grey lead into yellow gold."

On the other hand, Tolkien considers description central to the book's tone and style. His landscape descriptions are considered perhaps his greatest technique, unequalled in literature and similar to a landscape painting. He explains that he clearly visualized scenery and objects rather than artifacts like clothing.[73] Long passages describe the vegetation, terrain, weather, astronomy, buildings and cultural artifacts, and more. They also personify nature, as exemplified in lines such as "lines of unshaped stones marched." These passages have been subject to both criticism and high praise, however. Many argue that the description contributes to the realism and mythic tone, and mirrors the characters' moods. Long passages slow reading so that the reader's pace parallels that of the characters and simulates a journey rather than mere observation. Because Tolkien did not want to break the spell of the secondary world, he does not use direct religious references or imagery.

In contrast, Lewis's goal was to present the Gospels in a fresh way. Lewis's fantasy books are also more diverse than Tolkien's and thus his writing style varies. The Chronicles primarily use narrative ("this story is about") and dialogue. An omniscient narrator tells the story, but this perspective sometimes changes when the story is told from a character's point of view (e.g., Lucy, Edmund, Eustace, Trumpkin, Emeth, the Hermit). At other times, the narrator says he won't have the character tell the story, such as when he does not use the dwarf's words but only "the gist." Some details have been obtained from the characters themselves. The narrator often comments on events ("I agree with them" or "Now we come to one of the nastiest things in the story").

In general, in typical fairy-tale style, Lewis uses short sentences and a conversational style, mentioning himself ("I" or "we") or addressing the reader ("you"). The narrator often interrupts the narrative by addressing the reader. For example, he says you need to know port and starboard, or he asks, "Have you ever . . .?" The narrator also comments on his telling of the story. For example, he tells us he may explain about the islands in another book or that he had better finish the story of Rabadash. He says he could write pages and pages but "I will skip on," "I haven't time to tell it now," it would be dull to write down the details, or the story is almost over. The narrator especially has trouble describing Aslan's country: "It is as hard to explain how this sunlit land was different from the old Narnia, as it would be to tell you how the fruits of that country taste. . . . I can't describe it any better than that . . . the things that began to happen after that were so great and beautiful that I cannot write them." The narrative technique helps guides reader responses and reminds them this is a story.

Lewis is perhaps most successful when he uses powerful images in his stories to make spiritual concepts concrete. Lewis often uses striking scenes that provide images of Christian concepts. In *The Voyage of the "Dawn Treader,"* for example, Eustace's undragoning can only come from Aslan himself. As Eustace begins scratching, his scales begin falling off layer after layer. "You will have to let me undress you," says Aslan. When Aslan tears off the skin with his claws, it hurts worse than anything the boy has every felt, and then he tosses him into stingingly cold, clear water. "The cure had begun." This episode is an image of salvation and penetration to the true self. A similar image of salvation occurs in *The Silver Chair*. Jill Pole is desperately thirsty yet paralyzed with fright at Aslan's presence beside a stream. She pleads with him for a promise that he will not harm her and hopes to find another stream to drink from. "There is no other stream," the Lion replies.

Just as *The Lion* began with images, *Perelandra* grew out of recurring mental pictures of floating islands. Lewis most likely got this image from Stapledon's *Last and First Men*, which says, "In the early days of Venus men had gathered foodstuffs from the great floating islands of vegetable matter." The Green Lady is commanded not to sleep on the Fixed Land but rather on the floating islands. Like the command in Eden not to eat of the tree, the purpose of this restriction is simply so they may be obedient: "Only then can we taste the joy of obeying because his bidding is the only reason." Good is not the same on all worlds, Lewis suggests.

The floating islands have been interpreted as symbolic of God's will and our need to trust in his direction, instead of the security and legality of our own will: "Why should I desire the Fixed except to make sure—to be able on one day to command where I should be the next and what should happen to me?" asks the Green Lady. The purpose of the Fixed Land, in fact, is to lead them ultimately to their destined throne as rulers of Perelandra through their obedience and faith. Ransom finds a paradisal sweetness on these islands.

Ransom expects that the "cord of longing" for the floating islands was in him before the origins of time itself, a theme that recurs throughout Lewis's fiction.

LANGUAGE

Tolkien considers the languages and names to be the most important part "inextricable" from the stories, because the foundation of his work—a "linguistic aesthetic"—was inventing languages.[74] His primary goal was to create a world in which his languages could exist and to present it as history. Language is the key aspect of the cultural features, requiring a habitation and history to develop it.[75] Inventing languages is therefore closely linked to constructing and developing legends.[76] The stories came later and provided a world where he could express his love of language.[77]

There are other purposes for languages. Tolkien believes they give his story cohesiveness and consistency, as well as the "illusion of historicity" and "verisimilitude."[78] Thus he worked them out in great detail.[79] Tolkien also considers language diffusion important in sub-creation. Each rational species has its own language, and the Elves themselves have several languages. Two types of Elvish are Quenya (High-elven) and Sindarin (Grey-elven). Quenya becomes used for ceremony and song. Men of wisdom learn Quenya; the Dúnedain are the only race of Men who learn Sindarin and pass it on to their children as lore. The Riders of Rohan use poetry as an elegy to preserve the past. The language of the dwarves in the Third Age is a tongue of lore and treasure of the past. Tom Bombadil, who existed before art and nature became separate, speaks in verse. Evil beings, on the other hand, use language to control and enchant. For example, Saurman's voice sounds like an enchantment. Orcs do not have their own language, taking what they like from other languages and perverting it. Because they do not love words, they degrade language.

Tolkien also took great care in inventing names, considering it a private process that gave him pleasure and let him express his linguistic taste.[80] Names are primarily based on German or

Scandinavian and derived from Elvish languages. He also created the "cirth" or runes. Tolkien was irritated by commentators who attempted to find sources of his names in real languages rather than within the story itself.[81] He was also disturbed by attempts to translate the book into other languages that would destroy the original names he worked so hard to create.

Verlyn Flieger links language with the theme of light in the Bible and *The Silmarillion*. Genesis, for example, begins with the creation of light, while John begins with the creation of the Word (*Logos*). Tolkien's mythology similarly combines the creative principles of both Genesis and John.[82] Just as man as sub-creator is a fragment of the Light, words are fragments of the divine Logos. The fragmentation of Elvish languages parallels the idea of splintered light Tolkien mentions in "Mythopoeia." Like light, the Elvish language becomes modified and fragmented. The results of the Fall are splintered light and language. But humans can, in turn, use light and language to sub-create.

In the book of Genesis, because God is shown both creating and speaking, creativity is connected to language. Likewise, in *The Silmarillion*, Eru says "Eä," which means "It is" and "Let it be." His vision becomes realized through language. Just as God used words to create, so too humans create imaginary worlds from words. Sub-creation involves "combining nouns and redistributing adjectives."[83] In other words, as Tolkien explains in "On Fairy Stories," the writer separates adjectives and then reconnects them in new combinations (e.g., "green sun"). The creative mind that has this power can also imagine magical things, such as the ability of heavy objects to fly.

Mary Zimmer argues that because language first created reality, language affects things and can re-create material reality. The "*nous*" or Word in Christianity is both creation's eternal and ideal structure as well as a willed act of creation.[84] Throughout *The Lord of the Rings*, both the magic of incantations and names express the idea that names are analogous to divine ideas. Because creation proceeds through language, language is used in re-creation. [85]

Lewis develops his languages with much less detail than Tolkien. One of the great symbols for evil and man's pride resulting in diverse languages has been the Tower of Babel, and Lewis draws on this story as related in Genesis 11:1–9. This tower made of bricks in the plain of Chaldea in what was later Babylon was one of the ancient wonders of the world. Its purpose was to make a name for the people by creating a structure that would reach to the heavens and give them great power. At that time, all men spoke one language. But when God saw their vanity, he gave them all different languages and spread them over the Earth. This is thus the origin of our word *babble*.

The title of *That Hideous Strength* comes from Sir David Lyndesay's description of the Tower in his medieval poem "Ane Dialog" (The Monarche): "The Shadow of that hyddeous strength sax myle [six miles] and more it is of length." According to Lindsay, Nimrod, a strong hunter of huge stature and bulk, became king. He introduced idolatry and proposed building a city and a tower to the stars to dethrone God—a tower five and one-half miles high and ten miles around.

Like the Tower of Babel story, in Lewis's mythology, there was originally one common speech (Hlab-Eribol-ef-Cordi) for all rational creatures of the planetary system except Earth, where it was lost because of the Fall. Now there is no human language in the world descended from it. But it is the language of the hrossa (Hressa-Hlab), of Perelandra, and of Numinor. It was also known in fragments by old magicians of the Atlantean Circle, who repeated it to initiates. The words of Old Solar are polysyllabic and sound as if they are not "words at all but present operations of God, the planets, and the Pendragon." For this is the language spoken before the Fall. The meanings were not given to the syllables by chance, skill, or tradition but "truly inherent in them. . . . This was Language herself." Thus the names Lewis uses for the planets, except Thulcandra, are said to be their real names.

In the Space Trilogy, Ransom is a philologist, so many believe he is based on Tolkien. Lewis, however, claims that this profession makes his mastery of Old Solar more plausible. Dimble speaks the language spoken before the Fall, and on Perelandra, Weston speaks to the Green Lady in Old Solar. Whereas Weston was also previously ignorant of Old Solar, the evil eldila have since taught him the language.

Phonetic elements of Old Solar words are not based on actual language. Instead, Lewis invented new words by connecting syllables for their emotional suggestiveness.[86] Rather than inventing new words, Lewis obtained words from a variety of sources. Lewis notes that use of the Malacandran words *har* (mountains) and *sorn/seroni*, which declined like *hoken* in Arabic, and *handramit*, which resembles *handhramaut* in Arabic, is accidental and shows how hard it is to invent something that does not already exist.[87] Lewis's names are often more awkward than Tolkien's. For example, "Devine" is a play on "divine." Many of the names in his trilogy and Narnia books are borrowed from other writers. For example, *hross* comes from the root of wal*russ* (whale-horse), *ros*marine (in Spenser), and *hors*hwael (horse-whale) in K. Aelfred's version of Orosius. The Chronicles use similar types of derivations. Lewis found the name *Aslan*, the Turkish word for "lion," in the *Arabian Nights*. Many speculate that he obtained the name *Narnia* from over seven references in Latin literature.

All three Malacandran hnau speak the same language—the speech of the hrossa (Hress-Hlab or Old Solar)—but also speak their own, less ancient tongues at home. Hrossan is similar to Old Norse with its initial "h." They have no words for forgive, shame, or fault, and their speech cannot be translated into English. Hrossa have "furry" names. Pfifltriggian language is reminiscent of Turkish. Sorn (Surnibur) language is a relatively modern speech, developed probably within our Cambrian period. It is "big sounding," can be translated, and has a different vocabulary than hrossan.

Lewis recommends that names be "beautiful, suggestive, and strange." "Spelling counts" as much as sound. In his correspondence with fans, he provides advice on selecting effective words:[88]

- Write clearly; you may not have told the audience something that is clear to you.
- Use plain and direct words.
- Know the meaning of every word.

- Use words that fit the size of the subject; for example, reserve big words for big topics.
- Use concrete nouns.
- Avoid adjectives and adverbs to describe how you feel; instead, describe.
- Write with the ear rather than the eye.

A central theme in the Space Trilogy is the inadequacy of language. In *Perelandra*, Ransom tells the narrator about his experiences but laments that words are vague: "The reason why the thing can't be expressed is that it's too *definite* for language." But those at St. Anne's experience the presence of Viritrilbia (Mercury), the god of language himself. Ransom experiences the heart of language and white-hot furnace of speech. They speak puns, paradoxes, fancies, anecdotes, eloquence, melody, "toppling structures of double meaning," and "sky rockets of metaphor and allusion."

Tolkien and Lewis, then, differ in the detail used to portray their secondary worlds. These worlds, however, also have a "purpose": to convey Truths that readers can apply to the primary world. This topic is discussed in the next chapter.

6

Allegory and Applicability

Many find similarities to the real world in Tolkien's and Lewis's fantasy works. However, they have different views about the "meaning" of their fiction. This chapter describes their views about the "message" to be conveyed in fantasy and about allegory. It then presents their alternative terms for their techniques: applicability and supposition. Finally, it compares Tolkien and Lewis as "Christian" writers.

HEROES

Lewis calls "never-never land" appropriate for making a serious comment about the real life of humans. In describing *The Lord of the Rings*, Lewis points out that Tolkien wanted to show the "mythical and heroic quality" of a man. Tolkien accomplishes the "character delineation" usually found in realistic works by making his characters Elves, dwarves, and hobbits: "The imagined beings have their insides on the outside; they are visible souls. And Man as a whole,

Man pitted against the universe, have we seen him at all till we see that he is like a hero in a fairy tale?"[1]

This element conveys a positive view of man and shows that the most insignificant person can be a hero. Lewis asserts that both people and events that are "local" and "material" "can reveal transcendent glories and convey that glory into the most ordinary aspects of our lives."[2] Reader identification is effective when the protagonists are not superheroes but rather common people like ourselves. Lewis advises that the more "unusual" the scenes and events, the more "ordinary" and "typical" the characters should be.

The typical mythic heroes in fairy tales and fantasy must accomplish specific tasks. These characters, often children, are often empowered with special "gifts" and traits (like bravery, beauty, kindness) that make them superior to normal children. However, they are also fairly flat and undeveloped, lacking complexity and emotions such as fear and doubt. Aiding their tasks are supernatural powers and magical characters. Although subject to trials and evil characters, they succeed at their tasks and return to ordinary life, where adults once again take control.

Good characters are especially difficult to make interesting because the reader must see them from the inside.[3] The reader can only imagine characters with their best moments prolonged.[4] In addition, readers subconsciously want to find them incredible.[5] For example, Lewis calls the Green Lady a difficult character to portray, because she must combine the characteristics of a pagan goddess and Virgin Mary.[6] Tolkien writes something similar about Elves. His story had to shift from elvish myth and history (*The Silmarillion*) to men (*The Lord of the Rings*). Because we do not know Elves inwardly, we cannot write stories *about* them, even if we convert them into men.[7]

While good versus evil is the plot of most fantasy, in religious fantasy, good wins because God is considered the sovereign and absolute power. In addition, the hero chooses the side of good, often after a long inner battle. Because this moral struggle is the primary focus of the story, the character's journey is often symbolic of a spiritual quest. While Tolkien calls the physical journey a technical device, a thread to string things together, the quest is also symbolic of an inner journey.[8] Ursula LeGuin calls fantasy the natural language "for recounting of the spiritual journey, the struggle of good and evil in the soul."[9] Reader identification with characters is thus an effective technique for encouraging changes in the reader's own attitudes and values. For this reason, characters are often converted or morally changed.

MORAL LAWS

If the reader identifies with good characters, he can learn through their lessons and experiences. In the introduction to his translation of *Sir Gawain and the Green Knight*, Tolkien admires the author for being able to weave elements from diverse sources into his own work.[10] On the surface is a good story—a fairy tale for adults—with the faerie element adding peril and potency. On a deeper level, the author is able to make the story a vehicle for his own moral values, such as rejection of adultery. Gawain is still presented as a living, credible person.

Many critics observe that although the Christian elements in Tolkien's works are not as explicit as in Lewis's, there is an inherent morality in the books. Tolkien did not want his own mythology to be a lie but rather wanted it to express his moral view of the universe. So he did not set it in the real world, which would remove the imaginative aspect. While a story may contain a different world or creatures, the morals must remain the same as our world, thus encouraging a moral response in the reader. One goal of the writer, says Tolkien, is elucidating Truth and encouraging good morals by embodying them in unfamiliar ways so they are brought home.[11] However, says Tolkien, if a reader reads a work and perceives faith, sanctity, and light pervading it, then these elements come from him rather than the writer.[12]

Because fantasy maintains the same moral laws, it must show man as fallen; for Tolkien, all stories are about the Fall, thus Tolkien emphasizes the consequences of it.[13] Because man is fallen, not all man's creations are good or beautiful. However, fairy tales have a happy ending, and they fulfill many of the desires that resulted from the Fall. Chesterton agrees that every "deep or delicate treatment of the magical theme . . . will always be found to imply an indirect relation to the ancient blessing and cursing," and the work must be moral, not moralizing.[14] He suggests that the Fall in Eden can be compared to a fall from the spiritual world of fairyland to the real world.

Like Tolkien, George MacDonald cautions that there should be "no invention" by the author in the moral aspects of the created world. The writer must not create new moral laws but rather carry them into the invented world.[15] A fairy tale cannot help but have meaning and, if genuine and truer art, will mean many things.[16] Man's work, unlike God's, must always mean more than he meant. God's creation has layers of "ascending significance" and is there for man to use, modify, and adapt. Thus a work may have meaning that the writer cannot foresee: "A man may well himself discover truth in what he wrote; for he was dealing all the time with things that came from thoughts beyond his own."[17] But each reader will get different meanings depending upon his nature and development. Tolkien agrees that the reader will not perceive any religious feeling unless it is in him as well.[18] The best thing you can do for a reader, then, is to "wake things up that are in him" or to "make him think things for himself."[19]

According to Lewis, the "moral" should arise from the "cast" of the author's mind, as well as any "spiritual roots" within the reader. Because fantasy should be read primarily for pleasure and not edification, every reader will get different meanings depending on his/her spiritual background, nature, and development. Even authors can never know the meaning of their own works.[20] Every type of fiction uses forms from the real world. Because readers then interpret these forms, they may mean more than the artist intended. So what readers get out of a work depends upon what they bring to it.[21] Even viewing a work as real or fantasy also depends upon readers.[22] Readers, in turn, should read the work for the author's purpose rather than infecting it with theological, ethical, or philosophical references.[23]

Thus if a story does not show a moral, the reader shouldn't put one in. For example, when one child correspondent referred to the books as "silly stories" without a point, Lewis replied that "looking for a point" may keep a reader from getting the real effect of the story itself.[24] The intent is to convey meaning without rational explanation so that the message or religious echoes "wake up" things already in the reader. Like a picture, says Lewis, the story should trigger the reader's imagination and emotion. In fact, there are dangers in trying to find parallels: "Within a given story any object, person, or place is neither more nor less than what the story effectively shows it to be."[25]

Lewis writes that his own works catch readers unaware and trigger varied responses through fiction and symbol.[26] Because these elements draw on several referents at once and simultaneously carry several levels of meaning, they can communicate different meanings to different readers. In *A Preface to Paradise Lost*, Lewis praises Milton's use of images to arouse the reader's imagination rather than simply describe his own. Instead, he uses language to control what already exists in our mind. The artist should similarly regard the audience's needs and capacity as part of his material.[27]

In *An Experiment in Criticism*, Lewis writes that it is wrong to believe that good books give us knowledge and teach Truths about life. He distinguishes between using and receiving a work of art. The former is subjective and internal; the latter is objective and external. Most readers *use* art but few *receive* it.[28] You do something with the work of art rather than being open to what it can do to you. Get yourself out of the way and attend to the object itself. Words should not be pointers or signposts to content. They should also not be valued primarily for morals we can draw from them.[29]

ALLEGORY

Tolkien and Lewis differ about how clearly expressed the Christian meaning in their works should be. While all art must reflect and contain elements of moral and religious Truth, Tolkien believes it must not be "explicit as in the real world."[30] By exemplifying good morals in unfamiliar ways, the author can encourage them in the real world as well.[31] Tolkien considers sub-creation an end in itself (art for God's sake), whereas Lewis clearly desires to communicate his views.

There is a fine line between conveying ideas and using obvious allegory. *Allegory* is a story in which there is a one-to-one correlation between characters or events and a single abstract meaning such as psychological or spiritual experiences that they represent. The author intentionally plans these correspondences between the real and the immaterial or the intangible. Tolkien defines allegory as an account of events; symbolism is using visible things to represent objects or ideas.[32] Allegory makes the reader submit to the author's domination. To be an allegory, a work should have one event that the narrative and details coherently and consistently support. Lewis defines allegory as a pictorial or literary composition in which "immaterial realities are represented by feigned physical objects." The nature of thought and language is to represent the immaterial in picturable terms. When you begin with the immaterial and invent visible things to express them, the result is allegory.[33]

An example of allegory is *Pilgrim's Progress*. In his "Apology," John Bunyan lists several defenses for using allegory: it is like a fisherman's bait; Bible writers use biblical types, symbols, and metaphors; its aim is to convert, not entertain; and, unlike sermons and lectures, stories are like "burrs" that stick with us. *Pilgrim's Regress* (1933), Lewis's first published work of fiction in the same vein as Bunyan, was an attempt to explain his own conversion to Christianity, although he says not everything is autobiographical. It is "concerned solely with Christianity as against unbelief" by portraying a journey through various religious, political, and artistic movements and ideologies. However, Lewis admits that it contains "needless obscurity," especially because of the private meaning given to Romanticism. George MacDonald states that "he must be an artist indeed who can, in any mode, produce a strict allegory that is not a weariness to the spirit."[34]

Allegory's "aim and method are to dramatize a psychological experience so as to make it more vivid and more comprehensible," explains Sayers.[35] Parable and fable often do the same thing; each tells a complete story that is also similar to a spiritual or psychological experience. In "On Fairy Stories," Tolkien considers the beast fable related to fairy tales in that the sense of the marvelous comes from men speaking to living things. But beasts' speaking like humans destroys the magic; the animals are simply a substitute for humans.

In *The Allegory of Love*, Lewis traces the history of allegory. Once there were two worlds from which the artist could create his work: the actual world (*nature*) or religion (*supernature*). But the rise of literary allegory introduced the "other world" of "pure fancy."[36] When religion was an integral part of the universe, literature presented the universe as a unified whole. Although people believed that the Bible spoke literally of sacred history, they also felt it described events within man's soul. As a result, fictional forms became used to express spiritual ideas allegorically.

One of the earliest allegorical works was by Bernard Silvestris (*Cosmographia*, 1147), who used personification to present metaphysics. He was a major influence on Lewis's Space Trilogy. In the Middle Ages, mythography was the allegorical interpretation of pagan myths. Lewis uses this technique in *Till We Have Faces* as he presents the story of Cupid and Psyche.

One of Lewis's favorite books was Edmund Spenser's *The Faerie Queene*. His Fairy Land inhabited by heroes and monsters is a Christian allegory. Spenser uses the symbolism of Revelation to describe the Incarnation and inward quest of all Christians. Redcrosse knight must rescue Una, who stands for Truth or True Church, from oppression by a great dragon. This poem, says Lewis, is a fusion of medieval allegory and romantic epic—an ideal form for presenting a "Platonized Protestantism." But, Lewis adds, the use of pictorial images is also important. Because Spenser is more interested in a character's inner state than the outward story or action, the narrative story is the surface expression of the inner life.[37]

In the Middle Ages, there were four types of allegory, a method primarily used to explain discrepancies between the Old and New Testament (Table 6.1).

Table 6.1 Types of Allegory

Type of Allegory	Purpose of Events in the Story
Literal	Be interpreted literally
Typological	Show connection between Old and New Testaments
Tropological	Present morals
Anagogical	Present spiritual and mystical as they relate to eschatology and final judgment

To give an example of the anagogical, Dante uses Psalm 114, which mentions historical facts that should be interpreted literally. However, if the passage is interpreted spiritually, it signifies God's higher eternal glory. So the historical event is true but means more. In the literal sense, Israel becomes free from Egypt. In the typological sense, Christ frees us from sin. In the moral or tropological sense, the soul journeys from sin to grace. In the anagogical sense, there is an exodus of the soul from slavery of sin to eternal glory.

Dante also explains the multiple levels of meaning in his *Divine Comedy*. When he presented the work to his patron Can Grande della Scala, he also provided a letter containing his commentary. The work has more than one meaning (*polisignificante*) and is made of many senses or allegories (*polysemous*). In speaking as a prophet for God, Dante saw his purpose as urging readers to live a moral and religious life to prepare for Heaven. Lewis describes the *Divine Comedy* as "a high, imaginative interpretation of spiritual life" and the father of Wells and Verne.[38] However, Dante believes the universe was God's mirror, whereas Lewis describes it as a shadow, not a reflection. Madeleine L'Engle similarly defines anagogical as the "level of a book which breaks the bounds of time and space and gives us a glimpse of the truth, that truth which casts the shadows into Plato's cave, the shadows which are all we mortals are able to see."[39] The greatest writers do not even consciously use this technique.

According to Dante, allegory works on two senses: the literal and mystical or allegorical. The allegorical level can be read on three "senses" or methods. The *literal* sense does not go beyond the surface of the letter. The *allegorical* sense goes beneath the literal "cloak." The *moral* sense is the method that teachers should seek in the Scriptures. Finally, the *anagogical* sense ("sense beyond") goes beyond the senses, which refers to the transcendent meaning. Dante defines this sense as occurring "when a scripture is expounded in a spiritual sense which, although it is true also in the literal sense, signifies by means of the things signified a part of the supernal things of eternal glory."[40]

While some people consider allegory a "disguise" because it says "obscurely what could have been said more clearly," good allegory reveals rather than hides and makes the inner world tangible by imaginary concrete embodiment. It is best when it is grasped with the imagination and thus approaches myth, says Lewis.[41] In a better type of writing, which Lewis calls the "symbolic story," the meaning lives in the story and cannot be stated conceptually because it emanates from the whole story rather than the parts.[42] The greatest pleasure thus comes from symbolic or mythical stories.[43] While the allegorist talks about fiction, that which is less real, the symbolist attempts to find "that which is more real." The world we think is reality is only a "flat outline" of that which is "in all the round of its unimaginable dimensions."[44] Lewis compares allegory to a simile. An allegory is a continued simile that works backward; that is, you begin with the point.[45]

Lewis believes that even though a reader can find allegory and read any meaning in almost every story, most stories are not written to be allegorized.[46] Everything in art and nature can be allegorized if the reader desires it.[47] Reviewers, for example, found allegorical meanings in his stories that he never intended and even some he wished he had thought of.[48] The author is not the best judge of a book's meaning. He cannot be sure that it has all the meanings he intended, and readers may even find different meanings in it. A good work, Lewis argues, is more than just what happened, because a reader can reread it and still be moved. You can read a good book a number of times and find more in it, as well as continued delight.

Tolkien concedes that any attempts to explain the purpose of a myth or fairy tale inevitably must use allegorical language.[49] The more life a story has in it, the more it will lend itself to allegorical interpretation. Allegory and Story start out from opposite ends of a spectrum and meet somewhere in Truth (Figure 6.1). If an allegory is consistent, it can be read as a story; if it is closely woven and has "life," readers can find allegory in it.[50]

TOLKIEN AND "APPLICABILITY"

Throughout his letters and in the preface to *The Lord of the Rings*, Tolkien adamantly describes his work as "mythical" and "imaginative invention" because he disapproves of "conscious and intentional allegory."[51] *The Lord of the Rings* "is not about anything but itself" and is not intended to be allegorical in any way, including "topical, moral, religious, or political."[52] Tolkien clearly disliked allegory and preferred true or feigned history with varied "applicability" to the reader's thoughts and experiences and present times.[53] Allegory is the domination of the author, whereas applicability is the freedom of the reader. While any worthwhile tale has a moral, this quality also does not make it allegory. Fairy tales have a different and more powerful way of reflecting Truth than allegory or realism.[54]

Nevertheless, Tolkien writes that his "romance" grew out of allegory. It is actually impossible to write a story that is not allegory because we all embody "universal truth and everlasting life."[55] The wars, for example, are drawn from the allegorical "inner war" of good and evil.[56] However, he notes that the war and atomic bomb

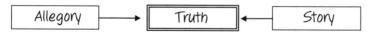

Figure 6.1 Tolkien's "sprectrum" of allegory versus story

had no influence on anything in the book except, perhaps, the land-scape.[57] If the Ring represents the atomic bomb, then the Ring would be seized and used against Sauron.[58] In addition, he wrote the work before the bomb was invented.[59] Similarly, Tolkien notes that comparing Sauron to Stalin is ludicrous because he wrote the book long before the Russian revolution. Placing Mordor in the east was required for the narrative and geography.[60] Humphrey Carpenter believes real events actually conformed to Tolkien's invention rather than the opposite.[61]

While Tolkien insists the work is not allegory and makes no po-litical references, it does have some basis in experience.[62] Tolkien calls his work a "comment on the world" that was most easily and naturally expressed in the form he chose. That is not to say, how-ever, that the intent was didactic. The religious element and writer's reflections and values become worked into and absorbed in the story and symbolism.[63] Individual characters also exemplify but do not represent principles. He observes that each person and event has two levels: the history and development of the individual and the history of the world.[64]

Tolkien is careful to clarify that his story is "mythical" rather than a new kind of religion and is "built" on religious ideas but is not an allegory of them.[65] It is a fundamentally religious and Catho-lic work with religion "absorbed" in the symbolism.[66] With the exception of *The Silmarillion*, there is little religion in Tolkien's fic-tion. Shippey theorizes that his lifelong desire was to combine Christian religion and pre-Christian literature, so there are hints of the Christian message, but Tolkien doesn't simply repeat it.[67] Tol-kien did not feel obligated to fit his story to formal Christianity but rather made it "consonant" with Christian thinking and beliefs because he feared these ideas would be turned into allegory and thus propaganda.[68] Objecting to a critic's description of him as a "be-liever in moral didacticism," he firmly replied, "I neither preach nor teach."[69] Yet he was annoyed when other critics wrote that *The Lord of the Rings* has no religion.

Tolkien showed Clyde Kilby an unpublished paper by a British professor, which said that many misunderstood *The Lord of the Rings* and did not see Christ's redemption of the world in it. Tolkien remarked that the statement was true except that this "scheme" was not consciously in his mind before or while he wrote. Instead, his aim was to unite religion and myth so that Christianity would come to the reader as "shock" or "romance." Because a writer cannot make a narrative out of nothing and finds it impossible to "rearrange the primary matter in secondary patterns" without showing his feelings and opinions about his material, the writer's own reflections and experience inevitably will get worked in.[70] In fact, when asked his motive, Tolkien replied that because he is a Christian, his writings reflect that viewpoint.[71]

As a devout Catholic, Tolkien wanted the core element of Christianity in his mythology. Tolkien writes that even though things that are not theologically sound can be acceptable in an imaginary world, they can still "elucidate" Truth.[72] Bradley Birzer argues that "if Tolkien wanted to renew Christendom it was in the sense of an ethic encoded in the natural and divine law."[73] Hence, "Middle-earth is a sub-creation that represents true Creation in which Rivendell best represents living with nature, the Shire represents the agrarian use of nature, and Orthanc and Mordor represent the exploitation, domination, and, consequently, the destruction of nature."[74]

Because Tolkien did not want to break the spell of the secondary world, he does not use direct religious references. He refers to *The Lord of the Rings* as a "monotheistic" and "sub-creational mythology."[75] At the same time, although Tolkien did not feel obligated to make his story fit Christian theology, he still uses many biblical themes and echoes much of its wording so that religion is in the "background." In a BBC interview, for example, Tolkien was asked if God was the One, and Tolkien answered, "The One, yes." Tolkien identifies a key conflict in *The Lord of the Rings* as God's sole right to honor.[76] However, Eru remains distant in all of Tolkien's works. Tolkien says the Creator is not embodied in the story or mythology.[77] During the time period of his stories, the wise know Eru exists, but only the Valar can approach him, or those descended from the Númenóreans can remember him in prayer.[78] Tolkien notes that God and the angels do "peep through" in certain places, such as Gandalf's statement that there is something at work beyond the Ring-maker's design.[79] There is continual mention of a divine plan behind the events.

Tolkien not only expands on, rewrites, and changes the Genesis story but also considers his myth a supplement to the Bible. In *The Silmarillion*, for example, Tolkien tells the story of a creation, a fall, redemption, and apocalypse. Tolkien's views about sub-creation are also illustrated in the creation of Middle-earth. Unlike the Bible, Tolkien focuses on the Silmarils. He describes his tales as new rather than derived from other myths and legends. However, they do contain some ancient elements because legend and myth are made of Truth, and all stories are about the Fall.[80] There is a fall of Angels, but it is different from Christian myth.[81] In addition, Edenic allusions can be found in Valinor, the Blessed Realm, and Lothlórien.

According to Tolkien, there are several differences between his mythology and the Bible. First, this mythology has three falls: that of Morgoth, Elves, and Men. In the Bible, the Fall of man is a consequence of the Fall of the angels, and evil is brought into the world by Satan. Second, there is a rebellion of created free-will rebels before Eä created the World.[82] Another example is Gandalf's "incarnation" after his death. Tolkien mentions that while one might be reminded of the Gospels, it isn't the same thing because God's Incarnation is greater than anything he could write about.[83]

Finally, Tolkien points out that his creation differs from the Bible; man was intended to live eternally, but mortality is a punishment for the Fall. In his mythology, Elves are immortal and men mortal. Mortality is blessing and gift to the Children of God because it is an escape from the weariness of time.[84] Men still do not find rest in the world and "seek beyond" it and the Music of the Ainur.[85]

Tolkien admits that the Virgin Mary was the basis for simple and majestic beauty. Consequently, characteristics of both Elbereth and Galadriel have been compared to Mary.[86] The hobbits and Elves often call upon Elbereth as a divine or angelic character. In addition, the Holy Eucharist is seen in the lembas that the Elves give to the hobbits to eat on their journey.[87]

Lewis states that Tolkien's work is not allegory, which has only one meaning; his work is more serious and "higher" than that.[88] Instead, *The Lord of the Rings* is "myth" because "there are no pointers to a specifically theological, or political, or psychological application."[89] Lewis compares allegory to a puzzle and a great romance to a flower with a smell you cannot identify. While you have a realistic story, the feel of it is not like the real world. The Orcs, Ents, and Elves are not like our world, "but the feel of it, the sense of a huge past, of lowering danger, of heroic tasks achieved by the most apparently unheroic people, of distance, vastness, strangeness, homeliness (all blended together) is exactly what living feels like to me."[90] Places like Lothlórien are "heart-breaking." The growing darkness and great deeds are just like the real world. Even though darkness keeps coming, it is never triumphant or defeated. The moral is the impermanence of any victory in this present world because of man's "unchanging predicament."

LEWIS AND SUPPOSITION

Lewis distinguishes allegory from "supposition." Each mixes the real and unreal in a different way. Lewis claims he was not exactly representing the real Christian story in symbols, but rather, things in his books are "like" biblical ones or "remind" us of them. Lewis insists that none of his stories began with a Christian message.[91] Instead, he calls his technique a "supposition." A supposition uses an original person or situation but doesn't change it. Thus Lewis is, in a sense, simply rearranging rather than creating. Supposals are ideal experiments that teach us about the things being experimented upon. If it succeeds, we will think, feel, and imagine "more accurately, more richly, more attentively" about the invaded world, the invader, or both.[92] When we say "what if," we can see ideas in new ways. The story exists even if we remove the theological elements.

For example, *The Great Divorce* (1946) was intended to have a moral. Lewis uses the dream narrative to describe a voyage to Heaven. It is an "imaginative supposal" about the afterlife to arouse curiosity rather than a "guess or speculation at what may actually await us."[93] The most successful aspect is the image of Heaven as "unbendable and unbreakable," an idea Lewis borrowed from a story in an American science fiction magazine. Imaginary voyages such as this, Lewis notes, became valued when the great age of real exploration died out, because they maintained the wonder and glory of exploration. Dream voyages show us Truth veiled in allegory.[94] Tolkien, however, discounts the dream device as fantasy. If the writer tells you the tale has been imagined, he cheats the "realization . . . of imagined wonder."[95]

Lewis also uses "supposition" in *The Chronicles of Narnia*. In several letters, Lewis insists the Narnia series is not exactly allegory but "overlaps" with it.[96] He told a fifth-grade class that they were wrong in thinking everything in *The Silver Chair* represents something as things do in *Pilgrim's Progress*. He didn't say, "Let's represent Jesus as a Lion in Narnia." Instead, "Let us *suppose* that there were a land like Narnia and that the Son of God, as He became a Man in our world, became a Lion there, and then imagine what would happen."[97] Suppose there was a world like Narnia that needed to be redeemed; then what would Christ's Incarnation, Passion, and Resurrection have been like?[98]

While it would be difficult to write a story specifically about God, it would be reasonable to imagine what God might do in another world, and "a story is only imagining out loud."[99] In the form of a Lion, Aslan can portray certain qualities of Christ: he is awesome, solemn, stern, and compassionate, a "terrible good." Aslan says the reason the children were brought to Narnia is "that by knowing me here for a little, you may know me better" in England. Ironically, most children who wrote to Lewis knew who Aslan really is, whereas most adults never saw the biblical connection.

Supposition restores our view of the commonplace. Chesterton observes that we do not know why certain images and metaphors are accepted by our imagination before reason can reject them. But fatigue has affected Christianity; because the facts are so familiar, it is almost impossible to make them vivid. He is convinced that if we retold the story of Christ by making him a Chinese hero and calling him the Son of Heaven, we would accept it better than concepts like atonement. We would "admire the chivalry of the Chinese conception of a god who fell from the sky to fight the dragons and save the wicked from being devoured by their own fault and folly."[100]

Another example of supposition is wondering what an unfallen race would be like and how we would affect it. In the preface to *Perelandra*, Lewis is careful to point out that the book is not an allegory (e.g., the Green Lady does not represent Eve). Instead, *Perelandra* shows that the Fall resulted from a free act of sin and could have been avoided. It supposes what would have happened if rational animals in another part of the universe did not fall.[101] In describing the Bent Oyarsa's tactics in great detail, Lewis expands on the Genesis account of the temptation. The book was thus the first science fiction work to present an unfallen paradise, working out Lewis's supposition: "Suppose, even now, in some other planet there were a first couple undergoing the same that Adam and Eve underwent here, but successfully."[102] Lewis feared that if humans were to meet aliens, we would infect them with slavery, deceit, and corruption. He enjoyed speculating about whether there are other races, and whether they are good or evil or have a redemption of their own.

LEWIS AND CHRISTIAN ELEMENTS

While some fairy tales transport you to a new world with its own laws, in others the real world is invaded by the fantastic.[103] To create convincing "other worlds," Lewis believed that he must draw on the only real "other world" he knew, that of the spirit. Lewis claims the Christian element welled up unconsciously into the narrative as he wrote, pushing itself in "of its own accord."[104] When he began *The Lion*, he did not foresee what Aslan was going to do and suffer. Lewis's goal was to strip the Christian message of its "stained-glass and Sunday school associations" and give it new form and meaning by putting all these things into an imaginary world.[105] By stealing past "watchful dragons" of inhibitions and traditional religious concepts and terminology, he could make them, for the first time, "appear in their real potency."

In a letter, Lewis tells a woman who misunderstood the duty of a Christian writer that "we needn't all write patently moral or theological work." Indeed, a work with latent Christianity "may do quite as much good and may reach some whom the more obvious religious work would scare away."[106] Before Lewis became converted to Christianity, he found certain expressions silly or shocking. Yet he did not mind the same ideas in story or mythic form because he was prepared to feel the myth's profound and suggestive meaning. Although we often feel that we ought to feel a certain way about God, "obligation to feel can freeze feelings." Lewis's goal was to present the Gospels in a fresh way. Purtill believes "Lewis's imaginative works reveal a mind which thinks naturally in Christian terms and can give these terms new imaginative life."[107]

Hooper and Green identify the "source book "for the Narnia tales as the Bible, but Lewis intended it to be subconsciously recognized.[108] A sort of "disguise" was part of Lewis's intention. Lewis was not exactly representing the real Christian story in symbols; rather, things in his books are "like" biblical ones or may "remind" us of them.[109] Consequently, we will not find a one-to-one relationship between stories and the Bible because he did not intend for us to. Hooper warns that trying to explain stories such as the Narnia Chronicles as one would decipher a code destroys their very purpose, so we should not search for analogies too closely or expect to find them. Sometimes it is not until later that the two worlds are joined in the mind. Artist Pauline Baynes, for example, told Walter Hooper that she was moved by Aslan's sacrifice but did not realize who he was meant to be until after she had illustrated *The Lion, the Witch and the Wardrobe*.

Lewis made Aslan a lion for several reasons: other animals are Talking Beasts, and the lion is king of beasts; Lewis had been having strange dreams about lions; and the Bible calls Christ the Lion of Judah. In explaining Aslan's other names, Lewis asked a child if she never heard of anyone in this world who arrived with Father Christmas, who said he was son of the Great Emperor, who gave himself for someone else, was mocked, came to life again, and is called a Lamb. "Don't you really know His name in this world?"[110] He was thankful that another girl recognized the "hidden story" in the Narnia books; children do and grown-ups rarely did.[111]

In his letters, Lewis identifies some of the differences and similarities between his Narnia stories and the Bible.

- *The Magician's Nephew* is about creation of a world, but not ours. Jadis's plucking the apple is not like Adam's sin because she had already fallen.
- In *The Lion, the Witch and the Wardrobe*, Aslan's crucifixion and resurrection are not exactly like Christ's; the Stone Table is a reminder of Moses's table. Edmund is like Judas, but he repents and is forgiven. There is a deeper meaning behind Aslan being killed by the White Witch.
- In *Prince Caspian*, old stories are disbelieved, and true religion is restored.
- *The Horse and His Boy* is about the conversion of heathen. The three replies to Shasta suggest a Trinity.
- *The Voyage of the "Dawn Treader"* is about the spiritual life, especially as seen in Reepicheep. When the children reach the End of the World, they see a Lamb who invites them to breakfast; he is so white they can barely look at him. Suddenly, he is changed, and they recognize him: "As he spoke his snowy white flushed into tawny gold and his size changed and he was Aslan himself, towering above them and scattering light from his mane." Similar "symbolism" is used in Revelation 5:5-6: "The Lion of the Tribe of Judah, the Root of David, has conquered, so that he can open the scroll and its seven seals. And between the throne and the four living creatures and among the elders, I saw a Lamb standing, as though it had been slain."
- *The Silver Chair* is about the war against darkness, and the old king is raised by a drop of blood.
- *The Last Battle* is about the reign of anti-Christ (Ape and Puzzle), the end of the world, and judgment.[112]

Although Lewis in places denies overt allegory, his books have many biblical overtones, for a good work, Lewis argues, is more than just what happened. Rather, the plot is "a net whereby to catch something else."[113] In life and art we are always trying to catch something that is not successive, an "elusive bird." It may be tangled in the net of time briefly so we can enjoy the plumage. The best literature, then, is a "handmaid" of religious or moral Truth.[114]

Lewis writes that "any amount of theology can now be smuggled into people's minds under cover of romance without their knowing it."[115] A Christian writer does not need to write moral or theological works. In fact, if the Christianity is less obvious, it may reach some audiences more effectively.[116] For example, he describes books by G. K. Chesterton and George MacDonald as traps for atheists.[117] George MacDonald's *Phantastes* "baptized" his imagination; similarly, Chad Walsh says that when he read *Perelandra*, "I got the taste and smell of Christian truth. My senses as well as my soul were baptized."[118] Lewis was pleased that most reviewers did not recognize that the "fall" of the Bent One was not his private invention. But this "great ignorance might be a help to the evangelisation of England."[119] The present task of the church is "to convert and instruct infidels."[120] Lewis calls *Pilgrim's Regress* and *Out of the Silent Planet* "almost propaganda" and admits that the trilogy as a whole became Christian.[121] Many of Lewis's statements like these appear to indicate a didactic or at least evangelistic motive for writing.

Moorman believes that the type of fiction Lewis wrote was affected by this purpose to propagate the faith.[122] Lewis often uses lengthy conversations or blunt statements to get his message across. For example, Ransom says outright, "I'm a Christian." Yet Lewis insists that Ransom is a "figura Christi" and simply plays the role of Christ as every Christian does or should.[123] Lewis also sometimes lapses into statements of his opinions. In *Perelandra*, for instance, Lewis states that Weston is obsessed with the idea that because humanity has corrupted our planet, it must spread itself to other planets. This idea is circulating in works of science fiction, "in little Interplanetary Societies and Rocketry Clubs," and in "monstrous magazines."

It is not surprising that because Lewis is a key Christian apologist, his fantasy fiction also contains Christian meaning. At a meeting of the Oxford Socratic Club on February 2, 1948, Lewis and philosopher G. E. M. Anscombe debated Lewis's book *Miracles*. Several writers believe that as a result, Lewis moved from writing apologetic works to "apologetic imagination."[124] Although Lewis claims that he did not place apologetics or moral values first in importance, his books have many biblical overtones and even evangelistic messages. According to Lewis, it wasn't the "liberal-minded" religious people who like his books; these are his worst critics.[125]

Many critics flatly dislike Lewis's moralizing tone, and some accuse him of using fiction to create a formal apology for Christian doctrine.[126] Lewis's fantasy works are often classified as "didactic" fantasy that aims to revise morality in line with cosmic Truth. Wrapping a didactic message in a fantasy stripped of traditional contexts to avoid stock responses makes it more palatable.[127] Lee Rossi describes Lewis's dilemma: Will he guarantee the Christianity of his writing, or will he concern himself primarily with "realizing" his fictional world? If the Christianity is too blatant, he ruins his imaginary world. But if he concentrates on the presentation, he may lose his point.[128] Dennis Quinn argues that in the Narnia books, "spectacles, scenes, and images" convey ideas in lieu of action where heroes defeat foes. Because the human actions exist only for the symbolism, they are "at best rhetoric, at worst propaganda."[129] Gunnar Urang emphasizes the tension that must exist between a story's controlling idea and the vehicle: "If the tension between the fiction and the idea collapses, then a heavier burden falls on belief." If the reader cannot accept the values of the hypothetical world, then "he will begin to examine Lewis' ideas in their own right. If he finds them unbelievable, he will find the novel unbearable."[130]

TOLKIEN AND LEWIS AS CHRISTIAN WRITERS

It is difficult to achieve believability and effectively integrate a "message" with the story, thus avoiding the extremes of either blatant allegory and didacticism or obscurity. Lewis's books are obviously perceived as more explicitly theological than Tolkien's. A. R. Bossert believes Lewis fell into a trap of making God subject to his imagination, thus making Christ unidentifiable.[131] Tolkien, in turn, avoided this trap in his own mythology. The problem lies with Lewis's claims that his book should not be read as allegory.

Yet there are numerous parallels in the story that require either reading the scene as allegory or being left with basic theological problems. The latter provides yet another explanation as to why Tolkien so strongly objected to the Narnia books. Eric Seddon cites the problem of Aslan's passion and crucifixion's lacking a Eucharist that Tolkien as Catholic would find necessary. "As a result, Lewis's Narnia would have repelled Tolkien for both its implications about the character of Christ and its lack of what Tolkien felt to be the most important thing in life—the Blessed Sacrament."[132] This problem comes from Lewis's blurring the borders between "myth as sub-creation and allegory as psychological projection" and his lack of awareness of it. Another example is the unorthodox view of Aslan's body. If Aslan is Christ in another world, then Lewis presents Christ with an illusory body.

The difference between Tolkien's Catholic view and Lewis's Evangelical Protestant views of Scripture affected their response to both Scripture and myth.[133] Tolkien responded similarly to sacred and secular literature. Religion and mythology "re-fuse" in fantasy literature, which can be valued for its own sake. But for Lewis, the Bible is true history and thus not to be "imaginatively enlarged upon."[134]

The Rev. Dwight Longenecker attributes the differences between Tolkien's and Lewis's works to deep theological differences between Catholicism and Protestantism. For Catholics, "Truth, while it may be argued dialectically, is essentially something not to be argued but experienced. The Truth is always linked with the mystery of the Incarnation, and is therefore something to be encountered." Catholics also believe that Jesus Christ is God's primary revelation. As a result, Tolkien's works incarnate Truths "in a complete, subtle, and mysterious way." Protestants, in contrast, view Truth as a dialectic, consisting of "abstract propositions to be stated, argued, and affirmed or denied." They argue that God's primary revelation is Sacred Scripture. Thus Lewis "produced works that were profound, worthy, and beautiful, but less than fully incarnational."[135]

Walter Hartt identifies two alternative views of art that Tolkien and Lewis demonstrate. Tolkien inclined to the "single art" alternative: Art is sub-creation when it is good art, regardless of whether or not it is thematically Christian. As a result, Tolkien's stories are just stories. In contrast, Lewis leaned toward the "both and" alternative: Art is sub-creation when it is both good art and thematically Christian. For Lewis, because religion conforms to a predetermined order, sub-creation is a restricted activity. There can be no "genuinely new" or "celebration of other stories." Tolkien's world is open and free, whereas Lewis's is closed off. While Tolkien looks forward to the story still being made, Lewis looks back to the Christian myth.[136]

While the word *fantasy* in common terms is usually associated with things that are made up and therefore untrue, Christian fantasy is presented as Truth. Because it can convey theological principles, Christian fantasy has been called "alternative theology," a phrase Chesterton used to describe George MacDonald's books, or "romantic theology," a phrase Lewis used to describe Charles Williams's works. The "message" is ideally conveyed through fantasy images, symbols, characters, and events. According to Lewis, Christian literature is best written about serious subjects rather than being frivolous art valued for its own sake and simply for the need to be "creative."[137] At the same time, Lewis believes that for art to teach well, both the doctrine and art must be good.[138] He cautions that we must realize that works of art are both something said and something made. We must treat them as objects that we receive instead of trying to draw ideas from them. Nevertheless, fantasy has many effects on the reader. Besides the moral values found in their fiction, Tolkien and Lewis believed there were several important advantages of fantasy, as discussed in the final chapter.

7

Advantages of Fantasy

I n "On Fairy Stories," Tolkien identifies the value of fairy tales as Recovery, Escape, and Consolation. This chapter describes Tolkien's and Lewis's views about the value of fantasy and myth.

RECOVERY

Recovery is regaining a "clear view" of things, thereby strengthening our relish for real life.[1] It is not seeing what things are but rather as we are meant to see them. It also helps us view things as separate, unique entities apart from ourselves and our possessiveness. For example, when Tom Bombadil spends the day talking to the hobbits, they begin to understand the "lives of the Forest, apart from themselves." In "On Fairy Stories," Tolkien writes that things appear trite when we have "appropriated" or possessed them, locking them up in our hoard and ceasing to look at them. Creative fantasy uses fantastic elements to help make things new, unchained, free, and wild. It unlocks the hoard and lets the "caged birds" fly away in freedom.

If we clean our "windows," we can free ourselves from viewing things as trite and familiar. Frodo and Sam see the light in Mordor "like a pale morning through the grimed window of a prison." In contrast, Frodo views Lothlórien as if "through a high window that looked on a vanished world." Language has no name for the light falling on that world. The shapes are so clear that it is as if they had just been thought of and then drawn the minute his eyes are uncovered. Colors are those he knows, but they are fresh, as if he is perceiving them for the first time and giving them new, wonderful names. Even though there is a set pattern to things, that does not mean we should become bored or find things distasteful. For example, paintings require curved or straight lines and a fixed set of primary colors. In "I Sit beside the Fire and Think," Tolkien considers things he has yet to see: "in every wood in every spring / there is a different green." In addition, escaping from the familiar does not mean works should become misshapen, drab, or silly.

The secondary world helps us see the primary world again by placing things in a different setting.[2] Chesterton says fairy tales create a "certain way of looking at life" and help us see the world as a "wild, startling, delightful place." They provide "elementary wonder" and touch the nerve of astonishment.[3] Lewis says that if one tires of looking at a landscape he should try looking at it in a mirror.[4] It helps the reader to rediscover reality and see things more clearly.

Lewis explains how secondary world fantasy changes our view of the primary world. Fiction containing another planet, parallel universe, or Earth in the distant past or future is "good for" spiritual adventures because such books satisfy the craving of our imaginations, suggest "otherness," and convey "wonder, beauty, and suggestiveness."[5] We may be more willing to enter a secondary world and accept what happens there, thus being more open to ideas in the story. Recognizing that the work is fantasy, we willingly suspend disbelief and accept the other world's laws. For instance, the main characters are taken to another world and experience anything without straining credibility. When they return to earth, they apply the things they learned. Because the secondary world is a mirror or metaphor for our own, things that happen in that world can be applied to our world. By showing us things in a different way, the other world sheds light on our world and helps us return to it with renewed vision.

In *The Abolition of Man*, Lewis argues that seeing through things is not the same as seeing.[6] We cannot "see through" or explain away things forever. When we simply see through things, the world becomes transparent and thus invisible. In reading George MacDonald's *Phantastes*, for example, Lewis found a work that did not make the real world seem dull. Instead, the "bright shadow" came into the world and transformed common things, thus "baptizing" his imagination.[7] Fairy land gives the actual world "a new dimension of depth" and sends us back to the real world with renewed pleasure, awe, and satisfaction.

The triteness of ordinary objects such as stone, wood, iron, trees, grass, fire, and bread is transformed to wonder. Tolkien cites the example of "MOOR EEFFOC," or COFFEE ROOM viewed from the inside of a glass door.[8] Chesterton uses this idea from Charles Dickens to describe how trite things look when suddenly seen from a new perspective or when really looked at for the first time. But Tolkien believes this type of fantasy is limited because it only gives the reader a fresh vision. It is comparable to a "time-telescope" used to view London in the past or future and thus focused on just one spot. In contrast, "creative fantasy" creates things anew. Other types of writing can provide recovery, but the core of fantasy in fairy stories is the most thorough at achieving it.

In his essay on Tolkien, Lewis writes that the value of myth is that it takes ordinary things and restores to them a significance that "the veil of familiarity" has hidden.[9] "The boy does not despise real woods because he has read of enchanted woods," writes Lewis; "The reading makes all real woods a little enchanted."[10] If a child pretends his cold meat is a buffalo he has just killed, he enjoys it more. Lewis contrasts this attitude with that of a Jungian psychologist, whose life had become so dreary that she was no longer able to feel pleasure, and her mental "landscape" was arid. Lewis asked her if she liked fantasies and fairy tales. With hands clenched and muscles tightened, she hissed, "I loathe them."[11]

Recovery thus renews our health and keeps us "childish." According to G. K. Chesterton, it is really adults who need fairy tales, not children, for children still have a sense of awe and wonder at the world simply as it is. He argues that young children do not need fairy tales—only tales—because life itself is interesting. Fairy tales describe nature using terms such as *charm*, *spell*, and *enchantment*. In fact, he believes children are the only readers who would not be bored by realistic novels.[12]

In Chesterton's story "The Coloured Lands," a stranger tells his story to a boy named Tommy who is bored with his world. The stranger has him try on both blue- and rose-colored glasses, and then tells his story. The man decided that things might look different if colors were different, so a wizard granted his wish. He then traveled to countries of different colors but found no peace or happiness in any of them. So the wizard asked him to construct a country that he would like. He ended up constructing, piece by piece, our same world. As a result of the story, Tommy stares at his cottage "with a new look in his eyes."

There is a need for the ability to wonder at the universe simply because it *is*. By expanding on creation, an author can glorify it. Chesterton wrote often about common objects like cheese or chalk because he was resolved to write against Pessimists and Decadents: "The object of the artistic and spiritual life was to dig for this submerged sunrise of wonder; so that a man sitting in a chair might suddenly understand that he was actually alive and be happy."[13] Stories of magic showed him that life is not only a pleasure but also "a kind of eccentric privilege."[14] They restore the kind of astonishment and wonder at the world that the ancients had, convincing him that this world is wild, startling, and delightful.[15] Even repetition such as the sun rising each day seemed to show the vitality in life rather than monotony. If man ever gets to the point that he cannot experience wonder and view things except as dull, then he must see them as things "entirely unfamiliar and almost unearthly."[16]

Tolkien's view of the restorative power of fantasy is seen at the end of "Leaf by Niggle" and in Lothlórien. Niggle's Parish, like Tolkien's work, becomes a place for holiday, refreshment, convalescence, and "the best introduction to the Mountains." People who visit there seldom have to return. Similarly, the company enters Lothlórien blindfolded. When their eyes are uncovered, they behold the beauty with wonder. Language is inadequate to give a name to the light. Frodo sees the colors gold, white, blue, and green in a fresh way, as if he is seeing them for the first time. When he touches a tree, he delights in the "living tree itself"—its wood and feel—rather than feeling it for how he might use it as a forester or carpenter. Sam notes that the magic is so deep you cannot lay your hands on it.

An example of "renewed vision" comes about in Lewis's *The Voyage of the "Dawn Treader"* when Caspian is amazed to hear that the children come from a round world. He had only read about them in fairy tales. "But I've always wished there were and I've always longed to live in one. . . . It must be exciting to live on a thing like a ball." "There's nothing particularly exciting about a round world when you're there," Edmund replies. Similarly, in *Out of the Silent Planet*, Ransom had always considered space cold, black, and dead. Now he sees it as an ocean of radiance. If he thinks of a hross as a man, it is disgusting; but if he sees it as an animal, it is delightful. He realizes that everything depends upon his point of view.

ESCAPE

Fantasy—"making or glimpsing of Other-worlds"—deals with what is real and fundamental and escapes the modern world. By *escape*, Tolkien does not mean "escapism" but rather escape from the ugliness of our world, from hunger, pain, and death and from industrialization, machines, and technology.[17] According to Lewis, what we escape in *The Lord of the Rings* is "the illusions of our ordinary life."[18] The charge of escapism is rooted in the confusion about what is real or the misconception that progress is better than the archaic. Tolkien once asked Lewis who would be hostile to the idea of escape. The answer was "jailers."[19]

In "On Fairy Stories," Tolkien distinguishes between the *Escape of the Prisoner* and *Flight of the Deserter*. The prisoner confined to a small cell thinks about the outside world and longs to go home. But that does not mean he is escaping his cell or that the outside world is less real than the cell. Rather, he desires to escape the Robot Age of technological and scientific power—of motor cars, factories, electric street lamps, machine guns, and bombs. Is a car more real than a horse or centaur? In a way, then, fantasy can be a flight *to* rather than *from* reality. In contrast, the Flight of the Deserter is a refusal to recognize sorrow and death and to escape duties and responsibilities.

In response to the charge of escapism in his own books, Lewis says that some accuse fairy tales of causing children to retreat into wish fulfillment. Fairy tales and realistic stories both present things we wish for. Lewis describes two kinds of fantasy. One type is simply wish fulfillment, such as being popular. This type of fantasy flatters the ego and sends one back to the world discontented.[20] For example, in *The Voyage of the "Dawn Treader,"* the Magician's Magic Book tempts Lucy to say a spell to make herself beautiful. Instead, she succumbs to the spell to learn what others think about her.

Then she comes across a "spell for the refreshment of the spirit" that is more like a story than a spell. Aslan promises that he will tell her that story—the loveliest she has ever read—for years and years. This is the second type of fantasy, which evokes a longing for fairy land and is a special kind of longing. For Lewis, marvelous literature satisfied his intense longing, which he calls "askesis," or a spiritual exercise.[21]

Lewis says we all have a desire for a "far off country" like an inconsolable secret—"a desire for something that has never actually appeared in our experience."[22] We mistakenly identify what we long for as beauty or a memory; but these are only the "scent of a flower we have not found, the echo of a tune we have not heard, news from a country we have never yet visited." Spells can both induce and break enchantments. "And you and I have need of the strongest spell that can be found to wake us from the evil enchantment of worldliness which has been laid upon us for nearly a hundred years."[23]

As described in his biography *Surprised by Joy*, Lewis all his life experienced this longing for a beauty that lies "on the other side" of existence. It began as a series of "aesthetic" experiences scattered through his younger years. Before Lewis was six years old, his older brother Warren made a miniature garden in the lid of a biscuit tin with moss, twigs, and flowers. This first experience with beauty made him see nature "as something cool, dewy, fresh, exuberant."[24] Similarly, the low line of the Castlereagh Hills that he could see from his nursery window—perhaps contoured like the mountains of Aslan's Country—taught him longing, or *Sehnsucht*. One day he stood beside a flowering currant bush, and the same sensation came over him—"a desire; but desire for what? . . . in a certain sense everything else that had ever happened to me was insignificant in comparison."[25] Later in his life, an Arthur Rackham illustration from *Siegfried and the Twilight of the Gods* and a line from this retelling of the Norse myth engulfed Lewis in what he described as "Pure Northernness," and he felt a return of the sense of distant joy for which he had long searched.

In Narnia, the things longed for are associated with the North, Aslan, the distant mountains of Aslan's Country, and the islands of the Utter East. For Reepicheep, questing valiantly for the End of the World, the spell of Aslan's Country has been on him all his life. In *The Last Battle*, Jewel the Unicorn, upon reaching the new Narnia of Aslan's Country, stamps on the ground and cries, "I have come home at last! This is my real country! I belong here. This is the land I have been looking for all my life, though I never knew it till now. The reason why we loved the old Narnia is that it sometimes looked a little like this."

A similar theme runs throughout Tolkien's works in the form of a fascination with seas ("sea-longing"), unknown lands, and the vanished past.[26] He was haunted his whole life by dreams of a great wave destroying the isle of Atlantis. As a result, the longing for a lost Eden runs throughout his tales. The Elves long for Valinor, but the beauty of this world is no longer accessible from this world. These longings for a heavenly realm can be interpreted as a "recollection of a desire for transcendent beauty that can no longer be fulfilled in this world."[27]

Our true longing is not simply for things that do not exist; for example, you would not want to exchange imaginary objects or creatures for real ones (e.g., hross for humans).[28] Rather, they are for a transcendent world. A correspondent with Lewis so fell in love with the worlds in *Out of the Silent Planet* and *Perelandra* that she felt they were more real than our world. Lewis replied that what she wanted will "never be in any finite *here* or *now*."[29] A person who reaches Heaven will find that "the kernel of what he was really seeking even in his most depraved wishes will be there, beyond expectation, waiting for him in 'the High Countries.'"[30] Someday he will find that he has either attained or lost "the unattainable ecstasy" that has hovered just beyond his grasp.[31]

Are fairy stories merely escapism or wish fulfillment, then? No, says Lewis. Instead, their true significance lies in their ability to arouse in one's mind a longing for something: "It stirs and troubles him (to his life-long enrichment) with the dim sense of something beyond his reach and, far from dulling or emptying the actual world, gives it a new dimension of depth. . . . This is a special kind of longing."[32]

FULFILLMENT OF DESIRES

In "On Fairy Stories," Tolkien writes that fairy stories are concerned with "desirability" rather than possibility. If they awaken, satisfy, and whet it "unbearably," they succeed. The enjoyment of a story does not depend on believing whether things could happen in real life. They satisfy a number of desires that increase in scale from simply experiencing new things to living forever. They satisfy our desires to make or glimpse other worlds, explore time and space, visit the sea, and fly. More important, they also fulfill our desires to escape death and to communicate with other living things by understanding their language.

Escape from Death

Tolkien calls our "oldest and deepest desire" the Great Escape, the Escape from Death.[33] It is not surprising, then, that a central theme

of *The Lord of the Rings* is death, immortality, and power—mortal
men and the deathless Elves, not Power and Domination.[34] In "On
Fairy Stories," Tolkien writes that the stories of Elves are about the
escape from Deathlessness and the burden of endless serial living.
Because they love the mortal world, they resist going to the Undy-
ing Lands but confuse immortality with unlimited serial longevity.[35]
The Elves who do not return to Valinor but remain on Middle-earth
will thus fade and diminish. For men, death is a gift; however, Melkor makes it seem a curse. Deathlessness is not immortality but prolonged life. For example, the One Ring allows the wearer to not die,
but life becomes stretched until it becomes "weariness." In contrast,
escape from death is eternal life.

Both Tolkien and Lewis write about the need to accept change,
and they relate it to possessiveness. Tolkien compares the Elves' refusal to accept change to a reader's settling down in one favorite
chapter of a book. They fall under Sauron's deceit by wanting to
have power over things by preserving them and keeping them "fresh
and fair." Yet they do not want to dominate other wills.[36] In *Out of
the Silent Planet*, the Oyarsa says they do not fear death. But the Bent
One, lord of earth, makes humans waste their lives fearing death.
The Bent Oyarsa is said to have clung to the old good for so long
that it became evil. Lewis suggests that the root of all evil may be
the itch to have things over again, like eating the same fruit or hearing the same symphony twice in one day. When an experience or
object gratifies us (e.g., gluttony versus hunger), it becomes a
"Need-Pleasure."[37] Rather, the fruit we are given to eat, and the
wave rolled toward us at each moment, is the best of all.

Many critics believe that Tolkien's mythology only shows glimpses of a happy ending in the future. Instead, it shows the need to
persevere even though defeat is certain in this world. Lewis's *The
Chronicles of Narnia*, on the other hand, have the fairy-tale ending
Tolkien describes. In *The Lion, the Witch and the Wardrobe*, we have
a foreshadowing of the victory over death when the Stone Table
cracks and Death starts "working backwards." In *The Magician's
Nephew*, Digory feeds his dying mother the Apple of Life that heals
her. In *The Silver Chair*, we join the children in a wonderful glimpse

of the afterlife in Aslan's Country and the means by which one can truly experience it. During Caspian's funeral in Narnia, the children are taken to Aslan's Mountain to walk by the stream. Eustace is told to drive a thorn into Aslan's paw, and the blood splashes onto the dead Caspian. The miraculous change begins as we see death truly working backward, fulfilling the Deeper Magic. His white beard, sunken cheeks, and wrinkles vanish; his eyes open. Suddenly, he leaps up and stands before them. Knowing he has died, they think he is a ghost, just as Lucy and Susan had thought Aslan a ghost when he appeared before them after his sacrifice. But "one can't be a ghost in one's own country." This is Caspian's real home now, and the children are promised that they too will come here to stay one day.

Although these have all been glimpses of Aslan's Country, the only way to enter is by dying.[38] The Chronicles have one of the most unusual endings in children's books: The children and their parents die in a railway accident in England. Aslan tells the children that all of them are as it is called "in the Shadow-lands—dead." The children's end on Earth is the beginning of an even greater and never-ending Story. The children "all lived happily ever after. But for them it was only the beginning of the real story."

Communication with Animals

When a writer uses animals in fantasy, he/she creates a world we wish were true: an Eden where lion and lamb can lie down together and where animals talk. The Fall severed communication with other creatures. Tolkien says man has broken off relations with animals so that he sees them from a distance and is at war with or in an "uneasy armistice" with them.[39] By making trees and animals talk, the fantasy writer shows a return to a right relationship with nature. However, the writer does not ignore the real world. Tolkien notes that one must be able to distinguish between frogs and humans in order to write fairy stories about frog kings.

The Elves desire to talk to everything because of their sympathy for other beings. Thus, they teach the Ents to talk. Because Tolkien believed trees were nature's most significant creatures, it is no surprise, then, that his Ents speak in long, sonorous tones in an "unhasty" pace. Many believe the Ents to be one of Tolkien's best creations by merging qualities of trees and humans.

Lewis identifies the presence of beings other than humans, who behave humanly—"giants and dwarfs and Talking Beasts"—as a central element in all fairy tales. Fairy tales contain not only terrible figures but also comforters and aides. Lewis considers it important to have such protectors side by side with terrible creatures.[40] He observes that "giants, dragons, paradises, gods, and the like" express basic elements in our spiritual experience. Thus he likens them to words of a "language which speaks the else unspeakable."[41] Because we want to be united with and to receive beauty, "we have peopled air and earth and water with gods and goddesses and nymphs and elves—that although we cannot, yet these projections can, enjoy in themselves that beauty, grace, and power of which Nature is the image."[42] Such creatures depict an ancient reality we have forgotten, a visionary view of nature and man, and hierarchy and cosmic order. According to Lewis, creatures higher than ourselves must be represented symbolically and are usually human because that is the only rational creature we know.[43]

Lewis describes several ways to write about animals. First, animals might talk and act like humans, but their relationships to each other and humans are the same. Another type of fantasy depicts another creation with different animals and different relationships.[44] Animals have the advantage of being like children, without cares or domestic responsibilities. They can also be like adults by doing what they please and going where they wish.[45] In addition, animals can portray personality types most succinctly to a wide audience. While in medieval beast fables animals served to satirize human foibles and teach morals, in fantasy they can convey psychology and character types more briefly and to a wider audience. Lewis gives the example of Mr. Badger in *The Wind in the Willows*. Any child who has met Mr. Badger gains knowledge about humanity and English social history that he could not have gotten any other way.[46] Where do we see courage more clearly than in the swashbuckling Reepicheep, a two-foot mouse, proudly and fearlessly defending and jabbing with his small sword?

As mentioned, Tolkien does not believe beast fables can be considered true fairy tales. In beast fables, there are no humans, so animals essentially speak for humans. In contrast, in fairy tales, humans can understand the language of animals, fulfilling our desire to commune with other living things. He classifies Beatrix Potter's tales as being on the border of Faërie—not because of her talking beasts but because of the strong moral elements.

Tolkien desired dragons "with a profound desire." He wrote his first story—a poem about a dragon—when he was just seven.[47] His essay "Beowulf: The Monsters and the Critics" (1936) is one of the definitive critical works on the story. His goal is to counter the criticism that the poem focuses on unimportant things and places the important on the edges. He also focuses on the monsters, Grendel and the dragon. This essay provides insights into both Tolkien's views of creatures in fantasy and techniques he believes are effective, particularly the power of myth.

Tolkien uses an analogy to negatively depict literary critics. A man inherits a field containing old stones from which he builds a house and a tower that looks out over the sea. His friends arrive but do not even climb the steps. Believing that the stones belonged to an older building, his friends push over the tower hunting for hidden carvings and inscriptions, the source of the stones, and coal deposits. While they believe the tower is interesting, they consider it a "muddle." Even the man's descendants call the tower "nonsensical." Here Tolkien criticizes those who overlook the work as a whole and focus on sources and influences.

Tolkien praises the ability of *Beowulf*'s author to make appealing the dark antiquity and melancholy behind the narrative by touching upon "poignant and remote" sorrows. Despite the fact that the poem is not historic, it presents a self-consistent picture of Denmark or Sweden in AD 500. This type of detail both shows design and creates the illusion of depth by surveying a significant, sorrowful past. The poet makes his theme explicit, incarnate in history and geography, and merges elements of Scripture with the pagan past and northern mythology. These are all qualities Tolkien achieves in his own mythology.

Some have criticized the trivial theme of *Beowulf*, but Tolkien believes that the author's selection of material indicates that he had a design in mind. First, the theme matches the style. Tolkien says that the historical allusions in *Beowulf* give the "impression of reality and weight" and the idea that the story is "part of the solid world" rather "in the air." He also praises the high and lofty tone, which contrasts the "low" theme: The hero is a man on Earth battling a hostile world and inevitable defeat in this world. The author depicts the past struggles of fallen and unsaved man; Tolkien describes him as "disgraced but not dethroned," the same phrase he uses in "Mythopoeia."

Tolkien believes the power of myth is its ability to move readers, but they may mistakenly attribute the effect to the wrong element, such as the style. Their interest and pleasure from the story may, in fact, lie in the ogres and dragons. The monsters are fundamental to the underlying ideas of the poem. The fact that Beowulf's foes are inhuman makes the story large and significant, for it goes beyond history and becomes a story about man's fate. There is a difference between a monster that brings temporal death and a spirit of evil that aims at the soul and therefore brings eternal death. When monsters take on human shape, they become symbolic of sin, God's adversaries. Grendel is a different type of enemy than a political one because he threatens fellowship and joy. Overcoming Grendel is important because he is a monster, thus giving the story a fairy-tale quality.[48]

Beowulf's final foe is a dragon—a creature that the imagination has made for such a purpose, says Lewis. According to Lewis, Phaedrus (first century AD) was the first to write about a dragon, and this creature has remained a powerful archetype.[49] Tolkien calls the dragon legend a potent and fascinating creation of men's imaginations. Dragons are identified with the powers of evil and enemies of God and mankind, and usually personify evil, greed, and destruction. Tolkien does not consider the dragon in *Beowulf* "frightfully good" because he is not a "plain pure fairy-story dragon."[50] Charles

Moorman argues that Tolkien and Lewis share the same creative methods toward their ends but that their worldviews differ, as illustrated by their views of death and struggles against such evil. Lewis's fiction is clearly Christian, while Tolkien's is more pagan. It is similar to *Beowulf* by expressing a pessimistic heroic pattern that shows the tragic effects of struggling against evil.[51]

MYTH

In his essay on *Beowulf*, Tolkien distinguishes between folk tales and myth, or the "mythical imagination." Analytical reasoning cannot pin on paper the significance of myth. Rather, it is at its best when a poet like the Beowulf author "feels" rather than makes his theme explicit and when he "makes it incarnate" through history and geography.

Tolkien and Lewis have a unique definition of *myth. Myth* usually means something that is not true; for Tolkien and Lewis, it means the opposite. Myth, fairy stories, and all art reflect elements of religious and moral Truth. Thus fairy stories should be presented as "true."[52] Recurring legends and myths also contain Truth, presenting aspects of Truth that can only be received this way.[53] Fairy tales, legends, and myths are the best way to express Truth because they use images and action rather than explanation. In fact, Tolkien ends "On Fairy Stories" with the statement that all tales may come true, although they may differ from the forms we give them.

The value of myth is key not only to Tolkien and Lewis's relationship but also to their views about the highest form of fantasy. The story begins with their disagreement about mythology and its relationship to Christianity. In *Surprised by Joy*, Lewis writes that when he became interested in Norse mythology in about 1919, he believed such tales were true. But he had "two hemispheres" of his mind: the imaginative life of poetry and myth versus shallow rationalism and intellect. While he loved the imaginary, he thought the real grim and meaningless.[54] In a letter from 1916, Lewis calls religion mythology grown up, simply man's invention.[55] At that time, he believed Christ existed, but he equated beliefs about his virgin birth and healings to mythology.[56] Legends about him simply contain kernels of Truth, similar to legends of King Arthur and Oden. G. K. Chesterton helped Lewis see that Paganism was the childhood of religion.[57] Paganism is an attempt to reach divine reality through only the imagination. Chesterton likens mythology and philosophy to rivers that run parallel until they meet in Christianity.[58]

Tolkien also influenced Lewis's conversion to Christianity, primarily through his arguments about myth. When he was fifteen, Lewis read Sir James Frazer's *The Golden Bough* (1922), which describes the many pre- and post-Christian civilizations that had myths about a god who dies and comes back to life. Lewis considered Christianity just another myth of such a god. Even before his conversion, Lewis realized that pagan stories hinted at Truth that later became history in the Incarnation. Lewis notes that it is not accidental that pagan mythology resembles Christian Truth because some tellers were guided by God.[59] Good elements in mythology can be preparation for the Gospel for people who don't know where they are being led.[60] Lewis calls myth "at its best, a real though unfocussed gleam of divine truth falling on human imagination."[61] Yet he could not understand the purpose of Christ, the Crucifixion, and the Resurrection.

On September 19, 1931, Lewis, Tolkien, and Hugo Dyson discussed myth. Tolkien observed that mankind historically conveyed belief through mythology. It would then follow that God would reveal himself in the form of a true myth. Christianity is thus a perfect myth because it not only has all the characteristics of other myths but is also true, whereas other myths merely reveal fragments of God's Truth. Lewis argued that myths are lies. Tolkien countered that because man comes from God, imaginative inventions must also come from God and contain some Truth. Myth is a medium of divine revelation, helping us understand what cannot be known through facts or history. Tolkien believed as well there are glimpses of religion in mythology: divinity, power, and worship.

Tolkien and Dyson convinced Lewis that if he accepted the idea of a sacrifice in a pagan story, he could accept Christ's sacrifice.[62] "Now the story of Christ is simply a truth myth." It affects us the same way as other myths except *"it really happened."* It is God's rather than man's myth. Whereas pagan poets use images that allow God to express Himself, in Christianity, God expresses himself through real things. Although we can get doctrines from pagan myths, they are less adequate than the Incarnation, Crucifixion, and Resurrection.[63] Lewis decided that the Christian story is a myth like other great myths except the Bible is myth become fact. In his essay "Myth Became Fact" (1944), Lewis writes, "If God chooses to be mythopoeic . . . shall we refuse to be *mythopathic?*"[64] Tolkien was influenced by this essay, noting that Lewis shows that not only does the Christian story's beauty have some permanent value but also provides nourishment. Lewis helped him not feel ashamed of or doubtful about the Eden "myth." Even though it is not as well documented as the New Testament, Eden did exist, and we long for it.[65] This longing for an Edenic past is a theme throughout Tolkien's mythology.

Lewis believed as well that pre-Christian pagan myths prefigured Christian Truth. In *The Discarded Image*, Lewis suggests that pagans and early Christians had much in common. It is not surprising, then, that in *The Chronicles of Narnia*, he blends classical mythology with Christian allusions rather than creating a new mythology, as did Tolkien. P. H. Brazier writes, "The Narnian stories are like pagan myths for Lewis; they do not exist in their own right to point to their own internal reality and logic—they exist to point to the single historic event in our reality."[66]

An intriguing idea occurs quite frequently in Lewis's works—that what is myth and legend in our world may be factual reality in another. Central to Lewis's story in the Space Trilogy is the fact that Earth is in a "bent" and "silent" state as a result of the Fall in Eden. The consequence has been a separation of myth, Truth, and fact; body and soul; matter and spirit; God and man. On Malacandra, Ransom wonders if the "distinction between history and mythology might be itself meaningless outside the earth." On Perelandra, he again suspects that things that are mythology on Earth or other worlds might be fact in another. He recognizes that "the triple distinction of Truth from myth and of both from fact—was purely terrestrial—was part and parcel of that unhappy division between soul and body which resulted from the Fall." Yet he is also aware that the division is not final because the Incarnation was the beginning of its disappearance.

Since the Fall in the Garden of Eden, man has separated subject from object, the phenomenal from the invisible numinous world, and how he experiences from what he experiences. The first result of this split was the demythologization of the physical world, which has taken us further and further away from the meaning of objects. In *The Silmarillion*, the world was flat until the Fall. It then changed to round as divine punishment. This detail illustrates Tolkien's view that we have been cut off from the supernatural and Edenic ideal. Demythologization similarly removes mythical elements from stories so that only historical fact remains. Both Lewis and Tolkien aimed to recombine them again.

In his preface to D. E. Harding's *Hierarchy of Heaven and Earth*, Lewis describes the ancient worldview in which every tree was a nymph and every planet a god. The universe eventually became emptied of gods, colors, smells, sounds, tastes, and solidity.[67] The naturalist, Lewis warns, begins to then further strip the universe of its significance by telling us that nothing really exists behind Nature either.[68] In this way, our present world has been drained of qualities of the supernatural and the wonderful. But a worse result is that man himself has been emptied of all meaning. The "masters of the method" claimed humans do not have souls, selves, or minds, just as trees do not have dryads. "We, who have personified all other things, turn out to be ourselves mere personifications."[69]

Eventually, the separated will become reunited. In *Miracles*, Lewis writes, "Nature and spirit, matter and mind, fact and myth, the literal and the metaphorical, have to be more and more sharply separated, till at last a purely mathematical universe and a purely subjective mind confront one another across an unbridgeable chasm. . . . Those who attain the glorious resurrection will see the dry bones clothed again with flesh, the fact and myth re-married, the literal and metaphorical rushing together."[70]

Until that time, because man will always be limited in his knowledge due to the gap between experience and perception, he needs both reason and imagination. Lewis suggests that the only way to unite these two modes of experience is through metaphor, the most perfect form of which he defines as *myth*. Despite the conventional ways of using this term, Lewis defines *myth* in his own way. Myth contains what man does not know and could not know in any other way; it provides meanings that vary and grow for different readers.[71] Because reality is much "larger" than the rational or what can be observed through the senses, myth allows man to rise above it. Myth is a form of literature, the purpose of which is thus to express and help us understand what we cannot rationally or intellectually know, thus serving as a bridge between thought and the real world. "In the enjoyment of a myth we come closest to experiencing what can otherwise only be understood as an abstraction."[72] At the heart of myth, in fact, is actually a revelation of God.

In *An Experiment in Criticism*, Lewis gives an example of what he means by myth. He tells the basic plot of the Orpheus and Eurydice story, plus the summaries of two other stories. Orpheus plays the harp and enchants beasts and trees with his music. When his wife dies, he goes to the land of the dead and plays for the King of the Dead. The King agrees to let him take his wife back to Earth if he agrees not to look back. However, Orpheus looks back, and his wife vanishes forever.[73]

While the Orpheus and Eurydice story makes a powerful impression on most readers, the other two stories are dull and boring. Lewis then identifies six characteristics of myth that explain the appeal:

- It exists despite the narrator because it is independent of literary form and details.
- The narrator's skill in creating suspense or surprise is also not important. The work is enthralling for its own sake and has a contemplative purpose.
- We only observe the characters rather than identify with them, as in most stories, because "they are like shapes moving in another world."

- It contains fantasy elements: creatures, the supernatural, the impossible, and the out-of-the-ordinary. These sentient animals or characters are larger than life.
- It is solemn and grave, and never comic.
- The experience is grave, awe-inspiring, and "numinous."

In *The Problem of Pain*, Lewis also uses the word *numinous*, identifying it as an element in religion. He obtained this term from Rudolph Otto's *The Idea of the Holy* (1917). Holiness inspires the numinous, a feeling of awe, wonder, joy, or enchantment that cannot be defined or expressed in language but can be evoked in symbols. Otto writes that fairy stories have both the element of the "wonderful" and miraculous events by infusing the numinous. This feeling, says Lewis, is as old as humanity. He distinguishes the numinous from fear, much like the difference between being told there is a mighty spirit or a tiger in the next room. Lewis's search for Joy his whole life is similar to searching to find the source of this indescribable sensation. Both Lewis and Tolkien locate the source of the numinous as "other," beyond this world, in Heaven. It nevertheless still transforms our view of reality here on Earth. The function of myth is to provide the experience of the numinous for the reader.

Because it is so much "larger" than words, myth allows us to go beyond the limitations of language. According to Lewis, in myth the imaginary events are the body and the inexpressible is the soul. The body can take any form—words, film, pictures—but these are "not much more than a telephone."[74] The real theme usually has no sequence and is "more like a state or quality."[75] It is the quality of the unexpected that delights us. Thus the "surprise" in reading fantasy is different from simply finding out what happens. It is the presence of the "Other."

Lewis says that in enjoying a myth, we come close to experiencing the abstract as concrete. For example, let's assume we are trying to understand an abstract concept—how "tasted reality" fades and vanishes if we try to grasp it with "discursive reason." But then if we hear the story of Orpheus and Eurydice, we can imagine this principle.[76] While human intellect is abstract, experiences are concrete. If we try to intellectually apprehend an experience such as love, pleasure, or pain, we are no longer experiencing them. We can either taste and not know or the opposite. Thinking cuts us off from reality. In other words, once we begin to examine our experience of reality, we are cut off from the object and left with only an abstraction, a mental construct. Myth is a solution to this dilemma because it helps readers come near to concretely experiencing abstraction and allows them to think and experience simultaneously. In other words, myth connects the peninsula of thought with the continent of reality, the physical and the spiritual.

The appeal of the Orpheus story is something beyond its literary form, because only the plot can strike and move us deeply. "Myth does not essentially exist in *words* at all but as 'a particular pattern of events.'"[77] What delighted Lewis about the myth of Balder is the pattern of events rather than the medium.[78] This pattern is important, not how the events are told. For example, in a novel by James Fenimore Cooper, if a pistol were substituted for a tomahawk, it would ruin the story, says Lewis. The reason is because we want the entire world sustained. The value of myth, then, is independent of its embodiment and not dependent upon words. Once the reader has grasped the "soul" of the story, the myth itself, he or she can do away with the vehicle that contained it. But the moment we state the meaning, we are back in the abstract world. "It is only while receiving the myth as a story that you experience the principle concretely."[79]

Lewis points out that because we do not look for an abstract "meaning" in this myth, we may find it surprising that he seems to be doing so. By our tacking on meaning, the story becomes not myth but allegory. Myth cannot be analyzed and dissected; otherwise, one may kill it and be left simply with allegory. Because the moral should not be abstracted, expressed, or restated but rather inherent in the myth, Lewis considers myth "higher" than allegory. While allegory has one meaning, myth has varying meanings that "will grow for different readers and in different ages."[80] The story has several different and true meanings that cannot be separated from the framework: "What flows into you from myth is not truth but reality (truth is always *about* something, but reality is that *about which* truth is) and therefore every myth becomes the father of innumerable truths on the abstract level."[81]

Myth goes beyond the expression of things we have already felt. It arouses in us sensations we have never had before or anticipated having. Lewis calls the "mythopoeic" a "mode of imagination which does something to us at a deep level."[82] "It gets under our skin, hits us at a level deeper than our thoughts or even our passions, troubles oldest certainties till all questions are re-opened, and in general shocks us more fully awake than we are for most of our lives."[83] Furthermore, it is as if "something of great moment had been communicated to us."[84]

Because abstract thinking is a "tissue of analogies," "demythologising" Christianity can become "re-mythologising" it—"substituting a poorer mythology for a richer."[85] Even the Scripture uses analogies. But we cannot get rid of the analogy to a literal Truth, for we would only substitute a theological abstraction. Are these likely to be more adequate, he asks, "than the sensours, organic, and personal images of Scripture—light and darkness, river and well, seed and harvest master and servant, hen and chickens, father and child? The footprints of the Divine are more visible in that rich soil than across rocks or slagheaps."[86]

Myth is not illusion or lies but a "real though unfocussed gleam of divine truth falling on human imagination." Just as God did not become less God by becoming a man, so too the "Myth remains Myth even when it becomes Fact."[87] That is, God expressed true myth in the form of the Incarnation, Crucifixion, and Resurrection. In the Incarnation, "what became Fact was Myth" and "carries with it into the world of Fact all the properties of a myth."[88] If a myth became fact and became incarnated, it would be like the Gospel story: "Here and here only in all time the myth must have become fact."[89] The Bible is the Myth God chose from countless Myths to carry spiritual Truth.[90] The Truth first appeared in mythical form and eventually became incarnate as History.

Christ's story demands "an imaginative response" because it is directed to the inner child, poet, savage, conscience, and intellect, thus serving to break down walls. According to Brazier, Lewis is stating that the Gospel story should have the effect of myth: "In the case of those who have consciously heard the Gospel narrative, the story of the Incarnation, Passion and Resurrection should operate on us in a perlocutionary way: awareness of the narrative is important because of the event it represents.[91] Victoria Nelson believes that our culture is undergoing a shift from the logic of Aristotelian thinking to Platonism, which views the religious dimension as non-rational. Religion is not found in churches but rather in imaginative works that "recycle" religious expression.[92] This is one reason why today mythopoeic works may be so appealing to those searching for religious meaning.

In *Pilgrim's Regress*, a voice speaks to John: "Child, if you will, it *is* mythology. It is but truth, not fact: an image, not the very real. But then it is My mythology. . . . But this is My inventing, this is the veil under which I have chosen to appear even from the first until now. For this end I made your senses and for this end your imagination, that you might see My face and live."[93]

EUCATASTROPHE

The Gospels are not fairy stories but true recorded history. They fuse Truth and symbol, history and legend, the divine and human. Tolkien writes that within them is a fairy story containing the essence of all fairy stories—marvels that are peculiarly artistic, beautiful, and moving, and "mythical" in their perfect, self-contained significance. This story has entered History and the primary world; the desire and aspiration of sub-creation has been raised to the fulfillment of Creation. The fairy story in the Gospels contains the essence of all fairy stories. It is Primary Art and pure Creation. The Author is God, the Lord of angels, men, and Elves, and the "supreme Artist and Author of Reality."[94] The Primary Miracle is the Resurrection, which gives us a glimpse of Truth and light shining through the "chinks" of the universe.[95] It produces a tearful Christian joy by mingling Joy and Sorrow. A fundamental principle is that this story begins and ends in joy. It has preeminently the "inner consistency of reality." There is no tale ever told that man would rather find was true.[96] This Gospel story that entered history and the primary world begins and ends in Christian "Gloria."

Tolkien calls the "Happy Ending" *consolation*. Fantasy does not deny "dystastrophe" (sorrow and failure); instead, the highest function of fairy stories is *eucatastrophe*, or good catastrophe, "a sudden glimpse of the underlying reality or truth" and a "sudden joyous turn" of events when good triumphs.[97] Christ's birth is the eucatastrophe of earth's history; the Resurrection is the eucatastrophe of the Incarnation; and the Great Eucatastrophe is God's future kingdom.

The turn in a fairy tale comes right before eucatastrophe; the reader catches his breath and feels his heart lifted, and the joy "is a sudden and miraculous grace" that one can never count on to recur.[98] A good fairy story has the peculiar quality of this turn, but it is difficult to achieve, and some tales may only partially succeed. A successful story lets the gleam come through the frame or web of the story, providing a glimpse of joy and the heart's desire. The story is on one plane; the literary "truth" is on the second plane.

In a letter to his son Christopher, Tolkien tells the true story of a young boy near death from tubercular peritonitis being taken away on a train. The boy suddenly sat up and demanded to talk to a little girl he noticed. He then arose, played with the girl, and declared that he was hungry. This "unhoped-for happy ending" moved Tolkien with an emotion he describes as like no other. Tolkien believes that *The Lord of the Rings* has a true fairy-tale ending because the hero is subjected to an evil power too great for him to overcome. The "cause," however, triumphs because of pity, mercy, and forgiveness.[99]

Fairy stories can bring a piercing joy that brings tears; our natures that have been chained by death feel suddenly relieved, as if all our limbs were once out of joint and have been snapped back.[100] Tolkien believes fantasy has a happy ending because the religious view perceives real consolation occurring after death or the end of the world. If the story has literary Truth, it perceives that our natures really were made for the Great World. For Tolkien, this emotion comes through in *The Hobbit* when Bilbo cries "The Eagles!

The Eagles are coming."[101] Tolkien calls it *evangelium* (Latin for "gospel" or "good news") that gives a fleeting vision of joy.[102] Shippey suggests that the Greek word for New Testament is *euangelion*, which contains the word *angel*. It means "the good message," translated into Old English as "gód spell," the good story or Gospel. Today, "spell" does not mean "story" but appropriately, "enchantment."[103]

THE GREAT STORY

The Great Story of the Gospels, which is both myth and fact, contains all elements of the perfect fairy tale. Each of us is also a character in the Story. In turn, our sub-creative works are stories within this Story. Both Tolkien and Lewis mention stories within stories in their novels, reminding readers that they exist outside the work itself but are part of a greater narrative.

The Lord of the Rings has a number of references to legends, tales, and stories. For example, in *The Two Towers*, on the slopes of Mount Doom, Sam and Frodo discuss tales about brave deeds. Sam used to think that brave people in the stories went out and looked for adventures because life was dull. But in the tales that really matter or stay in your mind, the heroes just land in them, and their paths are laid out for them. They may not even have a good ending. Happy endings are the best tales to be in but not necessarily the best ones to hear. Because Sam knows that they are in a tale, he wonders if their story will be put into words and what type of story they've fallen into. Frodo replies that you don't know what type of tale you are in, and the characters don't know either. Sam asks, "Don't the great tales never end?" The answer is that they never end as tales, and people go when their part has ended.

Tolkien ends "On Fairy Stories" with the idea that stories and fantasy still go on and should go on. "Evangelium" (the Gospel) has not abolished but rather has hallowed legends, especially the happy ending. Tolkien refers to The Writer of the Story—both the Great Story and even his own mythology—as someone other than himself.[104] The Christian has a purpose because he can help enrich creation, and "all tales may come true." Tolkien writes to his son Christopher, who was serving in World War II, that writing would give him relief about good and evil, help rationalize it, and prevent it from festering. He likens Christopher's situation to being "inside" a great story and that all stories give you that feeling when you are "in" them.[105] We are to move forward in time, to continue the story. According to Tolkien, the weakness of the Elves is their unwillingness to face change and move on, just like a reader of a long book who refuses to continue and settles down in a favorite chapter.[106]

Lewis also writes of the Great Story. In *The Voyage of the "Dawn Treader,"* Lucy enters the Magician's House and reads his Magic Book. She comes across a spell "for the refreshment of the spirit," a wonderful story about a cup, sword, and green hill that hints of the Gospel story. She begins to feel that she is living in the story as if it was real. But she cannot go back and read it or remember it. All good stories ever since remind her of the forgotten story. This example echoes Lewis's ideas about pagan stories' containing hints of the myth that becomes fact. It also echoes Niggle's Parish, which is a place of renewal, "refreshment," and the best introduction to the mountains. Aslan, who is behind all the stories, promises to tell Lucy the story. At the end of the Narnia tales, we are told that life in the real world and adventures in Narnia had been only the cover and title page of the real story. They were now beginning the first chapter of the Great Story that no one has read, that goes on forever, and that gets better with each chapter.

Lewis defines a story as a series of events—a plot. But the plot is a net composed of time and events intended to catch something that is not sequential: a process, state, or quality like "otherness." Seldom does the net catch the bird, the image of Truth. Tolkien similarly says that faerie cannot be caught in the "net of words" because it is indescribable. Life is also like a story, a succession of events. We search to find an embodiment of a sheer state of being that we desire and search for, but we fail. In both life and art we try to catch in the net "something that is not successive." Stories are almost able to succeed and are thus worth creating. In the end, perhaps "either the meshes will become fine enough to hold the bird,

or we will be so changed that we can throw our nets away and follow the bird to its own country."[107]

Myth can put us in touch with the Great Story. Both Tolkien
and Lewis believe that while art is unable to fulfill our desires or
expectations, it can refresh the spirit, create beauty, be an act of
worship, express the inexpressible, and renew our vision. The mythopoeic vision results in a renewed perspective on nature, individual
objects, and man himself. Lewis likewise describes a road that leads
outside the self to something that is "sheerly objective," "the naked
Other" that we desire and that our imagination salutes with hundreds of images.[108]

Influenced by Coleridge and Tolkien, in *An Experiment in Criticism*, Lewis defines a work of art as not just something *said* (*Logos*)
but something *made* (*Poiema*). As *Logos*, it tells a story, expresses
emotion, persuades, describes, and so on. As *Poiema*, it is an "objet
d'art" shaped to satisfy rather than a means to an end or vehicle of
Truth. As a complex, carefully crafted object, it simply "is."[109] Tolkien likewise calls for us to view each created object as it was meant
to be, before the Fall, as something "other," outside the self.

The artist creates a pattern by arranging events in an order and at
a tempo. The Logos and Poiema rely on each other. The Logos helps
present the Poiema, the imaginations, emotions, and thoughts that
arouse a reaction in the reader. When reading imaginative works,
the reader should thus be less worried about changing his opinions
but "entering fully" into the opinions and experiences of others.
The purpose of reading is to enlarge our being and be admitted to
experiences different from our own. "Literature as Logos is a series
of windows" and doors that lead us out of ourselves. It lets the
reader transcend himself to become a thousand men and yet become
more himself.[110]

The true artist and craftsman delights in creation for its own sake;
appreciates "otherness" and the freedom of objects, people, and nature from ourselves; and finally releases the created object. In *Smith
of Wootton Major*, the Faery Star is kept in a compartment of an old
black spice box but is removed when it comes time to pass it on to
the next child. Similarly, Frodo tells Sam that one must give up

things and lose them so others may keep them. Once Tolkien completed *The Lord of the Rings*, he did not believe it belonged to him. Rather, he describes it as having "been brought forth" and going its "appointed way in the world."[111] The power to make is a gift from the Creator and requires stewardship. Creative power, like other types of power, can be abused, such as to dominate others or to selfishly hoard.

For Tolkien and Lewis, fairy stories, myth, and fantasy are imperfect glimpses and shattered reflections of the Truth God tells in the Great Story. Nevertheless, the gift of making in God's image allows the fantasy writer to recombine, rearrange, remythologize, reenvision, reenchant, resacralize, and, at last—to relinquish.

Notes

INTRODUCTION

1. J. R. R. Tolkien, *The Letters of J. R. R. Tolkien*, ed. Humphrey Carpenter (Boston: Houghton, 1981), 231.

2. Ibid., 400.

3. C. S. Lewis, *A Preface to Paradise Lost* (London: Oxford University Press, 1977), 89.

CHAPTER 1

1. C. S. Lewis, *Collected Letters of C. S. Lewis*, Vol. I, ed. Walter Hooper (San Francisco: HarperCollins, 2004), 202.

2. Ibid., 104.

3. Ibid., 970.

4. Ibid., 169, 254, 281, 905; C. S. Lewis, *Collected Letters of C. S. Lewis*, Vol. II, ed. Walter Hooper (San Francisco: HarperCollins, 2004), 96.

5. J. R. R. Tolkien, *The Letters of J. R. R. Tolkien*, ed. Humphrey Carpenter (Boston: Houghton, 1981), 351.

6. Humphrey Carpenter, *Tolkien: A Biography* (Boston: Houghton Mifflin, 1977), 242.

7. Lewis, *Letters*, Vol. II, 709.

8. C. S. Lewis, *Surprised by Joy* (New York: Harcourt, 1955), 179.

9. Lewis, *Letters*, Vol. I, 901.

10. C. S. Lewis, *Collected Letters of C. S. Lewis*, Vol. III, ed. Walter Hooper (San Francisco: HarperCollins, 2007), 1458.

11. Lewis, *Surprised*, 72–73.

12. Lewis, *Letters*, Vol. II, 34.

13. Ibid., 747; Carpenter, *Tolkien*, 129.

14. Lewis, *Surprised*, 21, 23.

15. Tolkien, *Letters*, 78.

16. Ibid., 378.

17. Ibid., 211.

18. Lewis, *Letters*, Vol. II, 96.

19. Tolkien, *Letters*, 342, 347.

20. Ibid., 209.

21. Ibid., 378.

22. Ibid., 212.

23. Ibid., 261.

24. Ibid., 144.

25. Ibid., 314.

26. Ibid., 345.

27. Ibid., 377.

28. Ibid., 218–219.

29. Ibid., 345.

30. Ibid., 215, 219.

31. Ibid., 346.

32. J. R. R. Tolkien, Interview by Philip Norman, *New York Times*, "The Prevalence of Hobbits," January 15, 1967.

33. Tolkien, *Letters*, 31, 144.

34. Ibid., 297.

35. Ibid., 219 note.

36. Ibid., 218.

37. Ibid., 346.

38. Ibid., 31.

39. Lewis, *Letters*, Vol. II, 96.

40. C. S. Lewis, "The Hobbit," in *On Stories and Other Essays on Literature*, ed. Walter Hooper (New York: Harcourt Brace Jovanovich, 1982), 81.

41. Tolkien, *Letters*, 346.

42. Ibid., 215.

43. Ibid., 38.

44. Ibid., 41.

45. Ibid., 216.

46. Ibid., 412.

47. Ibid.

48. Ibid., 362.

49. Ibid., 303.

50. Lewis, *Letters*, Vol. III, 1458.

51. Tolkien, *Letters*, 68.

52. Ibid., 362.

53. Lewis, *Letters*, Vol. III, 824.

54. Tolkien, *Letters*, 209.

55. Ibid., 36.

56. Ibid., 38.

57. Ibid., 376.

58. Lewis, *Letters*, Vol. III, 856, 980; "Tolkien's *The Lord of the Rings*," in *On Stories*, 83.

59. Lewis, *Letters*, Vol. III, 383.

60. Lewis, *Letters*, Vol. II, 990.

61. Lewis, *Letters*, Vol. III, 980.

62. Ibid., 383.

63. Lewis, *Letters*, Vol. II, 261; Vol. III, 575.

64. Lewis, "Unreal Estates," in *On Stories*, 144.

65. Lewis, *Letters*, Vol. II, 183.

66. Lewis, *Letters*, Vol. III, 923.

67. Lewis, *Surprised*, 17.

68. Ibid., 54.

69. Lewis, *Letters*, Vol. I, 95.

70. Lewis, *Surprised*, 15.

71. Roger Lancelyn Green and Walter Hooper, *C. S. Lewis: A Biography* (New York: Harcourt Brace Jovanovich, 1974), 241.

72. George Sayer, *Jack: C. S. Lewis and His Times* (San Francisco: Harper and Row, 1988), 25.

73. Green and Hooper, 241.

74. Sayer, 189.

75. Carpenter, 138.

76. Lewis, *Letters*, Vol. II, 631.

77. Carpenter, 223–224.

78. Green and Hooper, 241.

79. Joe R. Christopher, *C. S. Lewis*. Twayne English Authors Series. (Boston: Twayne, 1987), 118.

80. Sayer, 313.

81. Carpenter, 151.

82. Tolkien, *Letters*, 32–33.

83. Ibid., 33.

84. Tolkien, *Letters*, 316.

85. Diana Pavlac Glyer, *The Company They Keep* (Kent, OH: Kent State University Press, 2007), 125.

86. Carpenter, 170.

87. Colin Duriez, *Tolkien and Lewis: The Gift of Friendship* (Mahwah, NJ: Paulist Press, 2003), 81; Tolkien, *Letters*, 209, 361–362.

88. Eric Seddon, "Letters to Malcolm and the Trouble with Narnia: C. S. Lewis, J. R. R. Tolkien, and Their 1949 Crisis," *Mythlore*, Fall-Winter, 2007, 352. http://www.accessmylibrary.com/coms2/summary_0286-33496441_ITM.

89. Carpenter, 151.

90. Ibid., 241.

91. Tolkien, *Letters*, 341, 349.

92. Joseph Pearce, *Tolkien: Man and Myth* (San Francisco: Ignatius Press, 1998), 80.

93. Gareth Knight, *The Magical World of the Inklings* (Longmead, UK.: Element Books, 1990), 112.

94. Tolkien, *Letters*, 104, 258.

95. Wayne G. Hammond, "'A Continuing and Evolving Creation': Distractions in the Later History of Middle-earth," in *Tolkien's Legendarium*, eds. Verlyn Flieger and Carl F. Hostetter (Westport, CT: Greenwood, 2000), 18.

96. Tolkien, *Letters*, 220, 231.

97. Ibid., 231.

98. Tolkien, *New York Times* interview.

99. Tolkien, *Letters*, 145.

100. Ibid.

101. Ibid., 334.

102. Carpenter, 198.

103. Tolkien, *Letters*, 216–217.

104. Clyde S. Kilby, *Tolkien and the Silmarillion* (Wheaton, IL: Harold Shaw, 1976), 53.

105. Tolkien, *Letters*, 189.
106. Ibid., 145, 212 note, 289.
107. Carpenter, 4.
108. Tolkien, *Letters*, 232.
109. Ibid., 252–253.
110. Ibid., 413.
111. Ibid.
112. Ibid., 122.
113. Ibid., 122–23.
114. Lewis, "Sometimes Fairy Stories May Say Best What's to Be Said," in *On Stories*, 45.
115. Lewis, *Letters*, Vol. III, 1132, 1213.
116. Lewis, "It All Began with a Picture," in *On Stories*, 53.
117. Lewis, *Letters*, Vol. III, 1214.
118. Ibid., 1109.
119. Walter Hooper, "Preface," in *On Stories*, xvii.
120. Lewis, *Letters*, Vol. III, 807.
121. Lewis, "It All Began with a Picture," in *On Stories*, 53–54.
122. Lewis, *Letters*, Vol. III, 162; "Unreal Estates," in *On Stories*, 144–145.
123. Lewis, *Letters*, Vol. III, 466.
124. Lewis, "On Three Ways of Writing for Children," in *On Stories*, 41.
125. Lewis, *Letters*, Vol. III, 683.
126. Lewis, "On Criticism," in *On Stories*, 134.
127. C. S. Lewis, *A Preface to Paradise Lost* (London: Oxford University Press, 1977), 3.
128. Lewis, "Sometimes," in *On Stories*, 46.
129. Ibid., 47.

CHAPTER 2

1. J. R. R. Tolkien, *The Letters of J. R. R. Tolkien*, ed. Humphrey Carpenter (Boston: Houghton, 1981), 220.
2. J. R. R. Tolkien, "On Fairy Stories," in *The Tolkien Reader* (New York: Ballantine, 1966), 2.
3. Ibid., 9.
4. Ibid., 32.
5. G. K. Chesterton, "The Ethics of Elfland," in *Orthodoxy* (New York: Image Books, 1959), 56.

6. Tolkien, "On Fairy," *The Tolkien Reader*, 20.

7. C. S. Lewis, "On Three Ways of Writing for Children," in *On Stories and Other Essays on Literature*, ed. Walter Hooper (New York: Harcourt Brace Jovanovich, 1982), 37.

8. C. S. Lewis, *Collected Letters of C. S. Lewis*, Vol. III, ed. Walter Hooper (San Francisco: HarperCollins, 2007), 515.

9. Ibid., 517.

10. C. S. Lewis, *Collected Letters of C. S. Lewis*, Vol. II, ed. Walter Hooper (San Francisco: HarperCollins, 2004), 802.

11. Lewis, "Sometimes," in *On Stories*, 46.

12. Ibid., 47.

13. Tolkien, "On Fairy," in *The Tolkien Reader*, 34; *Letters*, 220.

14. C. S. Lewis, *An Experiment in Criticism* (Cambridge, UK: Cambridge University Press, 1961), 70.

15. Lewis, "On Stories," in *On Stories*, 14; Tolkien, *Letters*, 209.

16. Jack Zipes, "Breaking the Disney Spell," in *The Classic Fairy Tales*, ed. Marla Tatar (New York: Norton Critical Edition, 1999), 335.

17. Margaret Blount, *Animal Land: The Creatures of Children's Fiction* (New York: Avon, 1974), 55.

18. Stephen Prickett, *Victorian Fantasy* (Bloomington: Indiana University Press, 1979), 10–11.

19. Tolkien, *Letters*, 209.

20. Ibid., 297.

21. Ibid., 310.

22. Ibid., 298.

23. Lewis, "On Three," in *On Stories*, 34.

24. Lewis, *Letters*, Vol. III, 396.

25. Tolkien, *Letters*, 297–298.

26. Ibid., 136.

27. Lewis, *An Experiment*, 67.

28. Tolkien, "On Fairy," in *The Tolkien Reader*, 38.

29. G. K. Chesterton, *The Common Man* (New York: Sheed and Ward, 1950), 56–57.

30. Lewis, *Letters*, Vol. III, 93.

31. Lewis, "On Three," in *On Stories*, 39–40.

32. G. K. Chesterton, *Tremendous Trifles* (New York: Sheed and Ward, 1955), 85–86.

33. Ibid., 86.

34. Lewis, *Letters*, Vol. II, 171.

35. Madeleine L'Engle, *A Circle of Quiet* (Greenwich, CT: Fawcett, 1972), 236–237.

36. Lewis, "Sometimes," in *On Stories*, 48.

37. Lewis, "On Three," in *On Stories*, 32.

38. Lewis, "On Juvenile Tastes," in *On Stories*, 49, 51.

39. Ibid., 51.

40. Lewis, "On Stories," in *On Stories*, 14.

41. Lewis, *Letters*, Vol. III, 807.

42. Lewis, "Sometimes," in *On Stories*, 47–48.

43. Lewis, "On Three," in *On Stories*, 34.

44. George MacDonald, "The Fantastic Imagination," in *The Gifts of the Child Christ*, Vol. I, ed. Glenn Sadler (Grand Rapids, MI: Eerdmans, 1973), 25.

45. Madeleine L'Engle, *Walking on Water: Reflections on Faith and Art* (Wheaton, IL: Harold Shaw, 1980), 74.

46. Lewis, *An Experiment*, 71.

47. Diana Waggoner, *The Hills of Faraway* (New York: Atheneum, 1978), 10.

48. Roger Lancelyn Green and Walter Hooper, *C. S. Lewis: A Biography* (New York: Harcourt Brace Jovanovich, 1974), 163.

49. Lewis, *Letters*, Vol. II, 918.

50. Lewis, "Unreal Estates," in *On Stories*, 144.

51. Lewis, "A Reply to Professor Haldane," in *On Stories*, 71.

52. C. S. Lewis, "The Seeing Eye," in *Christian Reflections*, ed. Walter Hooper (Grand Rapids, MI: Eerdmans, 1967), 173–174.

53. Lewis, *Letters*, Vol. II, 236–237.

54. Lewis, "On Science Fiction," in *On Stories*, 64–66.

55. C. S. Lewis, *Surprised by Joy* (New York: Harcourt, 1955), 36.

56. Lewis, "On Science," in *On Stories*, 64.

57. Lewis, *Letters*, Vol. III, 1178.

58. L'Engle, *Walking*, 134–135.

59. Tolkien, *Letters*, 34.

60. Lewis, *Letters*, Vol. II, 630, 753; Vol. III, 314.

61. Lewis, *Surprised*, 35.

62. Lewis, "On Science," in *On Stories*, 63.

63. Lewis, "On Stories," in *On Stories*, 11–12.

64. Tolkien, *Letters*, 278.

65. Lewis, *Letters*, Vol. II, 456.

66. Lewis, "*De Futilitate*," in *Christian Reflections*, 61.

67. C. S. Lewis, *Collected Letters of C.S. Lewis*, Vol. I, ed. Walter Hooper (San Francisco: HarperCollins, 2004), 952.

68. Tolkien, *Letters*, 258, 377.

69. Ibid., 377.

70. Ibid., 220.

71. Tolkien, "On Fairy," in *The Tolkien Reader*, 47.

72. Ibid., 54–55.

73. Ibid., 46–47.

74. Donald E. Glover, *C. S. Lewis: The Art of Enchantment* (Athens: Ohio University Press, 1981), 30, 37.

75. Lewis, *An Experiment*, 50.

76. Ibid., 52.

77. C. S. Lewis, "Preface," *George MacDonald: An Anthology* (New York: Macmillan, 1947), 12; Lewis, *An Experiment*, 56.

78. Lewis, "The Language of Religion," in *Christian Reflections*, 134.

79. C. S. Lewis, *The Discarded Image* (New York: Cambridge University Press, 1964), 207.

80. Lewis, *Letters*, Vol. III, 759.

81. Lewis, *Letters*, Vol. I, 762.

82. C. S. Lewis, "Bluspels and Flalansferes: A Semantic Nightmare," in *Rehabilitations and Other Essays* (London: Oxford University Press, 1939), 265.

83. Owen Barfield, *A Barfield Reader*, ed. G. B. Tennyson (Middletown, CT: Wesleyan University Press, 1999), 56.

84. Ibid.

85. Owen Barfield, *Poetic Diction: A Study in Meaning* (New York: McGraw-Hill, 1964), 27.

86. Ibid., 112.

87. Ibid., 131.

88. C. S. Lewis, *Letters to Malcolm: Chiefly on Prayer* (New York: Harcourt, 1964), 140.

89. C. S. Lewis, *Miracles* (New York: Macmillan, 1974), 72.

90. C. S. Lewis, *Mere Christianity* (San Francisco: HarperCollins, 2001), 173.

91. Lewis, "The Language of Religion," in *Christian Reflections*, 138–139.

92. Lewis, *Letters*, Vol. III, 1613.

93. Lewis, *Letters to Malcolm*, 86.

94. Lewis, *Letters*, Vol. III, 683.

95. Ibid., 684.

96. Tolkien, "On Fairy," in *The Tolkien Reader*, note E.

97. Tolkien, *Letters*, 319.

98. Humphrey Carpenter, *The Inklings* (Boston: Houghton Mifflin, 1979), 206

99. Lewis, *Letters*, Vol. I, 933.

100. C. S. Lewis, *The Problem of Pain* (New York: Macmillan, 1971), 150.

101. Lewis, *Letters*, Vol. I, 670.

102. Ibid., 671.

103. Lewis, *Miracles*, 74.

104. C. S. Lewis, "The Weight of Glory," in *The Weight of Glory and Other Addresses* (Grand Rapids, MI: Eerdmans, 1975), 6.

105. Lewis, "Transposition," in *The Weight of Glory*, 29.

106. Tolkien, "On Fairy," in *The Tolkien Reader*, 22.

107. Tolkien, *Letters*, 260.

108. Ibid., 188.

109. Samuel Taylor Coleridge, *Biographia Literaria*, ed. George Watson (London: Everyman's Library, 1965), 174.

110. Tolkien, "On Fairy," in *The Tolkien Reader*, 48.

111. Tolkien, *Letters*, 145.

112. Orson Scott Card, "How Tolkien Means," in *Meditations on Middle-earth*, ed. Karen Haber (New York: St. Martin's Press, 2001), 162.

113. Maisie Ward, "Introduction," in G. K. Chesterton, *The Coloured Lands* (New York: Sheed and Ward, 1938), 15.

114. Tolkien, "On Fairy," in *The Tolkien Reader*, 54.

115. Ibid., 55.

116. Lewis, "The Mythopoeic Gift of Rider Haggard," in *On Stories*, 99.

CHAPTER 3

1. J. R. R. Tolkien, *The Letters of J. R. R. Tolkien*, ed. Humphrey Carpenter (Boston: Houghton, 1981), 148.

2. Ibid., 146.

3. Ibid., 333.

4. Ibid., 146.

5. Ibid., 284.

6. Ibid., 146.

7. Ibid., 284.

8. Ibid., 203.

9. Ibid.

10. Ibid., 284.

11. J. R. R. Tolkien, *The Silmarillion*, ed. Christopher Tolkien (Boston: Houghton Mifflin, 1977), 15.

12. Ibid., 42.

13. Ibid., 146.

14. Ibid., 285.

15. Ibid., 194.

16. Ibid., 235.

17. Ibid., 259.

18. Ibid.

19. Ibid., 176.

20. Ibid., 190.

21. Ibid., 287.

22. Ibid., 60.

23. Tolkien, *Letters*, 151.

24. Ibid., 204.

25. Ibid., 155.

26. Ibid., 149, note.

27. Ibid., 185.

28. Ibid., 145, note.

29. Ibid., 145, note, 188.

30. Ibid., 190.

31. Ibid., 176, 189, 192, 236.

32. Ibid., 197.

33. Ibid., 151–52; J. R. R. Tolkien, *The Fellowship of the Ring*, Book II, Chapter 8 (New York: Ballantine, 1965), 479.

34. J. R. R. Tolkien, Interview by Dennis Gerrolt, BBC Radio 4, "Now Read On," January 1971.

35. Tolkien, *Letters*, 149.

36. Ibid., 207.

37. Ibid., 151, 197.

38. Ibid., 152.

39. C. S. Lewis, *Collected Letters of C. S. Lewis*, Vol. II, ed. Walter Hooper (San Francisco: HarperCollins, 2004), 570.

40. C. S. Lewis, *Collected Letters of C. S. Lewis*, Vol. III, ed. Walter Hooper (San Francisco: HarperCollins, 2007), 868.

41. Tolkien, *Letters*, 361.

42. C. S. Lewis, unpublished letter to Miss Jacob, July 3, 1941.

43. W. H. Lewis, *C. S. Lewis: A Biography*, unpublished. Letter to Charles Moorman, June 12, 1957 (Marion Wade Collection, Wheaton College, Illinois), 414.

44. C. S. Lewis, *The Four Loves* (New York: Harcourt, 1960), 32.

45. Tolkien, *Letters*, 106.

46. Ibid., 195.

47. Ibid., 191.

48. Ibid., 195.

49. Ibid., 190.

50. Ibid., 146.

51. T. A. Shippey, *J. R. R. Tolkien: Author of the Century* (Boston: Houghton Mifflin, 2001), 241.

52. J. R. R. Tolkien, *The Two Towers*, Book III, Chapter 8 (New York: Ballantine, 1965), 204.

53. Lewis, *Letters*, Vol. III, 1303.

54. Tolkien, *Letters*, 145.

55. Ibid., 146.

56. Ibid., 192.

57. J. R. R. Tolkien, "On Fairy Stories," in *The Tolkien Reader* (New York: Ballantine, 1966), 53.

58. Tolkien, *Letters*, 146.

59. C. S. Lewis, *English Literature in the Sixteenth Century Excluding Drama* (London: Oxford, 1954), 7.

60. C. S. Lewis, *Miracles* (New York: Macmillan, 1974), 137.

61. Lewis, *Letters*, Vol. II, 841.

62. John Granger, *Looking for God in Harry Potter* (Salt Lake City, UT: SaltRiver, 2006), 7.

63. C. S. Lewis, "The Weight of Glory," in *The Weight of Glory and Other Addresses* (Grand Rapids, MI: Eerdmans, 1975), 5.

64. G. K. Chesterton, "The Ethics of Elfland," in *Orthodoxy* (New York: Image Books, 1959), 61.

65. C. S. Lewis, *Letters to Malcolm: Chiefly on Prayer* (New York: Harcourt, 1964), 103–104.

CHAPTER 4

1. M. H. Abrams, *The Mirror and the Lamp* (New York: W.W. Norton, 1953), 6.

2. Kathryn Hume, *Fantasy and Mimesis: Responses to Reality in Western Literature* (New York: Methuen, 1984), 9.

3. Abrams, 273.

4. Ibid.

5. Ibid., 32.

6. Ibid., 34.

7. Ibid., 36.

8. Ibid., 15.

9. Ibid., 15.

10. Sir Philip Sidney, "An Apology for Poetry," in *Criticism: The Major Texts*, ed. Walter Jackson Bate (New York: Harcourt, 1970), 85.

11. Ibid., 86.

12. Abrams, 274.

13. Ibid., 42.

14. C. S. Lewis, *English Literature in the Sixteenth Century Excluding Drama* (London: Oxford, 1954), 321.

15. Abrams, 274.

16. Ibid., 275.

17. Ibid., 42.

18. Ibid., 69.

19. Ibid., 160–161.

20. Ibid., 162.

21. Ibid., 277.

22. C. N. Manlove, *Modern Fantasy: Five Studies* (Cambridge, UK: Cambridge University Press, 1975), 259.

23. Ibid.

24. Percy Bysshe Shelley, "A Defence of Poetry," in *Shelley's Poetry and Prose*, ed. Donald H. Reiman and Sharon B. Powers (New York: Norton, 1977), 487.

25. Abrams, 21.

26. Ibid., 23.

27. Ibid., 23.

28. Ibid., 48.

29. Ibid., 60, 283.

30. Samuel Taylor Coleridge, *Biographia Literaria*, ed. George Watson (London: Everyman's Library, 1965), 167.

31. Ibid.

32. Ibid.

33. Rolland Hein, *The Harmony Within* (Grand Rapids, MI: Christian University Press, 1982), 114.

34. George MacDonald, "Imagination: Its Function and Culture," in *A Dish of Orts* (London: Edwin Dalton, 1908), 3.

35. George MacDonald, "The Fantastic Imagination," in *The Gifts of the Child Christ*. Vol. I, ed. Glenn Sadler (Grand Rapids, MI: Eerdmans, 1973), 23–24.

36. MacDonald, "Imagination," 2.

37. Ibid.

38. Hein, 55.

39. Ibid., 154.

40. Kerry Dearborn, *Baptized Imagination: The Theology of George Mac-Donald* (Hampshire, UK: Ashgate, 2006), 75.

41. Ibid., 85, 89.

42. C. S. Lewis, *The Discarded Image* (New York: Cambridge University Press, 1964), 27.

43. C. S. Lewis, *Collected Letters of C. S. Lewis*, Vol. II, ed. Walter Hooper (San Francisco: HarperCollins, 2004), 576.

44. C. S. Lewis, *Collected Letters of C. S. Lewis*, Vol. III, ed. Walter Hooper (San Francisco: HarperCollins, 2007), 940.

45. Lewis, *Discarded*, 116.

46. Ibid., 163.

47. Ibid., 116.

48. C. S. Lewis, *The Problem of Pain* (New York: Macmillan, 1971), 150.

49. J. R. R. Tolkien, *The Fellowship of the Ring*, Book II, Chapter 6 (New York: Ballantine, 1965), 455.

50. C. S. Lewis, *Mere Christianity* (San Francisco: HarperCollins, 2001), 153.

51. C. S. Lewis, *Studies in Medieval and Renaissance Literature* (London: Cambridge University Press, 1966), 54.

52. Lewis, *Discarded*, 119.

53. Ibid., 112.

54. Ibid., 58, 75.

55. Lewis, *English*, 3.

56. J. R. R. Tolkien, *The Letters of J. R. R. Tolkien*, ed. Humphrey Carpenter (Boston: Houghton, 1981), 257.

57. Ibid., 113, 320.

58. Ibid., 110–111.

59. Ibid., 328.

60. Ibid., 113, 195, 320.

61. Ibid., 321.

62. Ibid., 189, 342.

63. Ibid., 313.

64. Ibid., 131, 238.

65. Ibid., 321.

66. Ibid., 419.

67. Clyde S. Kilby, *Tolkien and the Silmarillion* (Wheaton, IL: Harold Shaw, 1976), 62.

68. Tolkien, *Letters*, 216.

69. Ibid., 257.

70. Ibid., 145.

71. Ibid., 110–111.

72. Ibid., 412.

73. Ibid., 321.

74. J. R. R. Tolkien, "On Fairy Stories," in *The Tolkien Reader* (New York: Ballantine, 1966), 56.

75. Tolkien, *Letters*, 409.

76. Ibid., 56.

77. Ibid., 73.

78. Ibid., 335.

79. Ibid., 402.

80. Ibid., 194.

81. Ibid., 145.

82. T. A. Shippey, *J. R. R. Tolkien: Author of the Century* (Boston: Houghton Mifflin, 2001), 274.

83. C. S. Lewis, *Pilgrim's Regress* (Grand Rapids, MI: Eerdmans, 1976), 135.

84. Ibid., 152–153.

85. Ibid., 156.

86. J. R. R. Tolkien, *Smith of Wootton Major*, ext. ed., Verlyn Flieger (London: HarperCollins, 2005), 61.

87. Humphrey Carpenter, *Tolkien: A Biography* (Boston: Houghton Mifflin, 1977), 243; Tolkien (ed. Flieger), *Smith*, 65.

88. Robert Murray, "A Tribute to Tolkien." Obituary, *The Tablet* (September 15, 1973), 879.

89. Tolkien (ed. Flieger), *Smith*, 135.

90. Tolkien, *Letters*, 281.

91. Tolkien (ed. Flieger), *Smith*, 81.

92. Ibid., 101.

93. Ibid., 70, 84–85, 100.

94. Tolkien, *Letters*, 133.

95. C. S. Lewis, *Surprised by Joy* (New York: Harcourt, 1955), 7.

96. C. S. Lewis, "Myth Became Fact," in *God in the Dock*, ed. Walter Hooper (Grand Rapids, MI: Eerdmans, 1970), 66.

97. Tolkien, *Letters*, 99.

98. Tolkien, "On Fairy," in *The Tolkien Reader*, 54.

99. Tolkien, *Letters*, 148, note.

100. Ibid., 148.

101. Ibid.

102. Ibid., 146.

103. Ibid., 417.

104. Ibid., 149.

105. Ibid., 385.

106. J. R. R. Tolkien, *The Silmarillion*, ed. Christopher Tolkien (Boston: Houghton Mifflin, 1977), 141.

107. J. R. R. Tolkien, *The Return of the King*, Book VI, Chapter 2 (New York: Ballantine, 1965), 244.

108. Tolkien, *The Silmarillion*, 83.

109. Ibid., 84.

110. J. R. R. Tolkien, *The History of Middle-earth*, Vol. 10, ed. Christopher Tolkien (Boston: Houghton Mifflin, 1993), 400.

111. Tolkien, *Letters*, 211.

112. Ibid., 194.

113. Christopher Brawley, "The Sacramental Vision" (Ph.D. diss., Florida State University, 2003), 109.

114. C. S. Lewis, *Miracles* (New York: Macmillan, 1974), 125.

115. C. S. Lewis, *Letters to Malcolm: Chiefly on Prayer* (New York: Harcourt, 1964), 91.

116. C. S. Lewis, "The Weight of Glory," in *The Weight of Glory and Other Addresses* (Grand Rapids, MI: Eerdmans, 1975), 13.

117. Lewis, *Surprised*, 217.

118. Ibid., 217.

119. C. S. Lewis, *The Four Loves* (New York: Harcourt, 1960), 175.

120. Lewis, "Meditation in a Toolshed," in *God in the Dock*, 212, 125.

121. C. S. Lewis, *Reflections on the Psalms* (New York: Harcourt, 1958), 112.

122. Lewis, *Pilgrim's Regress*, 177.

123. Kilby, *Tolkien*, 27–28.

124. C. S. Lewis, "The Language of Religion," in *Christian Reflections*, ed. Walter Hooper (Grand Rapids, MI: Eerdmans, 1967), 140.

125. H. G. Wells, *Best Science Fiction Stories of H. G. Wells* (New York: Dover Publications, 1952), 320.

126. Lewis, *Letters*, Vol. II, 870.

127. Lewis, *Miracles*, 33.

128. Lewis, *Letters to Malcolm*, 55–56.

129. Lewis, *Problem*, 42.

130. Lewis, "Christianity and Literature," in *Christian Reflections*, 5.

131. Lewis, *Letters*, Vol. II, 555.

132. Lewis, "Christianity and Literature," in *Christian Reflections*, 6.

133. Ibid.

134. Lewis, *Surprised*, 167.

135. Ibid.

136. Lewis, "Christianity and Literature," in *Christian Reflections*, 6.

137. Ibid., 7

138. Lewis, *Four*, 180.

139. Lewis, "The Weight," in *The Weight*, 12.

140. C. S. Lewis, "Wormwood," in *Poems* (Boston: Houghton Mifflin Harcourt, 2002), 87.

141. Lewis, *Mere Christianity*, 165.

142. Lewis, "Christianity and Literature," in *Christian Reflections*, 6–7.

143. Ibid., 7.

144. Lewis, "Bulverism," in *God in the Dock*, 276.

145. Lewis, *Letters to Malcolm*, 73, 203; *Letters*, Vol. II, 555.

146. Lewis, *Problem*, 102.

147. C. S. Lewis, *A Preface to Paradise Lost* (London: Oxford University Press, 1977), 49.

148. Dorothy Sayers, *The Mind of the Maker*, rev. ed. (New York: Harper, 1979), 29.

149. Ibid., 27–28, 213.

150. Lewis, *Letters*, Vol. III, 1602–1603.

151. C. S. Lewis, "Tolkien's *The Lord of the Rings*," in *On Stories and Other Essays on Literature*, ed. Walter Hooper (New York: Harcourt Brace Jovanovich, 1982), 90.

152. Lewis, "On Three Ways of Writing for Children," in *On Stories*, 37–38.

153. Lewis, *Letters*, Vol. II, 326.

154. Lewis, *Discarded*, 152.

155. Ibid., 67.

156. Walter Hooper. *"Past Watchful Dragons"*: *The Narnian Chronicles of C. S. Lewis* (New York: Collier, 1979), 123.

157. Lewis, *Miracles*, 95.

158. Anna Blanch, "A Hermeneutical Understanding of *The Chronicles of Narnia*," paper presented at the C. S. Lewis Today Conference, Sydney, Australia, May 4–6, 2006. http://www.cslewistoday.com/conference-2006/a-hermeneutical-understanding-of-the-chronicles-of-narnia.

159. Dennis Quinn, "The Narnia Books of C. S. Lewis: Fantastic or Wonderful," *Childrens' Literature* 12 (1984): 109.

160. Ibid., 119.

161. Gunnar Urang. *Shadows of Heaven: Religion and Fantasy in the Writing of C. S. Lewis* (Philadelphia: Pilgrim Press, 1971), 29.

162. Ibid., 37.

163. Ibid., 38.

164. Tolkien, "On Fairy," in *The Tolkien Reader*, 68.

165. Lewis, "The Weight," in *The Weight*, 13.

CHAPTER 5

1. C. S. Lewis, *Collected Letters of C. S. Lewis*, Vol. II, ed. Walter Hooper (San Francisco: HarperCollins, 2004), 103.

2. C. S. Lewis, *Pilgrim's Regress* (Grand Rapids, MI: Eerdmans, 1976), 5–6.

3. J. R. R. Tolkien, *The Letters of J. R. R. Tolkien*, ed. Humphrey Carpenter (Boston: Houghton, 1981), 414.

4. C. S. Lewis, *Collected Letters of C. S. Lewis*, Vol. III, ed. Walter Hooper. (San Francisco: HarperCollins, 2007), 502–503.

5. Tolkien, *Letters*, 233.

6. Ibid., 233, 267.

7. Lewis, *Letters*, Vol. III, 502–503.

8. C. S. Lewis, "On Science Fiction," in *On Stories and Other Essays on Literature*, ed. Walter Hooper (New York: Harcourt Brace Jovanovich, 1982), 66.

9. C. S. Lewis, "Christianity and Literature," in *Christian Reflections*, ed. Walter Hooper (Grand Rapids, MI: Eerdmans, 1967), 9.

10. Tolkien, *Letters*, 412; "On Fairy Stories," in *The Tolkien Reader* (New York: Ballantine, 1966), 70.

11. Tolkien, *Letters*, 298; "On Fairy," in *The Tolkien Reader*, 55, 59.

12. Tolkien, "On Fairy," in *The Tolkien Reader*, 48, 54.

13. Ibid., 82, note G.

14. Robert Scholes, *Structural Fabulation: An Essay on Fiction of the Future* (Notre Dame, IL: University of Notre Dame Press, 1975), 7.

15. Tolkien, "On Fairy," in *The Tolkien Reader*, 140, note H.

16. Tolkien, *Letters*, 87.

17. Verlyn Flieger and Douglas A. Anderson, *Tolkien on Fairy Stories* (London: HarperCollins, 2007), 111.

18. Tolkien, "On Fairy," in *The Tolkien Reader*, 37.

19. Samuel Taylor Coleridge, *Biographia Literaria*, ed. George Watson (London: Everyman's Library, 1965), 169.

20. Lewis, *Letters*, Vol. III, 880.

21. Gary Wolfe, "Symbolic Fantasy," *Genre* 8 (1975): 201.

22. Dorothy Sayers, *Further Papers on Dante* (London: Methuen, 1957), 7.

23. Tolkien, *Letters*, 160.

24. Ibid., 231.

25. Christina Scull, "The Development of Tolkien's Legendarium: Some Threads in the Tapestry of Middle-earth," in *Tolkien's Legendarium*, ed. Verlyn Flieger and Carl F. Hostetter (Westport, CT: Greenwood, 2000), 7–8.

26. Tolkien, *Letters*, 168.

27. Ibid., 177.

28. Ibid., 412.

29. Ibid., 188, 248.

30. Ibid., 304.

31. Ibid., 278.

32. T. A. Shippey, *J. R. R. Tolkien: Author of the Century* (Boston: Houghton Mifflin, 2001), xv.

33. Tolkien, *Letters*, 365.

34. C. S. Lewis, "Tolkien's *The Lord of the Rings*," in *On Stories*, 84.

35. Ibid.

36. Ibid.

37. Lewis, *Letters*, Vol. II, 96.

38. Tolkien, *Letters*, 175, 185.

39. Ibid., 333.

40. Ibid., 188, 196.

41. Ibid., 354.

42. Ibid., 360.

43. Ibid., 231.

44. Ibid., 178.

45. Ibid., 288.

46. Ibid., 221, 420.

47. Ibid., 235.

48. Lewis, "Tolkien's *The Lord of the Rings*," in *On Stories*, 84.

49. Tolkien, *Letters*, 250.

50. Ibid., 288.

51. Ibid., 398.

52. J. R. R. Tolkien, "Foreword," in *The Lord of the Rings*, 13.

53. Tolkien, *Letters*, 303.

54. Ibid., 220, 233, 239, 244, 283.

55. Ibid., 283.

56. Ibid., 376.

57. J. R. R. Tolkien, *The History of Middle-earth Vol. 10*, ed. Christopher Tolkien (Boston: Houghton Mifflin, 1993), 37.

58. Charles E. Noad, "On the Construction of 'The Silmarillion,'" in *Tolkien's Legendarium*, ed. Verlyn Flieger and Carl F. Hostetter (Westport, CT: Greenwood, 2000), 32.

59. Jane Chance, *Tolkien's Art: A Mythology for England*. rev. ed. (Lexington: University Press of Kentucky, 2001), 29.

60. Lewis, *Letters*, Vol. II, 1178.

61. Ibid., 575.

62. Lewis, *Letters*, Vol. III, 575.

63. Ibid., 87.

64. Richard Purtill, *Lord of the Elves and Eldils: Myth, Morality, and Religion* (Grand Rapids, MI: Zondervan, 1974), 60.

65. Tolkien, *Letters*, 159.

66. Ibid., 310–311.

67. Ibid., 226.

68. Ibid., 160.

69. Ibid., 226.

70. David C. Downing, "Sub-Creation or Smuggled Theology: Tolkien contra Lewis on Christian Fantasy." C. S. Lewis Institute. http://www.cslewisinstitute.org/cslewis/downing_theology.htm.

71. Tolkien, "On Fairy," in *The Tolkien Reader*, 80.

72. Ibid., 22.

73. Tolkien, *Letters*, 274.

74. Ibid., 214, 220.

75. Ibid., 174, 375.

76. Ibid., 387.

77. Ibid., 219.

78. Ibid., 143, 379.

79. Ibid., 175, 219.

80. Ibid., 380.

81. Ibid.

82. Verlyn Flieger, *Splintered Light: Logos and Language in Tolkien's World* (Kent, OH: Kent State University Press, 2002), 59.

83. Tolkien, "On Fairy," in *The Tolkien Reader*, 53.

84. Mary E. Zimmer, "Creating and Re-Creating Worlds with Words: The Religion and Magic of Language in *The Lord of the Rings*," in *Tolkien and the Invention of Myth*, ed. Jane Chance (Lexington: University Press of Kentucky, 2004), 53.

85. Ibid., 58.

86. Lewis, *Letters*, Vol. III, 1005.

87. Lewis, *Letters*, Vol. II, 264.

88. Lewis, *Letters*, Vol. III, 766, 881, 1108–1109.

CHAPTER 6

1. C. S. Lewis, "Tolkien's *The Lord of the Rings*," in *On Stories and Other Essays on Literature*, ed. Walter Hooper (New York: Harcourt Brace Jovanovich, 1982), 89.

2. Charles Williams and C. S. Lewis, *Taliessin through Logres, The Region of the Summer Stars, and Arthurian Torso* (Grand Rapids, MI: Eerdmans, 1974), 8.

3. C. S. Lewis, *Collected Letters of C. S. Lewis*, Vol. II, ed. Walter Hooper (San Francisco: HarperCollins, 2004), 245–246.

4. Ibid., 496.

5. C. S. Lewis, "The Novels of Charles Williams," in *On Stories*, 25.

6. Lewis, *Letters*, Vol. II, 496.

7. J. R. R. Tolkien, *The Letters of J. R. R. Tolkien*, ed. Humphrey Carpenter (Boston: Houghton, 1981), 285.

8. Ibid., 239.

9. Ursula LeGuin, *The Language of the Night: Essays on Fantasy and Science Fiction* (New York: Berkley, 1979), 59.

10. J. R. R. Tolkien, *A Tolkien Miscellany* (New York: Houghton Mifflin, 2002), 231.

11. Tolkien, *Letters*, 194.

12. Ibid., 413.

13. Ibid., 203.

14. G. K. Chesterton, *Sidelights*, rev. ed. (Freeport, NY: Books for Libraries, 1968), 260.

15. George MacDonald, "The Fantastic Imagination," *The Gifts of the Child Christ*, Vol. I, ed. Glenn Sadler (Grand Rapids, MI: Eerdmans, 1973), 14, 25.

16. MacDonald, "Fantastic," 25.

17. Ibid., 27.

18. Tolkien, *Letters*, 413.

19. Ibid., 25, 27.

20. Lewis, *Letters*, Vol. II, 555.

21. C. S. Lewis, *Collected Letters of C. S. Lewis*, Vol. III, ed. Walter Hooper (San Francisco: HarperCollins, 2007), 167.

22. Lewis, *Letters*, Vol. II, 456.

23. Ibid., 644.

24. Lewis, *Letters*, Vol. III, 388.

25. C. S. Lewis, *Studies in Medieval and Renaissance Literature* (London: Cambridge University Press, 1966), 39–40.

26. Lewis, *Letters*, Vol. III, 651.

27. Ibid., 1333.

28. C. S. Lewis, *An Experiment in Criticism* (Cambridge, UK: Cambridge University Press, 1961), 19, 74.

29. Ibid., 18, 82, 89.

30. Tolkien, *Letters*, 144.

31. Ibid., 194.

32. Tolkien, *Miscellany*, 234.

33. C. S. Lewis, *The Allegory of Love* (London: Oxford, 1936), 44; *Letters*, Vol. III, 1004.

34. MacDonald, "Fantastic," 25–26.

35. Dorothy Sayers, *The Whimsical Christian* (New York: Macmillan, 1978), 207.

36. Lewis, *Allegory*, 82.

37. C. S. Lewis, *Spenser's Images of Life* (Cambridge, UK: Cambridge University Press, 1967), 97, 124.

38. C. S. Lewis, *A Preface to Paradise Lost* (London: Oxford University Press, 1977), 114.

39. Madeleine L'Engle, *A Circle of Quiet* (Greenwich, CT: Fawcett, 1972), 82.

40. Dante Alighieri, *Convivio*, Book 2, Chapter 1. http://dante.ilt.columbia.edu/books/convivi/convivio2.html.

41. C. S. Lewis, *Pilgrim's Regress* (Grand Rapids, MI: Eerdmans, 1976), 13.

42. Lewis, *Letters*, Vol. II, 438.

43. Ibid., 439.

44. Ibid., 45.

45. Lewis, *Allegory*, 124–125.

46. Lewis, *Letters*, Vol. III, 815–816.

47. C. S. Lewis, "On Criticism," in *On Stories*, 140–141.

48. C. S. Lewis, *Reflections on the Psalms* (New York: Harcourt, 1958), 99.

49. Tolkien, *Letters*, 145.

50. Ibid., 121.

51. Ibid., 145, 262, 283.

52. Ibid., 220, 262, 298; J. R. R. Tolkien, *The Lord of the Rings*, Foreword (New York: Ballantine, 1965), x.

53. Tolkien, *Letters*, 262.

54. Ibid., 233.

55. Ibid., 212.

56. Ibid., 82.

57. Ibid., 303.

58. Tolkien, "Foreword," in *The Lord of the Rings*, x–xi.

59. Lewis, *Letters*, Vol. III, 815–816; "On Criticism," in *On Stories*, 132.

60. Tolkien, *Letters*, 307.

61. Humphrey Carpenter, *Tolkien: A Biography* (Boston: Houghton Mifflin, 1977), 190.

62. Tolkien, "Foreword," in *The Lord of the Rings*, xi.

63. Tolkien, *Letters*, 172, 233.

64. Ibid., 233–234.

65. Ibid., 283.

66. J. R. R. Tolkien, "On Fairy Stories," in *The Tolkien Reader* (New York: Ballantine, 1966), 172.

67. T. A. Shippey, *J. R. R. Tolkien: Author of the Century* (Boston: Houghton Mifflin, 2001), 210, 259.

68. Ibid., 355.

69. Ibid., 414.

70. Tolkien, *Letters*, 298; "Foreword," in *The Lord of the Rings*, x.

71. Clyde S. Kilby, "Mythic and Christian Elements in Tolkien" in *Myth, Allegory, and Gospel*, ed. John Warwick Montgomery (Minneapolis. MN: Bethany Fellowship, 1974), 140.

72. Tolkien, *Letters*, 189, 194.

73. Bradley J. Birzer, *J. R. R. Tolkien's Sanctifying Myth: Understanding Middle-earth* (Wilmington, DE: ISI Books, 2003), 137.

74. Ibid., 128.

75. Tolkien, *Letters*, 235.

76. Ibid., 243.

77. Ibid., 237.

78. Ibid., 387.

79. Ibid., 201.

80. Ibid., 147.

81. Ibid.

82. Ibid., 235–236.

83. Ibid., 237.

84. Ibid., 189, 205.

85. J. R. R. Tolkien, *The Silmarillion*, ed. Christopher Tolkien (Boston: Houghton Mifflin, 1977), 41.

86. Tolkien, *Letters*, 288, 407.

87. Ibid., 275.

88. Lewis, *Letters*, Vol., III, 789.

89. Ibid.; "Tolkien's," in *On Stories*, 85.

90. Lewis, *Letters*, Vol. III, 971–972.

91. Ibid., 503, 1004.

92. Lewis, "The Novels of Charles Williams," in *On Stories*, 23.

93. C. S. Lewis, *The Great Divorce* (New York: Macmillan, 1946), 8.

94. C. S. Lewis, *The Discarded Image* (New York: Cambridge University Press, 1964), 63.

95. Tolkien, "On Fairy," in *The Tolkien Reader*, 14.

96. Lewis, *Letters*, Vol. III, 1113.

97. Ibid., 479–480, 1460.

98. Ibid., 1113.

99. Ibid., 576.

100. G. K. Chesterton, *The Everlasting Man*, rev. ed. (New York: Doubleday, 1955), 20.

101. Lewis, *Letters*, Vol. III, 466.

102. Ibid., 1004.

103. Lewis, "Novels," in *On Stories*, 22.

104. Lewis, "Sometimes Fairy Stories May Say Best What's to Be Said," in *On Stories*, 46.

105. Ibid., 47.

106. Lewis, *Letters*, Vol. III, 502.

107. Richard Purtill, *Lord of the Elves and Eldils: Fantasy and Philosophy in C. S. Lewis and J. R. R. Tolkien* (Grand Rapids, MI: Zondervan, 1974), 149.

108. Roger Lancelyn Green and Walter Hooper, *C. S. Lewis: A Biography* (New York: Harcourt, 1974), 252.

109. Walter Hooper, *"Past Watchful Dragons": The Narnian Chronicles of C. S. Lewis* (New York: Collier, 1979), 106, 109–110.

110. Lewis, *Letters*, Vol. III, 334.

111. Ibid., 1474.

112. Ibid., 1113, 1158, 1244, 1245.

113. Lewis, "On Stories," in *On Stories*, 17.

114. Lewis, *Letters*, Vol. II, 390.

115. Ibid., 262.

116. Lewis, *Letters*, Vol. III, 502–503.

117. C. S. Lewis, *Surprised by Joy* (New York: Harcourt, 1955), 191.

118. Ibid., 180–181; Chad Walsh, "Impact on America," in *Light on C. S. Lewis*, ed. Jocelyn Gibb (London: Geoffrey Bles, 1965), 107.

119. Lewis, *Letters*, Vol. II, 262.

120. C. S. Lewis, "Christian Apologetics," in *God in the Dock*, ed. Walter Hooper (Grand Rapids, MI: Eerdmans, 1970), 94.

121. Lewis, *Letters*, Vol. II, 376.

122. Charles Moorman, "Fictive Worlds of C. S. Lewis and J. R. R. Tolkien," in *Shadows of Imagination*, ed. Mark. R. Hillegas (Carbondale: Southern Illinois University Press, 1969), 69.

123. Lewis, *Letters*, Vol. III, 313, 1005.

124. Ronald T. Michener, *Engaging Deconstructive Theology* (Hampshire, UK: Ashgate, 2007), 204.

125. Lewis, *Letters*, Vol. II, 707.

126. Lois Rose and Stephen Rose, *The Shattered Ring* (Richmond, VA: John Knox, 1970), 60.

127. Kathryn Hume, *Fantasy and Mimesis: Responses to Reality in Western Literature* (New York: Methuen, 1984), 103, 118.

128. Lee D. Rossi, *The Politics of Fantasy: C. S. Lewis and J. R. R. Tolkien* (Ann Arbor, MI: UMI Research Press, 1984), 30.

129. Dennis Quinn, "The Narnia Books of C. S. Lewis: Fantastic or Wonderful," *Children's Literature* 12 (1984): 114.

130. Gunnar Urang, *Shadows of Heaven* (Philadelphia: Pilgrim Press, 1971), 28.

131. A. R. Bossert, " 'Surely You Don't Disbelieve': Tolkien and Pius X: Anti-Modernism in Middle-earth," *Mythlore* 95/96 (Fall-Winter 2006): 72.

132. Eric Seddon, "Letters to Malcolm and the Trouble with Narnia: C. S. Lewis, J. R. R. Tolkien, and Their 1949 Crisis." *Mythlore* (Fall-Winter 2007).

133. Randel Helms, "All Tales Need Not Come True," *Studies in the Literary Imagination*, 14:2 (Fall 1981): 31.

134. Ibid., 35–36, 42.

135. Rev. Dwight Longenecker, "Tolkien's 'No' to Narnia," insidecatholic. com, May 15, 2008. http://insidecatholic.com/Joomla/index.php?option= com_content&task=view&id=3657&Itemid=48.

136. Walter F. Hartt, "Godly Influences: The Theology of J. R. R. Tolkien and C. S. Lewis," *Studies in the Literary Imagination* 14:2 (Fall 1981): 23, 25, 28.

137. C. S. Lewis, "Christianity and Literature," in *Christian Reflections*, ed. Walter Hooper (Grand Rapids, MI: Eerdmans, 1967), 10.

138. Lewis, *Letters*, Vol. II, 918.

CHAPTER 7

1. C. S. Lewis, "On Fairy Stories," in *On Stories and Other Essays on Literature*, ed. Walter Hooper (New York: Harcourt Brace Jovanovich, 1982), 57.

2. J. R. R. Tolkien, "On Fairy Stories," in *The Tolkien Reader* (New York: Ballantine, 1966), 59.

3. G. K. Chesterton, "The Ethics of Elfland," in *Orthodoxy* (New York: Image Books, 1959), 50, 53, 58.

4. Lewis, "Tolkien's *The Lord of the Rings*," in *On Stories*, 90.

5. Lewis, "On Science Fiction," in *On Stories*, 64.

6. C. S. Lewis, *The Abolition of Man* (New York: Macmillan, 1965), 91.

7. C. S. Lewis, *Surprised by Joy* (New York: Harcourt, 1955), 180–181.

8. Tolkien, "On Fairy," in *The Tolkien Reader*, 58.

9. Lewis, "Tolkien's," in *On Stories*, 90.

10. Lewis, "On Three Ways of Writing for Children," in *On Stories*, 38.

11. Lewis, "On Science," in *On Stories*, 67.

12. Chesterton, "Ethics," in *Orthodoxy*, 53–54.

13. G. K. Chesterton, *The Autobiography of G. K. Chesterton* (New York: Sheed and Ward, 1936), 91.

14. Chesterton, "Ethics," in *Orthodoxy*, 64.

15. Ibid., 58.

16. G. K. Chesterton, *The Everlasting Man*, rev. ed. (New York: Doubleday, 1955), 17.

17. Tolkien, "On Fairy," in *The Tolkien Reader*, 65.

18. Lewis, "Tolkien's *The Lord of the Rings*," in *On Stories*, 85.

19. Lewis, "On Science," in *On Stories*, 63.

20. Lewis, "On Three," in *On Stories*, 37.

21. Ibid., 39.

22. C. S. Lewis, "The Weight of Glory," in *The Weight of Glory and Other Addresses* (Grand Rapids, MI: Eerdmans, 1975), 4.

23. Ibid., 5.

24. Lewis, *Surprised*, 7.

25. Ibid., 16.

26. J. R. R. Tolkien, *The Letters of J. R. R. Tolkien*, ed. Humphrey Carpenter (Boston: Houghton, 1981), 110.

27. Matthew Dickerson and Jonathan Evans, *Ents, Elves, and Eriador: The Environmental Vision of J. R. R. Tolkien* (Lexington: University Press of Kentucky, 2006), 116.

28. C. S. Lewis, *Collected Letters of C. S. Lewis*, Vol. II, ed. Walter Hooper (San Francisco: HarperCollins, 2004), 754.

29. Ibid., 753–754.

30. C. S. Lewis, *The Great Divorce* (New York: Macmillan, 1946), 6.

31. C. S. Lewis, *The Problem of Pain* (New York: Macmillan, 1971), 148.

32. Lewis, "On Three," in *On Stories*, 38.

33. Tolkien, "On Fairy," in *The Tolkien Reader*, 67.

34. Tolkien, *Letters*, 246, 262, 284.

35. Ibid., 267.

36. Ibid., 236.

37. C. S. Lewis, *The Four Loves* (New York: Harcourt, 1960), 28ff.

38. C. S. Lewis, *Collected Letters of C. S. Lewis*, Vol. III, ed. Walter Hooper (San Francisco: HarperCollins, 2007), 480.

39. Tolkien, "On Fairy," in *The Tolkien Reader*, 66.

40. Lewis, "On Three," in *On Stories*, 40.

41. C. S. Lewis, *A Preface to Paradise Lost* (London: Oxford University Press, 1977), 57.

42. Lewis, "The Weight," in *The Weight*, 13.

43. C. S. Lewis, *The Screwtape Letters* (New York: Macmillan, 1961), viii.

44. Lewis, *Letters*, Vol. III, 970.

45. Lewis, "On Stories," in *On Stories*, 13–14.

46. Lewis, "On Three," in *On Stories*, 36.

47. Tolkien, *Letters*, 214, 221.

48. Ibid., 242.

49. C. S. Lewis, *The Discarded Image* (New York: Cambridge University Press, 1964), 147.

50. J. R. R. Tolkien, "Beowulf: The Monsters and the Critics," in *Modern Writings on Major English Authors*, ed. James R. Kreuzer and Lee Cogan (Indianapolis, IN: Bobbs-Merrill, 1963), 13.

51. Charles Moorman, "Fictive Worlds of C. S. Lewis and J. R. R. Tolkien," in *Shadows of Imagination*, ed. Mark. R. Hillegas (Carbondale: Southern Illinois University Press, 1969), 61–62.

52. Tolkien, "On Fairy," in *The Tolkien Reader*, 14.

53. Tolkien, *Letters*, 147.

54. Lewis, *Surprised*, 65–66, 169, 170.

55. C. S. Lewis, *Collected Letters of C. S. Lewis*, Vol. I, ed. Walter Hooper (San Francisco: HarperCollins, 2004), 231.

56. Ibid., 234.

57. Lewis, *Surprised*, 235.

58. Chesterton, *Everlasting*, 128–133.

59. C. S. Lewis, *Reflections on the Psalms* (New York: Harcourt, 1958), 107, 111.

60. Lewis, *Letters*, Vol. II, 453.

61. C. S. Lewis, *Miracles* (New York: Macmillan, 1974), 139.

62. Lewis, *Letters*, Vol. I, 976–977.

63. Ibid., 977.

64. C. S. Lewis, "Myth Became Fact," in *God in the Dock*, ed. Walter Hooper (Grand Rapids, MI: Eerdmans, 1970), 67.

65. Tolkien, *Letters*, 109–110.

66. P. H. Brazier, "C. S. Lewis & Christological Prefigurement," *The Heythrop Journal* 48 (2007): 765.

67. C. S. Lewis, "Preface," in *Hierarchy of Heaven and Earth*, by D. E. Harding (London: Faber, 1952), 9.

68. Lewis, *Miracles*, 10.

69. Lewis, "Preface," in *Hierarchy*, 9–10.

70. Lewis, *Miracles*, 167.

71. Lewis, *Letters*, Vol. III, 789–790.

72. Lewis, "Myth," in *God in the Dock*, 66.

73. C. S. Lewis, *An Experiment in Criticism* (New York: Cambridge University Press, 1961), 40.

74. C. S. Lewis, "Introduction," in *Phantastes and Lilith*, by George MacDonald (Grand Rapids, MI: Eerdmans, 1964), 10.

75. Lewis, "On Stories," in *On Stories*, 18.

76. Lewis, "Myth," in *God in the Dock*, 66.

77. C. S. Lewis, "Preface," in *George MacDonald: An Anthology* (New York: Macmillan, 1947), xxvi–xxvii.

78. Ibid., 26–27.

79. Lewis, "Myth," in *God in the Dock*, 66.

80. Lewis, *Letters*, Vol. III, 789.

81. Lewis, "Myth," in *God in the Dock*, 66.

82. Lewis, "On Science Fiction," in *On Stories*, 67.

83. Lewis, "Introduction," in *Phantastes*, 10–11.

84. Lewis, *An Experiment*, 44.

85. C. S. Lewis, *Letters to Malcolm: Chiefly on Prayer* (New York: Harcourt, 1964), 52.

86. Ibid., 51–52.

87. Lewis, *Miracles*, 139.

88. Lewis, "Myth," in *God in the Dock*, 67.

89. Lewis, *Surprised*, 236.

90. Lewis, *Letters*, Vol. II, 246.

91. Brazier, 770.

92. Victoria Nelson, *The Secret Life of Puppets* (Cambridge, MA: Harvard University Press, 2001), 9.

93. C. S. Lewis, *Pilgrim's Regress* (Grand Rapids, MI: Eerdmans, 1976), 171.

94. Tolkien, *Letters*, 100–101.

95. Ibid., 101.

96. Tolkien, "On Fairy," in *The Tolkien Reader*, 71–72.

97. Ibid., 70–71, 99.

98. Tolkien, *Letters*, 100.

99. Ibid., 252.

100. Ibid., 100.

101. Ibid., 100–101.

102. Tolkien, "On Fairy," in *The Tolkien Reader*, 68.

103. T. A. Shippey, *J. R. R. Tolkien: Author of the Century* (Boston: Houghton Mifflin, 2001), 260.

104. Tolkien, "On Fairy," in *The Tolkien Reader*, 252–253.
105. Tolkien, *Letters*, 78.
106. Ibid., 236.
107. Lewis, "On Stories," in *On Stories*, 19–20.
108. Lewis, *Surprised*, 221.
109. Lewis, *An Experiment*, 82, 132.
110. Ibid., 141.
111. Tolkien, *Letters*, 413.

Bibliography

Abrams, M. H. *The Mirror and the Lamp*. New York: W.W. Norton, 1953.

Alighieri, Dante. *Convivio*. http://dante.ilt.columbia.edu/books/convivi/.

Armitt, Lucie. *Fantasy Fiction: An Introduction*. New York: Continuum, 2005.

Barfield, Owen. *A Barfield Reader*. Edited by G. B. Tennyson. Middletown, CT: Wesleyan University Press, 1999.

——. *Poetic Diction: A Study in Meaning*. New York: McGraw-Hill, 1964.

Bate, Walter Jackson, ed. *Criticism: The Major Texts*. Ext. ed. New York: Harcourt, 1970.

Birzer, Bradley J. *J. R. R. Tolkien's Sanctifying Myth: Understanding Middle-earth*. Wilmington, DE: ISI Books, 2003.

Blanch, Anna. "A Hermeneutical Understanding of *The Chronicles of Narnia*," C. S. Lewis Today Conference, Sydney, Australia, May 4–6, 2006. http://www.cslewistoday.com/conference-2006/a-hermeneutical-understanding-of-the-chronicles-of-narnia.

Blount, Margaret. *Animal Land: The Creatures of Children's Fiction*. New York: Avon, 1974.

Bossert, A. R. "'Surely You Don't Disbelieve': Tolkien and Pius X: Anti-Modernism in Middle-earth." *Mythlore* 95/96 (Fall-Winter 2006): 53–76.

Bowman, Mary R. "The Story Was Already Written: Narrative Theory in *The Lord of the Rings*." *Narrative* 14:3 (October 2006): 272–293.

Brawley, Christopher Straw. "The Sacramental Vision: Mythopoeic Imagination and Ecology in Coleridge, MacDonald, Lewis, and Tolkien." Ph.D. diss., Florida State University, 2003.

Brazier, P. H. "C. S. Lewis & Christological Prefigurement." *The Heythrop Journal* 48 (2007): 742–775.

Card, Orson Scott. "How Tolkien Means." In *Meditations on Middle-earth*, edited by Karen Haber, 153–173. New York: St. Martin's Press, 2001.

Carpenter, Humphrey. *The Inklings*. Boston: Houghton Mifflin, 1979.

——. *Tolkien: A Biography*. Boston: Houghton Mifflin, 1977.

Carter, Lin. *Imaginary Worlds*. New York: Ballantine, 1973.

Chance, Jane. *Tolkien's Art: A Mythology for England*. Rev. ed. Lexington: University Press of Kentucky, 2001.

Chesterton, G. K. *The Autobiography of G. K. Chesterton*. New York: Sheed and Ward, 1936.

——. *The Coloured Lands*. New York: Sheed and Ward, 1938.

——. *The Common Man*. New York: Sheed and Ward, 1950.

——. "A Defense of Nonsense." In *The Man Who Was Chesterton* edited by Raymond T. Bond. New York: Doubleday, 1960.

——. *The Everlasting Man*. Rev. ed. New York: Doubleday, 1955.

——. *Orthodoxy*. New York: Image Books, 1959.

——. *Sidelights*. Rev. ed. Freeport, New York: Books for Libraries, 1968.

——. *Tremendous Trifles*. New York: Sheed and Ward, 1955.

Christopher, Joe R. *C. S. Lewis*. Twayne English Authors Series. Boston: Twayne, 1987.

Coleridge, Samuel Taylor. *Biographia Literaria*. Rev. ed., edited by George Watson. London: Everyman's Library, 1965.

Cristobal, Spartan. "Neoplatonism and J. R. R. Tolkien." The One Ring. http://www.theonering.com/articles1-13678/NeoplatonismandJRR Tolkien.

Dearborn, Kerry. *Baptized Imagination: The Theology of George MacDonald*. Hampshire, UK: Ashgate, 2006.

Dickerson, Matthew, and Jonathan Evans. *Ents, Elves, and Eriador: The Environmental Vision of J. R. R. Tolkien*. Lexington: University Press of Kentucky, 2006.

Downing, David C. "Sub-Creation or Smuggled Theology: Tolkien contra Lewis on Christian Fantasy." http://www.cslewisinstitute.org/cslewis/downing_theology.htm.

Duriez, Colin. *Tolkien and Lewis: The Gift of Friendship*. Mahway, NJ: Paulist Press, 2003.

Flieger, Verlyn. *Splintered Light: Logos and Language in Tolkien's World*. Kent, OH: Kent State University Press, 2002.

Flieger, Verlyn, and Douglas A. Anderson. *Tolkien on Fairy Stories*. London: HarperCollins, 2007.

Glover, Donald E. *C. S. Lewis: The Art of Enchantment*. Athens: Ohio University Press, 1981.

Glyer, Diana Pavlac. *The Company They Keep: C. S. Lewis and J. R. R. Tolkien as Writers in Community*. Kent, OH: Kent State University Press, 2007.

Granger, John. *Looking for God in Harry Potter*. Salt Lake City, UT: SaltRiver, 2006.

Green, Roger Lancelyn, and Walter Hooper. *C. S. Lewis: A Biography*. New York: Harcourt, 1974.

Haldane, J. B. S. *Possible Worlds and Other Essays*. New York: Harper and Bros., 1927.

Hammond, Wayne G. "'A Continuing and Evolving Creation': Distractions in the Later History of Middle-earth." In *Tolkien's Legendarium*, edited by Verlyn Flieger and Carl F. Hostetter, 19–29. Westport, CT: Greenwood, 2000.

Hart, Trevor. "Tolkien, Creation, and Creativity." In *Tree of Tales: Tolkien, Literature, and Theology*, edited by Trevor Hart and Ivan Khovacs, 39–53. Waco, TX: Baylor, 2007.

Hartt, Walter F. "Godly Influences: The Theology of J. R. R. Tolkien and C. S. Lewis." *Studies in the Literary Imagination* 14:2 (Fall 1981): 21–29.

Hein, Rolland. *The Harmony Within*. Grand Rapids, MI: Christian University Press, 1982.

Helms, Randel. "All Tales Need Not Come True." *Studies in the Literary Imagination* 14:2 (Fall 1981): 31–45.

——. *Tolkien and the Silmarils*. New York: Houghton Mifflin, 1981.

Hooper, Walter. *"Past Watchful Dragons": The Narnian Chronicles of C. S. Lewis*. New York: Collier, 1979.

Houghton, John William. "Augustine in the Cottage of the Lost Play: The Ainudindalë as Asterisk Cosmogony." In *Tolkien the Medievalist*, edited by Jane Chance, 171–182. London and New York: Routledge, 2003.

Howard, Thomas. "The Uses of Myth." *Mythlore* 7 (March 1980): 20–23.

Hume, Kathryn. *Fantasy and Mimesis: Responses to Reality in Western Literature*. New York: Methuen, 1984.

Kilby, Clyde S. "Mythic and Christian Elements in Tolkien." In *Myth, Allegory, and Gospel: An Interpretation of J. R. R. Tolkien, C. S. Lewis, G. K. Chesterton, Charles Williams*, edited by John Warwick Montgomery, 119–143. Minneapolis, MN: Bethany Fellowship, 1974.

——. *Tolkien and the Silmarillion*. Wheaton, IL: Harold Shaw, 1976.

Knight, Gareth. *The Magical World of the Inklings: J. R. R. Tolkien, C. S. Lewis, Charles Williams, Owen Barfield*. Longmead, UK: Element Books, 1990.

LeGuin, Ursula. *The Language of the Night: Essays on Fantasy and Science Fiction*. New York: Berkley, 1979.

L'Engle, Madeleine. *A Circle of Quiet*. Greenwich, CT: Fawcett, 1972.

——. *Many Waters:* New York: Farrar, Straus & Giroux, 1986.

——. *Walking on Water: Reflections on Faith and Art*. Wheaton, IL: Harold Shaw, 1980.

Lewis, C. S. *The Abolition of Man*. New York: Macmillan, 1965.

——. *The Allegory of Love*. London: Oxford, 1936.

——. *Arthurian Torso*. Grand Rapids, MI: Eerdmans, 1974.

——. *Christian Reflections*. Edited by Walter Hooper. Grand Rapids, MI: Eerdmans, 1967.

——. *Collected Letters of C. S. Lewis*, Vol. I. Edited by Walter Hooper. San Francisco: HarperCollins, 2004.

——. *Collected Letters of C. S. Lewis*. Vol. II. Edited by Walter Hooper. San Francisco: HarperCollins, 2004.

——. *Collected Letters of C. S. Lewis*. Vol. III. Edited by Walter Hooper. San Francisco: HarperCollins, 2007.

——. *The Discarded Image*. New York: Cambridge University Press, 1964.

——. *Dymer*. London: Dent, 1926.

——. *English Literature in the Sixteenth Century Excluding Drama*. London: Oxford, 1954.

——. *Essays Presented to Charles Williams*. Grand Rapids, MI: Eerdmans, 1966.

——. *An Experiment in Criticism*. Cambridge, UK: Cambridge University Press, 1961.

——. *The Four Loves*. New York: Harcourt, 1960.

——. *God in the Dock*. Edited by Walter Hooper. Grand Rapids, MI: Eerdmans, 1970.

——. *The Great Divorce*. New York: Macmillan, 1946.

——. "Introduction." In *Phantastes and Lilith*, by George MacDonald. Grand Rapids, MI: Eerdmans, 1964.

———. *The Last Battle*. New York: Collier, 1976.

———. *Letters to Malcolm: Chiefly on Prayer*. New York: Harcourt, 1964.

———. *Mere Christianity*. San Francisco: HarperCollins, 2001.

———. *Miracles*. New York: Macmillan, 1974.

———. *On Stories and Other Essays on Literature*. Edited by Walter Hooper. New York: Harcourt Brace Jovanovich, 1982.

———. *Out of the Silent Planet*. New York: Macmillan, 1970.

———. *Perelandra*. New York: Macmillan, 1970.

———. *Pilgrim's Regress*. Grand Rapids, MI: Eerdmans, 1976.

———. *Poems*. Boston: Houghton Mifflin Harcourt, 2002.

———. "Preface." In *George MacDonald: An Anthology*. Edited by C. S. Lewis. New York: Macmillan, 1947.

———. "Preface." In *Hierarchy of Heaven and Earth*, by D. E. Harding. London: Faber, 1952.

———. *A Preface to Paradise Lost*. London: Oxford University Press, 1977.

———. *The Problem of Pain*. New York: Macmillan, 1971.

———. *Reflections on the Psalms*. New York: Harcourt, 1958.

———. *Rehabilitations and Other Essays*. London: Oxford University Press, 1939.

———. *The Screwtape Letters*. New York: Macmillan, 1961.

———. *The Silver Chair*. New York: Collier, 1976.

———. *Spenser's Images of Life*. Cambridge, UK: Cambridge University Press, 1967.

———. *Studies in Medieval and Renaissance Literature*. London: Cambridge University Press, 1966.

———. *Surprised by Joy*. New York: Harcourt, 1955.

———. *They Asked for a Paper*. London: Geoffrey Bles, 1962.

———. *The Weight of Glory and Other Addresses*. Grand Rapids, MI: Eerdmans, 1975.

Lewis, W. H. *C. S. Lewis: A Biography*. Unpublished. Letter to Charles Moorman, June 12, 1957. Marion Wade Collection, Wheaton College, Illinois.

Longenecker, Rev. Dwight. "Tolkien's 'No' to Narnia." insidecatholic.com, May 15, 2008. http://insidecatholic.com/Joomla/index.php?option=com_content&task=view&id=3657&Itemid=48.

MacDonald, George. *A Dish of Orts*. London: Edwin Dalton, 1908.

———. *George MacDonald: An Anthology*. Edited by C. S. Lewis. London: Bles, 1946.

———. *The Gifts of the Child Christ*. Vol. I. Edited by Glenn Sadler. Grand Rapids, MI: Eerdmans, 1973.

MacLeod, Jeffrey J., and Anna Smol. "A Single Leaf: Tolkien's Visual Art and Fantasy." *Mythlore* 103/104 (Fall-Winter 2008). http://findarticles. com/p/articles/mi_m0OON/is_/ai_n30956846.

Manlove, C. N. *Modern Fantasy: Five Studies.* Cambridge, UK: Cambridge University Press, 1975.

Menion, Michael. "Elves and Art in J. R. R. Tolkien's Aesthetics" (online commentary on the mythopoeia poem). *Firstworld* 2003/2004.

Michener, Ronald T. *Engaging Deconstructive Theology.* Hampshire, UK: Ashgate, 2007.

Moorman, Charles. "Fictive Worlds of C. S. Lewis and J. R. R. Tolkien." In *Shadows of Imagination*, edited by Mark. R. Hillegas, 59–69. Carbondale: Southern Illinois University Press, 1969.

Morrow, Jeffrey L. "J. R. R. Tolkien and C. S. Lewis in the Light of Hans Urs von Balthasar." *Renascence* 56:3 (Spring 2004): 181–196.

Murray, Robert. "A Tribute to Tolkien." Obituary. *The Tablet* (September 15, 1973): 879–880.

Nelson, Victoria. *The Secret Life of Puppets.* Cambridge, MA: Harvard University Press, 2001.

Noad, Charles E. "On the Construction of 'The Silmarillion.'" In *Tolkien's Legendarium*, edited by Verlyn Flieger and Carl F. Hostetter, 31–68. Westport, CT: Greenwood, 2000.

Otto, Rudolf. *The Idea of the Holy: An Inquiry into the Non-Rational Factor in the Idea of the Divine and Its Relation to the Rational.* New York: Oxford University Press, 1958.

Pearce, Joseph. *Tolkien: Man and Myth.* San Francisco: Ignatius Press, 1998.

Prickett, Stephen. *Victorian Fantasy.* Bloomington: Indiana University Press, 1979.

Purtill, Richard. *J. R. R. Tolkien: Myth, Morality, and Religion.* San Francisco: Harper & Row, 1984.

——. *Lord of the Elves and Eldils: Fantasy and Philosophy in C. S. Lewis and J. R. R. Tolkien.* Grand Rapids, MI: Zondervan, 1974.

Puttenham, George. "The Art of English Poesy." In *The Renaissance in England*, edited by Hyder E. Rollins and Herschel Baker, 640–646. Boston: Heath, 1954.

Quinn, Dennis. "The Narnia Books of C. S. Lewis: Fantastic or Wonderful." *Children's Literature* 12 (1984): 105–121.

Ready, William. *Understanding Tolkien.* New York: Warner Paperback Library, 1968.

Rose, Lois, and Stephen Rose. *The Shattered Ring*. Richmond, VA: John Knox, 1970.

Rossi, Lee D. *The Politics of Fantasy: C. S. Lewis and J. R. R. Tolkien*. Ann Arbor, MI: UMI Research Press, 1984.

Ryken, Leland. *How to Read the Bible as Literature*. Grand Rapids, MI: Zondervan, 1984.

———. *Triumphs of the Imagination*. Downers Grove, IL: InterVarsity, 1975.

Sayer, George. *Jack: C. S. Lewis and His Times*. San Francisco: Harper and Row, 1988.

Sayers, Dorothy. *Further Papers on Dante*. London: Methuen, 1957.

———. *The Mind of the Maker*. Rev. ed. New York: Harper, 1979.

———. *The Whimsical Christian*. New York: Macmillan, 1978.

Schakel, Peter. *Imagination and the Arts in C. S. Lewis: Journeying to Narnia and Other Worlds*. Columbia: University of Missouri Press, 2002.

Scheer, Andrew. "Malice in Wonderland?" *Moody Monthly* (July–Aug. 1985): 31–35.

Scholes, Robert. *Structural Fabulation: An Essay on Fiction of the Future*. Notre Dame, IL: University of Notre Dame Press, 1975.

Scull, Christina. "The Development of Tolkien's Legendarium: Some Threads in the Tapestry of Middle-earth." In *Tolkien's Legendarium*, edited by Verlyn Flieger and Carl F. Hostetter, 7–18. Westport, CT: Greenwood, 2000.

Seddon, Eric. "Letters to Malcolm and the Trouble with Narnia: C. S. Lewis, J. R. R. Tolkien, and Their 1949 Crisis." *Mythlore* (Fall-Winter 2007). http://www.accessmylibrary.com/coms2/summary_0286-33496441_ITM.

Shelley, Percy Bysshe. "A Defence of Poetry." In *Shelley's Poetry and Prose*, edited by Donald H. Reiman and Sharon B. Powers, 480–508. New York: Norton, 1977.

Shippey, T. A. *J. R. R. Tolkien: Author of the Century*. Boston: Houghton Mifflin, 2001.

Timmerman, John. "Fantasy Literature's Evocative Power." *Christian Century* (May 17, 1987): 533–37.

Tolkien, J. R. R. "Beowulf: The Monsters and the Critics." In *Modern Writings on Major English Authors*, edited by James R. Kreuzer and Lee Cogan, 1–32. Indianapolis, IN: Bobbs-Merrill, 1963.

———. *The History of Middle-earth*. Edited by Christopher Tolkien. Boston: Houghton, 1984–1996.

———. Interview by Dennis Gerrolt, BBC Radio 4, "Now Read On," January 1971.

——. Interview by Philip Norman, *New York Times*, "The Prevalence of Hobbits," January 15, 1967.

——. *The Letters of J. R. R. Tolkien*. Edited by Humphrey Carpenter. Boston: Houghton, 1981.

——. "Mythopoeia." In *Tree and Leaf* by J. R. R. Tolkien. London: Harper-Collins, 2001. http://home.ccil.org/~cowan/mythopoeia.html.

——. "On Fairy Stories." In *The Tolkien Reader* by J. R. R. Tolkien. New York: Ballantine, 1966.

——. *Roverandom*. Edited by Christina Scull and Wayne G. Hammond. New York: Houghton Mifflin, 1998.

——. *The Silmarillion*. Edited by Christopher Tolkien. Boston: Houghton Mifflin, 1977.

——. *Smith of Wootton Major*. Ext. ed. Edited by Verlyn Flieger. London: HarperCollins, 2005.

——. *Smith of Wootton Major & Farmer Giles of Ham*. New York: Ballantine, 1975.

——. *A Tolkien Miscellany*. New York: Houghton Mifflin, 2002.

Urang, Gunnar. *Shadows of Heaven: Religion and Fantasy in the Writing of C. S. Lewis, Charles Williams, J. R. R. Tolkien*. Philadelphia: Pilgrim Press, 1971.

Waggoner, Diana. *The Hills of Faraway*. New York: Atheneum, 1978.

Wain, John. *Sprightly Running: Part of an Autobiography*. New York: St. Martin's, 1963.

Walsh, Chad. "Impact on America." In *Light on C. S. Lewis*, edited by Jocelyn Gibb, 106–116. London: Geoffrey Bles, 1965.

Wells, H. G. *Best Science Fiction Stories of H. G. Wells*. New York: Dover Publications, 1952.

Williams, Charles, and C. S. Lewis. *Taliessin through Logres, The Region of the Summer Stars, and Arthurian Torso*. Grand Rapids, MI: Eerdmans, 1974.

Wolfe, Gary. "Symbolic Fantasy." *Genre* 8 (1975): 194–209.

Wood, Ralph C. "Conflict and Convergence on Fundamental Matters in C. S. Lewis and J. R. R. Tolkien, *Renascence* 55:4 (Summer 2003): 315–338.

Zimmer, Mary E. "Creating and Re-Creating Worlds with Words: The Religion and Magic of Language in *The Lord of the Rings*." In *Tolkien and the Invention of Myth*, edited by Jane Chance, 49–60. Lexington: University Press of Kentucky, 2004.

Zipes, Jack. "Breaking the Disney Spell." In *The Classic Fairy Tales*, edited by Marla Tatar, 332–352. New York: Norton Critical Edition, 1999.

Index

107–108; Platonism, 110, 113–114; search for, 172; transcendent vs. objective, 41, 63, 124, 183
heroes, 143–145
holiness, 2, 72, 183

illustrations, 3, 6, 11, 134
imagery, 41, 74, 97, 103, 134–135
imagination, 36–40, 69, 71, 72–73, 76, 109
imitation, 68, 107
Inklings, 2, 4

journey, 83–86, 114, 120, 135, 144–145, 148

Kalevala, 5

Lang, Andrew, 22
leaves, 87–88
Le Morte d'Arthur (Thomas Mallory), 2
L'Engle, Madeleine, 34, 150
Lewis, C. S.: animals, writing about, 175; children, writing for, 30–31; conversion, 179; didacticism, 161–162; fairy story genre, 24–30; form, 17–18; Great War, 37, 40, 104–105; imitation, 107, 109; influences, 3; joy, 97, 186; language, 138–141; Magician's Magic Book, 90, 113, 170, 189; map, 128; meeting Tolkien, 1; mother, 3; Myth of Deep Heaven, 52–55; names, 14, 140; opinion of *The Lord of the Rings*,

7–8, 123, 156, 169; publication of his books, 8–12; science fiction, 32–35; style, 25, 114, 120–121, 135–137, 140–141; words, 140–141; writing process, 17–18
Lewis, C. S., characters:
—Andrew, 62
—Aslan, 17, 157, 158, 159, 174
—Eustace, 30, 62, 90, 136, 174
—Jadis, 60, 62
—Lucy, 90, 113, 170, 189
—Maleldil, 52–56
—Ransom: 9, 34, 54, 56, 57, 58, 60, 75, 79, 81, 106; changed viewpoint, 82–83, 104, 130, 169; as a Christian, 161; effect of landscape on, 131–132, 136–137; as an instrument, 77; on myth, 180; as narrator, 14, 128–129, 141; as philologist, 139; Platonism, 112
Lewis, C. S., places: Aslan's Country, 97, 113, 125, 171, 174; Malacandra, 52–53, 57–58, 82, 120, 129, 130–131
Lewis, C. S., works:
—*Abolition of Man*, 10, 81, 167
—*The Allegory of Love*, 74, 149
—*Animal-Land*, 11
—*The Chronicles of Narnia*, 10–11, 127, 157, 160, 180
—*The Dark Tower*, 9
—*The Discarded Image*, 80, 111
—*English Literature in the Sixteenth Century*, 61–62
—*An Experiment in Criticism*, 28, 32, 147, 182, 190

About the Author

MARTHA C. SAMMONS is Professor of English at Wright State University, where she has taught since 1975. Her publications include *Document Design for Writers*, *The Longman Guide to Style and Writing on the Internet*, *A Guide Through Narnia: Revised and Expanded Edition*, *"A Far-Off Country": A Guide to C.S. Lewis's Fantasy Fiction*, *"A Better Country": The Worlds of Religious Fantasy and Science Fiction*, as well as articles on both fantasy fiction and teaching with technology.